The Uncrowned King of
MONT BLANC

D0474392

TGB circa 1952.
Photo: B. Goodfellow, Alpine Club Photo Library, London.

The Uncrowned King of
MONT BLANC

The life of T. Graham Brown,
physiologist and mountaineer

PETER FOSTER

bâton wicks

Bâton Wicks, Sheffield
www.v-publishing.co.uk/batonwicks

AUSTRIA

BERNINA ALPS *Piz Bernina*
ORTLER ALPS

Bolzano

Bormio

Disgrazia

Presanella
Adamello BRENTA DOLOMITES

Sondrio

Trento

Como Lecco

Milan

Verona

ITALY

THE EUROPEAN ALPS

Principal Alpine centres
and surrounding peaks

The Uncrowned King of

MONT BLANC

PETER FOSTER

First published in 2019 by Bâton Wicks, an imprint of Vertebrate Publishing.

Vertebrate Publishing
Omega Court, 352 Cemetery Road, Sheffield S11 8FT United Kingdom.
www.v-publishing.co.uk

Copyright © Peter Foster 2019.
Foreword copyright © Lindsay Griffin 2019.
Map by Simon Norris.

Front cover: the Brenva Face of Mont Blanc. Photo: Peter Foster.

Peter Foster has asserted his rights under the Copyright, Designs and Patents Act 1988
to be identified as author of this work.

This book is a work of non-fiction based on the life of T. Graham Brown. The author has
stated to the publishers that, except in such minor respects not affecting the substantial accuracy
of the work, the contents of the book are true.

A CIP catalogue record for this book is available from the British Library.

ISBN 978-1-898573-82-1 (Paperback)
ISBN 978-1-898573-83-8 (Ebook)

10 9 8 7 6 5 4 3 2 1

All rights reserved. No part of this work covered by the copyright herein may be reproduced or used
in any form or by any means – graphic, electronic, or mechanised, including photocopying, recording,
taping or information storage and retrieval systems – without the written permission of the publisher.

Every effort has been made to obtain the necessary permissions with reference to copyright material,
both illustrative and quoted. We apologise for any omissions in this respect and will be pleased
to make the appropriate acknowledgements in any future edition.

Design and production by Jane Beagley.
www.v-publishing.co.uk

Bâton Wicks and Vertebrate Publishing are committed to printing on paper from sustainable sources.

Printed and bound in the UK by T.J. International Ltd, Padstow, Cornwall.

Contents

Foreword by Lindsay Griffin

Dawn broke with an eerily green, almost luminescent hue, as three naive teenage climbers disconnected their primitive headlamps and began to ascend the great snow slope. Spirits were buoyed as they realised the rounded snow ridge, over which they had just walked, must have been the famous ice arête, one of the route's cruxes; the other, a complex sérac barrier, lay far above. By the time the team was beneath its menacing structure, thick woolly cloud had reduced the visibility to ten metres and the air was alive with snowflakes. It was only by pure chance that they happened upon a climbable break through the towering ice cliffs, emerging on to the col above in a blizzard. For one of the party, entirely ignorant of any Alpine history, let alone that of the mountain on which he now stood, this felt no more serious than a Lakeland fell in winter. It was fortunate his partners were better prepared. In their short span of visibility from the Brenva Spur, the eyes of these young climbers drifted across the expansive face to the left, a mélange of ribs, séracs and buttresses. They absorbed the details that would later become all too familiar from photographs and literature, vowing to return for one of the lines up the Brenva Face.

Four years later, one of the party had already retired from climbing, the second had sadly been killed in a road accident, but the third – myself – returned to the small refuge perched spectacularly on the Col de La Fourche, less naive but with considerably more anxiety about the outcome. By now I had devoured the books of Bonatti, Smythe and Graham Brown, and had the experience of many more Alpine ascents, showing me in no uncertain terms all that could possibly go wrong. It was late in the season. My partner and I were the only team on the vast Brenva Face. On this occasion dawn broke with a smile as we reached the safety of the rib of *Route Major*. Alarmingly, looking back over our lengthy approach from Col Moore, gathering light revealed that the majority of it had been seriously threatened by sérac fall, not just the crossing of the Grand Couloir as we had been led to believe. As we climbed the three successive ribs and upper slope,

I had ample time to trace the line taken by the adjacent *Sentinelle Rouge*. The objective danger appeared much higher than *Route Major* and the line less aesthetic: it didn't offer what I wanted in life. In the other direction lay *The Pear*, which I swiftly concluded had very little terrain throughout the entire ascent that was not exposed to sérac fall and avalanche. These three routes, forming the great triptych of the Brenva Face, had all been put up by a Scottish physiologist in the late 1920s and early 1930s. Who was this Thomas Graham Brown? Existing literature suggested a man of some fitness but with no great technical ability, who seemed to have a talent for making himself unpopular with most other climbers, notably his partner on the *Sentinelle* and the *Major*, the iconic, media-savvy Frank Smythe. Now while all this could have been true, it was also clear that Graham Brown had an uncanny eye for a line, and – wow – was he bold.

Peter Foster, much like Graham Brown, is a mountaineer, former consultant physician and Alpine Club member. For as long as he can remember he has been interested in alpinism of the period between the wars. While still a medical student he ticked many of the classics from that era, such as the north faces of the Dru, Badile and Dent d'Hérens, and was mesmerised by the Brenva Face, after seeing a magnificent photographic spread. By the time he retired Peter had already decided he wanted to pen something on the subject of alpinism during the 1920s and 1930s, but quickly realised that if he were to contribute anything substantially new, it would require the reading of copious material in various foreign languages, for which, by his own admission, his O-level French and German (failed!) were inadequate. Then, by chance, he stumbled upon the Graham Brown archive, held at the National Library of Scotland in Edinburgh. On his first visit he found himself carefully teasing apart the stuck pages of a tiny notebook written by Graham Brown in the Rishi Gorge en route for Nanda Devi. Peter discovered an entry explaining that the book had been soaked by rain and Graham Brown had had to dry it out in front of the campfire. As a researcher, Peter was in heaven! Over the subsequent five years he unearthed voluminous amounts of previously unpublished material and tracked down and interviewed or corresponded with Graham Brown's closest surviving relatives and friends who had known or climbed with him. His resulting biography is of direct interest to the mountaineer and general reader, although it does not ignore Graham Brown's significant contribution to neurophysiology. Many erudite articles have already celebrated this important part of his life, and Peter, eminently qualified to do so, has made that aspect accessible for the layman.

Almost thirty years after my ascent of the *Major* I was standing on the edge of the tundra, fending off giant mosquitoes. Just to my east lay the western upthrust of the Central Alaska Range and the third highest mountain in Alaska and the United States, Mount Foraker. On the skyline shimmered its huge north-west ridge. Graham Brown took part in a number of high-profile expeditions to the greater ranges, helping to put Odell and Tilman on the summit of Nanda Devi, the highest peak in the world climbed at that time, but, arguably, his greatest success, which is often overlooked today, was the first ascent of Foraker, via this same north-west ridge. After a chance meeting with the youthful but ambitious Charlie Houston at the Montenvers Hotel above Chamonix, Graham Brown was invited to bolster Houston's inexperienced American team, which planned to attempt Foraker. They reached the summit in a capsule-style – albeit prolonged – ascent, which convinced Graham Brown that the big peaks of the Himalaya could probably be climbed in the same way, an avant-garde view for the era. The sheer logistical battle of even gaining the foot of the north-west ridge, let alone climbing its substantial length, meant that a full fifty years after first being completed the ridge had received only two subsequent ascents and one of these involved a significant variation. The advent of bush pilot access to high glacier basins has resulted in today's normal route to the summit lying on the opposite side of the mountain, and Graham Brown's north-west ridge has slid into obscurity.

And what of his signature routes on the Brenva today? The traverse from Col Moore to the Grand Couloir was made substantially more difficult and dangerous in the late 1990s by a cataclysmic rockfall, resulting in both the *Major* and *Sentinelle Rouge* being abandoned for many years. The *Sentinelle* has been skied a couple of times in the last decade, while the *Major* is now being climbed as long as conditions on the traverse allow, normally when there is a heavy covering of consolidated snow. Vastly improved gear, fitness and climbing ability have inevitably eroded the reputation of most classic Alpine routes. Against this backdrop the *Major* has retained its status as a difficult route, and paradoxically has a far greater reputation than it did in the 1970s or 1980s. *The Pear* has always had a fearsome reputation. By the 1950s only a handful of parties had climbed it, and while it would see rather more ascents during the next couple of decades, current authorities report there has been no known ascent for years. Generally, far fewer people now climb long, technical, serious routes (Grandes Jorasses excepted) in the massif.

By reading this book I learnt that Thomas did not have a double-barrelled surname – there is no hyphen – and that his Alpine CV has far more depth and quality than I ever realised. And while this book does not disprove that he was a complex and cantankerous old sod, and one who likely would have made difficult company on any expedition, it does show that it is this aspect of his character, fuelled by the many criticisms from those who wrote about him, that has overshadowed one stark fact: Graham Brown was undoubtedly one of the foremost British mountaineers during the interwar period and indeed one of the most experienced alpinists of his generation.

Lindsay Griffin, 2018
President of the Alpine Club 2014–2017

Introduction

If ever a man were his own worst enemy it was Thomas Graham Brown. Over a long and combative life there would be many men who would contest that position, but time and again it was Graham Brown's difficult and acerbic character that stood between him and the recognition he deserved as a scientist and mountaineer of genuine distinction.

Graham Brown's career was marked by controversy. His tenure of the chair of physiology at University College, Cardiff was turbulent. He clashed with the authorities over the relationship of his department with University College and the nascent Welsh School of Medicine. His research placed him at odds with received opinion and it was the same story in the mountains. His battle with his climbing companion, Frank Smythe, over recognition of his role in the discovery and climbing of the original routes on the Brenva Face of Mont Blanc, was acrimonious and obsessive. His editorship of the *Alpine Journal* generated such disquiet within the Alpine Club that he was sacked. 'His was one of the most complex personalities I have ever known,' declared Lord Tangley, Graham Brown's friend of forty years and a former president of the Alpine Club:

> There was the rigorous scientist whose work in physiology earned him the fellowship of the Royal Society. There was a deep humility in the presence of great mountains, amounting to awe. There was a deep capacity for friendship. There was a soaring ambition which quite naturally made him wish that the world should know that the great Brenva climbs were his. There was also a touchiness which made him at times a difficult companion and resulted in interruptions of friendship.

As a mountaineer, Tangley reckoned Graham Brown's 'great strength was his ability to go on indefinitely without any apparent fatigue' and 'a will and imagination ... capable of transcending his own limitations and those of others.' 'There can be no doubt,' he concluded, 'that both in achievement and character Graham Brown was one of the most outstanding (perhaps the most outstanding) amongst British climbers in the Alps during the interwar period'[1] and his encyclopaedic knowledge of the mountain earned him the soubriquet 'the uncrowned King of Mont Blanc.'[2]

—❦—

A word on the material that lies behind this book: on his death, Graham Brown's personal papers – diaries, correspondence, extensive notes on mountaineering topics, pamphlets, newspaper cuttings and ephemera – were deposited in the National Library of Scotland. The collection and retention of this material was in itself a significant manifestation of his personality.

Graham Brown's first extant diary is from 1898 when he was a schoolboy. The entries record daily events and activities in microscopic but legible handwriting, a style he continued as an adult. He was not a habitual diarist and there are many gaps, but from 1924 he kept records of his climbing expeditions in tiny paperback notebooks. Writing in pencil, he meticulously noted start and finish times, duration of halts, prevailing weather and conditions, and the principal events of the climb. He also recorded details of the photographs he took, such as the subject or scene and the technical details of aperture and exposure time. All this information was recorded in real time, adding significantly to the duration of his ascents and irritating his companions who were eager to get on with the climbing. These notebooks provided the factual base for his journals, which he wrote up days, sometimes weeks, afterwards and are more reflective, containing impressions and comment. Some of the journals have been amended at a later date with additions and deletions, sometimes rendered totally illegible, suggesting a tendentious motive. Subsequently these climbing notebooks and journals were analysed repeatedly and reworked in extensive notes, lists and tables. These projects absorbed him for hours. He classified his climbs according to whether the ascent was guided or guideless, listed his companions, and noted his contribution to leading the route – a topic that kept him particularly preoccupied. He also tabulated times, rate of ascent and 'climbing effort', a measurement calculated using a formula he devised.

The archive contains hundreds of letters – it seems he never discarded any – many of which are mundane. The majority are incoming but Graham

Brown developed the habit of making copies of his own letters. Whilst at Cardiff the practice was almost routine, for he enjoyed the services of a secretary who typed his letters and made carbon copies. At other times he kept handwritten drafts. This habit meant he never lacked written evidence in any dispute – and there were many.

His collection of pamphlets and newspaper cuttings is concerned mainly with mountaineering topics and is the source for many of his scholarly articles on aspects of Alpine history. Surprisingly and inexplicably, there are also three bound volumes of cuttings dealing with murders, trials and executions in the second half of the nineteenth century. The cuttings have been retrieved from back numbers of *The Illustrated London News* and *The Times*, and are carefully pasted in under headings in his own handwriting. Graham Brown's retention of ephemera betrays the instinct of a hoarder. The items are numerous and varied. Just a sample includes: invitations, greetings cards, rail tickets, bills from mountain huts, bills from his tailor, scraps of paper on which he has scribbled train times, unused book tokens, unfranked postage stamps cut from envelopes for re-use and a sprig of dried heather from Nanda Devi.

This extraordinarily rich material forms the basis of the narrative that follows and, above all, it enables us to hear clearly Graham Brown's voice, querulous, opinionated and, to the discomfort of his adversaries, almost always right.

Chapter 1
Early Influences

Thomas Graham Brown was born on 27 March 1882 at 63 Castle Street, in the original New Town of Edinburgh, into the comfortable and respectable circumstances of an established and quietly distinguished family from the city's professional class.

For a man who never showed much enthusiasm for his siblings, Graham Brown was always keenly interested in his own ancestry. His father, John, had been born in Edinburgh in September 1853, 'the son and grandson of Presbyterian ministers of a family that sent its sons into medicine, or the church or to India'.[1] John was one of two boys and always styled himself John Graham Brown[a] to distinguish himself from his brother James Wood Brown. After qualifying in medicine in 1875, he succeeded to the practice established by his Wood grandfather and uncle.[b] He married Jane Thorburn, another product of Free Church Presbyterianism, and they had four children. Thomas's birth was followed by that of two more boys, David Thorburn and Alexander Wood, and a daughter called Jane. When Thomas was only nine, his mother died from bowel cancer. His chief memory of her is that she encouraged him to draw, but her death inevitably meant that his formidable father was his greatest influence.

By the time Thomas reached school age, his father was already on the path that would take him to the pinnacle of his profession, the presidency of the Royal College of Physicians of Edinburgh. A photographic family portrait provides a defining image of the late Victorian paterfamilias: grey-haired and bearded, an unruly full-set, pince-nez dangling on a cord. John is seated, surrounded by a chubby, fourteen-year-old Tom in knickerbockers; David,

---

a   Thomas followed suit, always signing himself T. Graham Brown, explaining 'there is no hyphen, but there are so many of us in the world that I like the two names – they are an old family combination' (15/1/36; NLS Acc 4338/6).

b   His uncle, Alexander Wood (1817–1884), was president of the Royal College of Physicians of Edinburgh in 1858–1861.

known as Thor, smartly dressed in a naval cadet's uniform; Alex wearing an Eton collar and a forced smile; a demure Janey, and the pet dog.

John Graham Brown can never have been the easiest of fathers. The son of a distinguished churchman and scientist[c] himself, he was not the man to expect less of his eldest son. Seventy-odd letters to Thomas written during the period 1898–1920 are extant, their tone humourless and almost invariably admonitory. 'Your letters are delightful reading but you do make a lot of mistakes in spelling,' he wrote to his sixteen-year-old son, and it was a tone he never lost.[2] 'You must stick hard into it,' he would tell him when he was a medical student learning anatomy, 'for it means a lot of very careful reading and memory work as well as the mere dissecting ... I hope you have been working hard at your bones.'[3] Even when Graham Brown was appointed to the chair of physiology at Cardiff, his father's congratulations were qualified by the hope that the post was 'only a stepping stone' to a more prestigious position.

From the first, Graham Brown had been inculcated with the need to succeed, but his schooldays were unexceptional and gave no hint of his abilities. In 1889, aged seven, he entered the recently established preparatory school of the Edinburgh Academy. Here he would have encountered the formidable Miss Wood, one of the original three dames engaged to teach at the school. She had arrived at the Academy from the Clergy Daughters' School at Casterton in Westmoreland where Charlotte Brontë had been a pupil, and which had been the model for Lowood School in *Jane Eyre*. She was a strict disciplinarian; silence reigned in her class and 'woe betide the offender who did not on every occasion come up to her high standard of neatness and accuracy', for he would receive 'such a torrent of rebuke as many an older person would have flinched under'.[4]

Three years later he proceeded to the upper school and, like the majority of pupils, attended as a day boy, his home in Chester Street in the city's West End being just a mile distant. The Edinburgh Academy had been founded in 1824 to provide an alternative to the high school, a sixteenth-century foundation, which was overcrowded and failing its pupils:

---

c   Thomas Brown (1811–1893) was appointed moderator of the general assembly of the Free Church of Scotland, its senior position. Remarkably, at a time when religious beliefs were being challenged by the work of Lyell and Darwin, he took a serious interest in science, his studies in geology and botany earning him election to the Fellowship of the Royal Society of Edinburgh.

[G]reat mobs of boys sat in long rows that rose upwards in tiers, with the cleverest at the top and the slower boys 'sitting boobie' on the lowest benches. They droned their Latin verbs and declensions en masse with 'ushers' (monitors paid by the masters out of their own pockets) 'hearkening' each row and helping to dispense punishment to the slow or inattentive.[5]

At the Academy, by way of contrast, class sizes were controlled and emphasis was placed on raising the standards of teaching, especially of Greek. From the outset, at the urging of Sir Walter Scott, one of the founder directors of the school, English was compulsory. However, study of the classics remained central to the curriculum until in 1866 it was organised into two separate schools: classical and modern. The modern side learned more English, French, German and Maths, less Latin and no Greek.

Graham Brown's time at the Academy coincided with the rectorship of R.J. Mackenzie (1888–1901). On assuming charge, Mackenzie had found the Academy in a parlous state with the school roll falling, morale 'low', 'discipline ragged, debts high and prospects poor'.[6] Espousing the principles of 'strict discipline, moral rectitude, and cleanliness of soul' that were dear to the heart of every Victorian parent and 'with a blend of determination, charm, enthusiasm and sheer hard work that inspired an extraordinary degree of loyalty and devotion in everyone connected with the school', he turned the school's fortunes around.[7] By 1895 the number of pupils had more than doubled.

Mackenzie put the teaching of science on a proper footing, building a science laboratory and appointing J. Tudor Cundall, who was only twenty-five but had already built a record as an able chemist, as special science master to organise the laboratory and devise a course of study. Cundall founded the school's Scientific Society. Its earnest meetings included guest lectures by distinguished scientists, demonstrations and papers given by the boys on topics that ranged from 'colour photography' to 'ants and their habits'; Graham Brown read one on 'Aluminium'. In addition, there were worthy educational visits to 'factories, power stations and other establishments of scientific interest', surely only of interest to an unusual species of teenage boy.[8]

Mackenzie also believed strongly in the educational value of sport, stating that 'vigorous exercise of some kind is, I think, a necessity for boys'.

He considered that participation in organised games could 'develop phy-sique, endurance, presence of mind, qualities of the highest value in prac-tical life ... [and] afford an education in public spirit', adding, 'if I were asked what was the most dangerous occupation for a boy's hours of leisure, I should at once name loafing'.[9] He introduced compulsory games on three afternoons a week; almost the whole of the upper school opted to play cricket and rugby rather than take the special course in gymnastics. Perhaps due to his short stature and difficulties with his eyesight, Graham Brown exhibited no sporting prowess, even failing to show in the sixty-yard sack race at the annual sports day. But like most schoolboys faced with the dreary task of letter writing, the results of matches provided ready subject matter: 'The Academy beat Fettes yesterday much to their disgust. I suppose they will get no jam for tea for at least a fortnight'.[10]

Outside school his enthusiasms were for 'old castles, the quest for secret chambers and underground passages; the "greyhounds" of the Atlantic; prehistoric forts; the yachts of the America's Cup race; fossil hunting; egg collecting; armour'.[11] Amongst his favourite books were Robert Louis Stevenson's *Kidnapped* and S.R. Crockett's *The Raiders*, a tale of outlaws and smugglers in Galloway in the early eighteenth century. He delighted in tracing and marking the heroes' routes on a map, a habit which 'taught me early the valuable art of map-reading'.[12] As an older boy:

> A phase of golfing holidays merged with the more serious business of fishing – bicycle, rod, and a .380 revolver, which was merciful to the rabbits. Spey, Tweed and Clyde were fished, and the small streams of the Lammermuirs and Lothians, Loch Leven and Loch Ard.[13]

There were family seaside holidays at Largo on the Fife coast, when he scrambled on the sea cliffs at nearby Elie, and, memorably, 'two long summers ... in my father's schooner amongst the Hebrides and along the Western coast'.[14]

In 1898 Graham Brown was removed from the Academy to spend four months in Germany. He was having trouble with his eyesight – the nature of the problem is unclear but his microscopic handwriting may have been a manifestation – and his father arranged for him to travel to Wiesbaden to consult an oculist whose prescription was to avoid reading. The visit also provided an opportunity for him to improve his German, in accordance with his father's wishes. Graham Brown was dutiful but unenthusiastic; his daily entries in the diary of his stay start with 'lessons as usual' and were soon replaced by a single, monotonous remark: 'nothing in particular'. He found Wiesbaden 'a dull place'.[15]

The following year Graham Brown had a sabbatical in Italy, which his father hoped would provide 'a great opportunity of enlarging your mind'.[16] He stayed with his uncle who had resigned his curacy because of ill health and retired to Florence to indulge his interest in Tuscan architecture and the paintings of the Italian primitives. Graham Brown spent 'happy days' sketching the interiors of churches and details of the monuments, and he made a careful study of the Church of Santa Maria Novella, producing an accurate ground plan that was published in his uncle's architectural and historical study of the church. He saw some 'splendid frescoes' and liked Botticelli's paintings. As a diversion from all this earnestness he took daily fencing lessons. The purchase of a sword provided a moment of excitement and pleasure: 'Went to get a rapier in morn[ing]. Saw (and bought) a beauty only £5. Fencing master delighted with it. Very flexible.'[17] His new enthusiasm caused him to overreach himself by advocating that his fencing master should come to Edinburgh. His father wrote reprovingly:

[F]irst of all to the fencing master. I do not know of any position here which he could get which would bring him in anything like the income he can make in Florence … Nor would I take the responsibility of recommending him to make such a move – and you should not do so either.[18]

After three months in Italy, Graham Brown returned to Edinburgh. Predictably, his father gave clear instructions how his seventeen-year-old son should proceed on the journey home:

I think you will manage your journey quite well alone. Uncle James will give you some money in addition to your ticket to London, for in London you will have to buy a 3rd class ticket from Euston to Edinburgh costing 32s 8d – If you have no change with you, you will need to get your money changed on board the steamer – take a cup of coffee and get a sovereign changed. This is because you will have to tip a porter 2d to get your luggage to a cab and you will have to pay the cabman. You will drive straight to Euston Station, and although you will have some time to wait there before the 10.15 morning train leaves for Edinburgh, I do not want you to leave the station. You will get some breakfast there and that will help to pass the time. Also when you get to Euston send me a telegram – Be very careful with your money on your journey. Don't spend more than is reasonable and keep a note of what you do spend. I leave the details to your common sense.[19]

Twelve months later Graham Brown was preparing for the entrance examination for Edinburgh University. 'I hope the tutor is satisfactory,' his father wrote, 'and that you feel you are getting ready for the conflict. I can barely fancy you a student at the university, but you will be that next month if all goes well.'[20] Graham Brown was successful, but his schooldays had not been marked by academic distinction and his father expected better in future: 'I dreamed last night that you had taken honours! So you must make sure that comes true.'[21]

Chapter 2
First Steps in Physiology

Following in his father's footsteps, Graham Brown enrolled to read medicine at Edinburgh in 1900, and here, for the first time, he began to show his formidable abilities.

The study of physiology was a necessary requirement for a medical qualification, although some medical teachers remained sceptical about its value in training doctors. 'When you first enter my wards, your first duty is to forget all your physiology,' Samuel Gee, physician at St Bartholomew's Hospital, told his students:

> Physiology is an experimental science – and a very good thing no doubt in its proper place. Medicine is not a science but an empirical art.[1]

The professor of physiology at Edinburgh was Edward Schäfer, an impressive and popular lecturer:

> Few things could be more dramatic than the sudden transition from the babble of two hundred voices to stillness as of the grave when Schäfer appeared at the door of his theatre and made his way slowly, and with characteristic step to the rostrum. Many a time the one o'clock gun went off as Schäfer was talking. In probably any other lecture theatre in the University that would have been the signal for pandemonium, but Schäfer was permitted to go on. The admiration of the student for Schäfer was mixed with fear, but to those who knew him he was, under the somewhat stern exterior, the kindliest and friendliest of men, with a keen sense of humour and a very charming smile.[2]

Years later Graham Brown would credit Schäfer with arousing his interest in physiology, but it was Noel Paton, superintendent of the research laboratory of the Royal College of Physicians, and Edwin Bramwell,[a] a physician with a special interest in neurology, who encouraged and guided him in a research project that remarkably resulted in a paper, published when Graham Brown was still a student. Paton wrote in a testimonial that Graham Brown was one of his 'ablest' students and Graham Brown justified the assessment by being awarded, in 1903, the degree of BSc *summa cum laude*, thus fulfilling his father's dream.

The focus of Graham Brown's studies now shifted to clinical medicine and surgery. His contemporary and friend, Murray Drennan,[b] outlined the daily routine of a conscientious student:

> Our first class begins at 8.00 a.m. so we have to be up betimes in the morning. From 8 to 10 I have anatomy and then at 11 I go over to the Infirmary; nominally we leave there about 1 p.m. but on operation days, twice a week at least, it is often 3 before I get away … After lunch the afternoon is taken up with anatomy till 5 p.m. … In the evening I have to be at the Infirmary at 7 and I get back here anytime between 8.30 and 11 depending on what is doing. We have a cup of coffee … and the rest of the evening is taken up with writing up notes and working at anatomy till about morning.[3]
>
> On 'waiting days', when the firm was on call for emergencies, all the new cases, accidents etc. come to our dressing rooms … there were a great many cut heads etc. to sew up.[4]

Graham Brown worked hard, attending his father's clinics assiduously. On 20 June 1906 he presented himself for his final examination, a *viva voce* in medicine. His examiners were the professor of medicine and his father – the stuff of nightmares: 'I never felt so bad in my life as before this oral.'[5] Properly his father withdrew, leaving Professor Wyllie alone to examine Graham Brown. He passed with honours but did not win a prize. Convinced that he had performed better than one of the prizewinners, he was disappointed and angry. 'I have been very badly treated … and I shan't forget it,' he complained, displaying a developing sense of self-esteem and attendant touchiness.[6] A few months later he suffered another disappointment when he failed to be elected senior president of the Royal Medical

---

a   Edwin Bramwell, FRCP, FRSE (1873–1952). In 1919 he succeeded Graham Brown's father as university lecturer in neurology and in 1922 was appointed to the chair of clinical medicine at Edinburgh.

b   A.M. Drennan (1884–1984). Professor of pathology at Edinburgh, 1931–1954.

Society, an historic and exclusive student club.[c] He came second in the poll and recorded that he was 'very glad that my friend AM D[rennan] is senior though would have liked it myself' and added suspiciously, 'a curious point – who did not vote for me?'[7]

In October he started work as an unsalaried, resident house physician at the Royal Infirmary. He made notes of his first day's schedule in his diary:

> Wards at 10. Visit and took one case. Dr James[d] arrived. Worked till 2.30 (catheterised case) and then lunch in the Residency. Then read till dinner and then wards again. All serene. Then worked till 11 and then supper. Then last ward visit to observation and other wards at 12.15 and to bed after 1.00 a.m.[8]

This six-month appointment would be Graham Brown's only experience of practising medicine until he had to resurrect his skills during the First World War, as an officer in the Royal Army Medical Corps.

In December he visited Professor Sherrington in Liverpool. Sherrington was at the forefront of research on the physiology of the nervous system and was a former colleague of Graham Brown's father, with whom he had remained on friendly terms. Sherrington received him warmly. On his first evening, after dinner, Graham Brown 'had a very interesting talk' with the professor, retiring to bed at midnight. The next day Sherrington showed him around his laboratory. Lunch was followed by 'another long talk' and the following day, he 'chatted all morning' with Sherrington before returning to Edinburgh in the afternoon. Graham Brown summed up his visit: 'I have never spent a more enjoyable time.' On his return home he had a 'long talk' with his father, for the visit had confirmed his wish to pursue a career as a physiologist rather than a physician, and Sherrington's advice was to visit Germany.[9]

During the second half of the nineteenth century medical education and physiological research in Germany had risen to pre-eminence in Europe, and a spell working in a German institution had become a rite of passage for

---

c   Founded in 1737, it was granted a Royal Charter by George III in 1779. Its rules are arcane and are enforced through a system of fines. The members met, as they still do, to read papers – dissertations – and present interesting cases to each other. The dissertations tended to be reviews of clinical topics such as pneumonia or the treatment of cardiac disease. Graham Brown's subject, 'Organic evolution', in which he examined the theories of natural selection, was unusual and, taken with his presidential address, 'A religion without faith', suggests a broader, philosophical interest that was out of the ordinary.

d   Alexander James MD, FRCPE (c1851-1932). Ordinary physician at the infirmary from 1892-1907 and Graham Brown's 'chief'.

the serious medical scientist. Graham Brown's father and Sherrington had both studied in Berlin. On completion of his residency, Graham Brown set out for Germany and the University of Strasbourg. Following the Franco-Prussian War of 1870, Strasbourg had been incorporated into Germany and two years later, in a display of Teutonic superiority and insensitivity, an imperial university and medical school were opened in the former French city and placed under the direct supervision of Otto von Bismarck. The new medical faculty, formally appointed by the kaiser himself, represented 'the cream of medical science'.[10]

Graham Brown arrived in Strasbourg in April 1907. He was affiliated to Professor Ewald's department of physiology where he was put to work investigating factors that influenced the contraction and relaxation of the gastrocnemius muscle of the frog. Graham Brown, however, had his own ideas and was unhappy with the project, writing to Sherrington and his father to express his doubts. Sherrington counselled him to accept Ewald's advice 'even against your own inclination'.[11] Graham Brown worked dog-gedly and his observations made during three months in Strasbourg resulted in two papers.

In October he returned to Scotland as assistant to Professor Paton, who had been appointed to the chair of physiology in Glasgow. Here he con-tinued investigating what was considered to be a form of epilepsy in the guinea pig – work that he had started as a medical student. For more than fifty years it had been known that in the guinea pig various lesions of the nervous system, particularly sectioning one of the sciatic nerves, would often lead to convulsive attacks resembling those of epilepsy. It had, how-ever, proved difficult to define the exact conditions under which the attacks could be induced reproducibly. This variability acted both as a hindrance to the investigator and a lure; it raised the hope of finding some variable factor which might lead to epilepsy in man as well as the guinea pig. This lure was all the temptation a character like Graham Brown needed, for as Lord Adrian[e] observed, he 'was a man of great determination'.[12] Graham Brown persevered for several years but his interests were shifting from the causes of epilepsy towards the general principles of the organisation of the nervous system, the chief concern of Sherrington's laboratory, and in 1910, supported by a Carnegie Fellowship, he moved to Liverpool.

---

e   E.D. Adrian (1889–1977), professor of physiology at Cambridge University. He shared the Nobel Prize with Sherrington in 1932. A keen mountaineer, he was made honorary member of the Alpine Club in 1955.

Chapter 3
Sherrington and Liverpool

Sir Charles Sherrington OM, GBE, FRS, Nobel laureate, was throughout his long life – he died in 1952, his ninety-fifth year – mentor and friend to Graham Brown. Sherrington's influence was such that Edward Cathcart, professor of physiology at the London Hospital Medical School, remarked to Graham Brown, 'You have taken Sherrington so openly as your model that people are apt to think you are a mere imitator.'[1] Graham Brown was not alone in falling under the spell of Sherrington, whose unaffected interest in his protégés and capacity for friendship endeared him to them; 'He loved young men and young-minded men and wanted to know their thoughts and problems.'[2] Sir John Eccles, who worked with Sherrington at Oxford, and subsequently also won a Nobel Prize, recalled 'his modesty, charm, vivacity and good humour' and that he was 'so human a person that his pupils' admiration was transmuted into love.'[3] Graham Brown paid his own tribute in an article published in the *British Medical Journal* on the occasion of Sherrington's ninetieth birthday:

> It was to those who worked in his laboratory that Sherrington gave most and showed most. The research student would enter it, timidly, with a mental picture of the author of *Integrative Action* as a man who must dwell in a sphere of his own making, difficult to attain or travel in – a man necessarily aloof and out of common reach, 'academic', coldly intellectual. But the disarming spirit of equality with which the recruit was received at once destroyed a mental barrier which could not in any case have for long withstood the sympathetic friendship which was offered by Sherrington and earned lasting friendship in return. There was no pomp … The laboratory life was a continuing adventure with always widening horizons.[4]

Sherrington had been appointed Holt professor of physiology at Liverpool in 1895. During his time there, he investigated the nature of the reflexes of the spinal cord and studied cerebral function in relation to movements. This research resulted in a major contribution to the understanding of the working of the nervous system and was synthesised in his influential book *The Integrative Action of the Nervous System*, published in 1906. In the first decade of the twentieth century Sherrington's department at Liverpool was a magnet for all physiologists interested in the central nervous system and received a stream of international visitors.

When Graham Brown arrived in Liverpool in 1910, Sherrington's assistant lecturers were Cyril Burt[a] and Herbert Roaf, a Canadian from Toronto, whose respective interests were in clinical psychology and chemical physiology (i.e. biochemistry); his research assistants were, unusually for the period, both women, one of whom was amongst the first six women to be elected members of the Physiological Society in 1915. Sherrington believed in a hands-on approach to experimental work and Graham Brown took note, proving to be a tireless and skilful experimenter. Without teaching and administrative responsibilities but with the advantage of Sherrington's guidance, his output during his time in Liverpool was greater than at any other time in his career as a physiologist.

The control of locomotion had aroused the curiosity of eighteenth-century 'natural philosophers', who had observed the macabre phenomenon of a decapitated chicken continuing to run until its circulation collapsed and also noted that a decapitated frog exhibited purposeful movements of its hindlimbs when the spinal cord was stimulated with a pin. Experiments performed at the end of the nineteenth century had revealed that after transection of their spinal cord, cats and dogs exhibited rhythmic movements of the limbs similar to the act of walking in the intact animal. Sherrington and others had investigated the neural control of these movements and, at the beginning of the twentieth century, the prevailing view was that walking was mediated by sequential reflexes: sensory input from pressure on the paw of the animal or stretching of a muscle would stimulate muscle contraction or relaxation, resulting in flexion (bending) or extension (straightening) of the limb and forward movement. But Graham Brown's observations,

---

a   Sir Cyril Burt (1883–1971), professor of psychology, University of London. His chief interest was in methods to measure intelligence and the influence of heredity on intelligence. His work underpinned the introduction of the 11-Plus examination. Shortly after his death, allegations that he had fabricated some of his data emerged, causing controversy which has still not been fully resolved.

made during his earlier work on anaesthetised guinea pigs, had suggested to him 'that the act of progression may, too, be essentially a central and not a peripheral phenomenon.'[5]

Adapting the experimental model and techniques devised by Sherrington, Graham Brown demonstrated that rhythmic movements of the hindlimbs occurred in a cat when the spinal cord had been transected *and* the sensory input from the limbs had been abolished by severing the nerves supplying them. This seminal observation made clear that stepping movements, sufficient for walking, could occur in the absence of command signals from the brain and sensory reflex feedback from the periphery, which implied the existence of circuits of nerve cells within the spinal cord that could generate a regular pattern of movement. Graham Brown developed the observation by studying the phenomenon of 'narcosis progression' in different animal models. At varying stages during induction of anaesthesia with ether or chloroform, animals displayed the rhythmic movements associated with locomotion: the wingbeat of a pigeon, the hopping of a rabbit and the galloping of a cat. His findings provided compelling evidence that the neural control of walking was an innate property of the spinal cord and he formulated the hypothesis that stepping movements were the product of mutually inhibitory connections between a pair of flexor and extensor 'half-centres' on each side of the spinal cord.

Some of the preliminary work formed the basis of the thesis that he submitted for the degree of Doctor of Medicine, which was awarded with a gold medal. Graham Brown presented his father with a set of his scientific papers handsomely bound in leather with a gilded title, eliciting a rare expression of praise: 'I'm very proud of Tom. The boy has done exceptionally well.'[6] But at the time, Graham Brown's novel concept, which is the basis of the now widely accepted model of central pattern generators in the control of locomotion, did not gain the recognition its importance deserved. His prolix and impenetrable writing style was a problem. His friend, Professor Cathcart, proffered some trenchant criticism:

> You bury your valuable material in what is generally considered to be a mass of verbiage ... I told you I had great difficulty in following you. Herein lies the trouble; people have not troubled to read your papers, you have never enunciated any point, which can readily be grasped and used, in clear and elementary language.[7]

Furthermore, his comprehensive review of the subject and exposition of his ideas, amounting to 484 pages, was published in German and, somewhat inopportunely, on the brink of and during the First World War. Graham Brown wrote ruefully:

> It seems to me a rich jest that the Germans translated and published my second *Ergebnisse* article since the outbreak of war, while my own people seem to care not a jot. Well, it can't be helped.[8]

But Sherrington had no doubt about his protégé's ability. In a glowing testimonial, he wrote:

> [Graham Brown] stands in the very front rank of our experimental neurologists today ... he combines freshness and independence of view and psychological insight. Earnestness, high aim and unusual power of sustained interest and endeavour are part of his nature ... His oral exposition is lucid and direct, the natural outcome of clear and orderly thinking ... he spares no pains to achieve the best ... and a high minded devotion to the advancement of knowledge are inalienable from Dr Graham Brown's character.[9]

It was not all work, though. 'High-mindedness' was in the air and perhaps it should not be as surprising as it is to find Sherrington's determined and industrious physiologist in a rather different environment. During his three years in Liverpool, Graham Brown was resident in the University Settlement, located in an area of slums close to the docks.[b] The settlement's warden, Frederick Marquis[c], 'a young socialist whose ideas were as challenging as the red tie he habitually wore',[10] had determined to recruit residents of 'sufficient quality, as well as interest' and 'instead of making a sentimental appeal to people to come and "help the poor"' would 'only take into residence people who had taken a good degree, preferably a first,

---

b   The University Settlement movement had been launched in 1883. Its founder, Samuel Barnett, vicar of a Whitechapel parish, exhorted university men to observe poverty at close quarters and develop practical solutions, adjuring 'they must do so in no spirit of patronage or asceticism; they must live normal lives, following their professions, making informal contacts with their neighbours, and their desire must be to know their new friends as fellow humans, hoping so to learn something of the social and economic causes of poverty'. (King, C.M. & H., *The Two Nations:* p. 4)

c   F.J. Marquis (1883–1964), first Earl of Woolton. In an act of apostasy, he resigned from the Fabian Society and, in 1945, joined the Conservative Party, becoming its chairman. Graham Brown was best man at his wedding.

in one of the universities'.[11] Graham Brown was one of the first in this cohort. Marquis described the atmosphere in the settlement at this time:

> [T]he place was pulsating with ideas that were thrashed out – often until the early hours of the morning – among young men with much idealism, but with minds tempered by training to careful and precise thinking.[12]

Few details of Graham Brown's involvement with the settlement's activities survive but it must be assumed that he took an active part and embraced its ideals.

It was also while Graham Brown was in Liverpool that he began to visit the Lake District for camping holidays when 'such time as could be spared from cooking and washing up was spent in hillwalking with much rough scrambling and many delightful bathes'.[13] His first visit seems to have been in August 1911 to Grange, near Keswick. Photographs taken during his holiday at Rosthwaite the following year show his friends doing camp chores, bathing in the nude and in one picture they appear to be in fancy dress, their headgear fashioned out of towels and resembling the headdress of a pharaoh.

In 1913 Sherrington left Liverpool for the chair at Oxford and Graham Brown was offered the newly created post of lecturer in experimental physiology at the Victoria University, Manchester. The stipend was £200, rising to £250 per annum after the first year, which his father considered niggardly but wrote, 'I know quite well that if you get all the other things you ask – particularly independence – you will not let the money question stand in your way.'[14] He was right, it was not the money Graham Brown baulked at. As well as independence in pursuing his research he wanted a minimal commitment to teaching and when asked to give some additional lectures he agreed only reluctantly. This lack of enthusiasm for teaching would lead to difficulties in the future.

Chapter 4
Physiologist at War

In August 1914 Graham Brown, aged thirty-two, was at the height of his powers as a scientist. During the twelve months since taking up the post of lecturer in experimental physiology at Manchester, he had published half a dozen papers based on the work he had done in Liverpool and embarked on a new and productive line of enquiry that developed the work done by Sherrington on the localisation of functions within the brain. The outbreak of war posed a dilemma. At a time when he might have hoped for professional advancement, should he continue his physiological research or volunteer for military service? Initially he resisted the patriotic fervour that resulted in friends scrambling for commissions or enlisting in Pals battalions. His youngest brother, Alex, immediately joined the ranks in the Honourable Artillery Company (he was commissioned into the Royal Engineers in 1915) and Thor was already serving as gunnery officer on HMS *King Edward VII*. In November 1914 he joined the Officer Training Corps and some months later his friend Cathcart, a keen Territorial, wrote, 'Joy it is to find you active in the OTC. It is splendid that you have at last taken to it … Sergeant Graham Brown. Hooray.'[1] At the beginning of 1915, however, he was still unsure what to do and requested advice from his father, who was in no doubt: 'My own view is that you should not delay any longer but try at once to get a commission … The RAMC seems to me the proper place.' He continued with an epistolary white feather:

> My chief reason is that it is your clear duty to do what you can – your bit of the job. A secondary and quite subsidiary reason is that in the years to come I don't think you would like to look back on this time of stress and to feel that you had not done your part. It might some time or another be disagreeable to you to have to admit that

you were not in it (even although your reasons for so doing were sound enough, from some points of view).

Graham Brown asked whether he could have the family sword to which his father replied jingoistically, 'Of course you can have the sword blade if you want but I would not myself care to carry steel made in Germany as that was.'[2]

Graham Brown was commissioned into the RAMC as a temporary lieutenant in March 1915. His mentor, Sherrington, wrote expressing approval of Graham Brown's decision and doubts about his own contribution to the war effort: 'Well, my dear Tom, I feel you are doing the right thing and I know you would not be happy otherwise. I have qualms that I myself am not.' Sherrington's department at Oxford had been all but emptied of staff and students who had enlisted, and he had offered to assist at the hospital where he was put to work in the bacteriology department. He considered this placement 'poor salve to my conscience'. In response to Graham Brown's pessimistic request to guard his posthumous reputation, Sherrington concluded:

> As to looking after your scientific papers I need not say I regard no trust more sacred. Rest satisfied about that. But may the need never arise: goodbye, all success be with you, and au revoir.[3]

Following training in Torquay, Graham Brown was posted to the 77th Field Ambulance near Winchester. Faced with the disconcerting prospect of life as a regimental medical officer, for which his limited practical experience of doctoring hardly fitted him, Graham Brown was determined to do neurological work. He lobbied to be sent to France because he recognised the opportunity afforded by injury from bullet, shrapnel and bayonet to study and localise pathways and functions within the brain and spinal cord. The muzzle velocity of bullets of the period had not reached the excessive levels that could destroy the brain with shock waves. Therefore, wounded soldiers might survive penetrating wounds of the brain with residual impairment of function, such as weakness or paralysis of a limb. Trench warfare led to a disproportionate number of head wounds as a result of soldiers exposing their heads above the parapet. The steel helmet adopted by the British in 1916 afforded some protection from low-velocity shrapnel but its design left the back of the head unprotected, and wounds to the posterior part (occipital lobe) and base of the brain were common.[a] However, general medical and surgical skills, rather than specialist neurology, were mostly required at the front, and the grim reality was that there were 'lots of men … waiting for a chance [to get to the front] – just as there are lots of RAMC officers at the front eager to get away from it'.[4] Instead, Colonel T.R. Elliott, consulting physician to the British Expeditionary Force, proposed an appointment in England and wrote flatteringly to Graham Brown, saying that he was 'the man who more than all the clinicians could help to analyse … these clear cut lesions of the spinal cord'.[5] But with the unfathomable logic of the military, Graham Brown was instead posted, in August 1915, to the Red Cross Military Hospital, Maghull, near Liverpool, the former Moss Side Asylum, which had been commandeered by the War Office to provide 300 beds for the treatment of soldiers with 'nervous shock'.

The shell shock epidemic of 1915 challenged the capacity and expertise of the British Army's medical services. Unsure about the nature of shell shock, the army's medical chief, Sir Alfred Keogh, was persuaded to send to Maghull a 'brilliant band' of academic psychologists and doctors to investigate the phenomenon and devise treatments.[6] Under the direction of the medical superintendent, Dr (temporary Major) R.G. Rows, 'a psychiatrist who had swung from a purely materialistic view of mental disease to the opposed view that mental tangles ought to be straightened by mental means',[7] Maghull became 'a running symposium on the mind, a society in which the interpretation of dreams and the discussion of mental conflicts formed the staple subjects of conversation'.[8] During 1915 there were probably as many opinions about the nature and treatment of shell shock as there were doctors on the staff, but by the end of that year a consensus that shell shock and its manifestations were forms of 'psychoneurosis' had begun to emerge. This provided a basis for strategies of treatment. It was at Maghull that W.H. Rivers[b] began to experiment with the techniques of psychotherapy, which he would later employ at Craiglockhart War Hospital. Its most famous patient, the poet Siegfried Sassoon, later described his experiences there in his fictionalised memoir, *Sherston's Progress*. However,

---

a   The occipital lobe receives visual information from the retina of both eyes via the optic nerve, which it organises into images that the brain can understand. Study of more than 400 cases of occipital gunshot wounds enabled Dr Gordon Holmes to construct a map of the cortical representation of the retina that remains fundamental to current knowledge of the visual pathway.

b   William H. Rivers, FRS (1864–1922), anthropologist, neurologist and psychologist.

in the early days at Maghull the efficacy of this approach was unclear. Graham Brown would later recall Rivers' confession that he 'could not be certain that any of his cases which got well did so because of the treatment'. Maghull Hospital was designated for 'other ranks', who were understandably suspicious of sympathetic questioning by an officer, and feared that their responses would either confirm their insanity and they would be incarcerated in an asylum or, if judged sane, would be sent back to the front or even accused of cowardice.

Graham Brown found himself trapped, surrounded by psychiatrists, psychologists and victims of shell shock who were hardly the colleagues or patients he would have chosen. However, he had a kindred spirit and an ideal collaborator in Roy Stewart, who after graduating with distinction from Edinburgh University Medical School in 1911, five years after Graham Brown, had trained in psychiatry and was deeply interested in neuropathology. Naturally taciturn and seemingly aloof, he was 'a thorough, though slow clinician' with 'infinite capacity for taking pains'.[9,10] Together they embarked on an elaborate clinical study of a patient with sensory impairment following a gunshot wound to the head, and this led to them becoming lifelong friends.

Before the war, Graham Brown and Sherrington had observed considerable recovery of function following experimentally induced lesions in the motor region of a chimpanzee's brain. Graham Brown was interested to explore whether similar recovery occurred following a destructive lesion in the sensory area of the brain and whether recovery might be improved by training. Their subject was a twenty-eight-year-old soldier, who had persistent impairment of sensation over the right arm following a wound of the left cerebral hemisphere. In October 1914, near Ypres, a rifle bullet had hit him; paralysed and unable to speak, he lay in his trench until he was removed on a stretcher under the cover of darkness. Six months later he was transferred to Maghull because although his strength and speech had improved, his recovery had been complicated by the development of delusions and auditory hallucinations. He believed he was Napoleon's grandson and 'a voice told him of his imperial rank'.[11] His delusions slowly resolved and by January 1916 he was able to co-operate intelligently with the study. A series of spots were marked on the front and back of the soldier's fingers and a corresponding set of marks were applied to the hand of a model – Graham Brown or Stewart. The subject passed his hand through a cover so that he was unable to see it. A spot, chosen at random, was stimulated by applying pressure with a fine rod or pricking with a pin and the subject localised the site of stimulation on the hand of the model. To determine the effect of training, a series of three spots on the same finger were stimulated repeatedly and the accuracy of localisation assessed at intervals. Observations were made over thirteen consecutive days and on one day accuracy was assessed seventeen times at half-hourly intervals, an arduous experimental protocol. The experiment generated a huge amount of data that took months to analyse. From the results, they concluded that training could improve sensory localisation long after any spontaneous recovery of function had occurred; this was an early example of the potential for neuro-rehabilitation. But Graham Brown was frustrated at Maghull. Opportunities to study cases of cerebral and spinal cord injury had been limited. He still wanted to do neurological work in France but even Sherrington's influence was insufficient to secure a posting for him there. He continued to pester the authorities with requests to be sent abroad and, in June 1916, he was transferred to the British Salonika Force.

After the failure of the landings at Gallipoli[c] and under pressure from the French to support Serbia, the British had eventually deployed 200,000 men in Macedonia. The first allied troops, a British and a French division, had arrived in the neutral Greek port of Salonika (modern day Thessaloniki) in October 1915. However, this show of support failed to deter the Bulgarians from joining in the Austro-German invasion of Serbia. The Serbian army recoiled, fleeing to Albania and then Corfu, while the Allies withdrew to Salonika for the winter. In May 1916 the reconstituted Serbian army began arriving in Salonika in the build-up to an offensive on the Serbo-Greek frontier. In anticipation of future casualties, the Serbian director of medical services appealed to the British Force to provide 7,000 hospital beds. Three British general hospitals, 36th, 37th and 38th, were despatched from England to be attached to the Serbian army and, on 24 June, Graham Brown and Stewart embarked on the hospital ship *Dover Castle* with the 38th.

---

c   Graham Brown's youngest brother, Alex, was amongst the last of the troops to be evacuated from Gallipoli and was responsible for devising automatic methods of firing to deceive the Turks that the trenches were still occupied. In addition to utilising 'clockwork' rifles 'worked by water dripping from one tin into another attached to the trigger', he 'invented a rough device which gave a very good imitation of rifle fire. It ... consisted of a box in which were two lighted candles through which fine string was threaded every quarter inch in height. To the string, cartridges in clips were attached. As each string was burnt through the cartridges went down a slide into a brazier ... by this means the sound of continuous intermittent firing was got.' (11/2/16; Imperial War Museum docs 15427)

Three weeks earlier Graham Brown's brother Thor, now first lieutenant and gunnery officer on HMS *Royal Oak*, had been in action at the Battle of Jutland, the biggest concentrated naval battle in history involving 250 ships, which he attempted to describe in a letter to his wife. Written in the immediate aftermath, it neatly illustrates the limitations of personal testimony of battle. 'I would not have missed it for worlds,' he wrote:

> Imagine bang bang bang, lurid flashes, quantities of smoke and many splashes and ... the occasional heavy concussion of our own guns going off – and you have it.[12]

Graham Brown's voyage to and through the Mediterranean was uneventful, despite the ship being lit up 'like a fairy palace' and the lurking threat of attack by enemy submarines. His diary contains some purple passages describing sunsets and famous landmarks; passing Cape St Vincent, he was moved to recall Robert Browning's lines from *Home-Thoughts, from the Sea*:

> Nobly, nobly Cape Saint Vincent to the North-West died away;
> Sunset ran, one glorious blood-red, reeking into Cadiz Bay;
> Bluish 'mid the burning water, full in face Trafalgar lay;
> In the dimmest North-East distance dawned Gibraltar grand and gray

More prosaically, Graham Brown thought the southern Pillar of Hercules might offer some good climbing and the islands of the Cyclades were 'very like those of the west coast of Scotland', the only difference being 'the absence of heather and the presence of olive trees'.

He arrived in Salonika on 4 July. The red roofs and white minarets viewed from the sea were 'most picturesque' and, away to the south-west, Mount Olympus was visible, 'splendid and big, with a snowcap on each summit'. *The Balkan News*, a single sheet of paper priced at two pence, carried news of the opening day of the Battle of the Somme, reporting with misplaced optimism that it 'goes well for France and England'. Following disembark-ation, the 38th General Hospital took up its position close to Mikra Bay, a few miles south-east of Salonika. The tented hospital was erected in an area used previously as horse lines and smelt strongly of ammonia. Graham Brown's tent was 'small and dirty' and had been used at Gallipoli but apparently never 'opened, cleaned or aired since'. It was insufferably hot:

107.8° Fahrenheit measured with a clinical thermometer suspended from a thread inside his tent. The occupant of the neighbouring tent was 'a great infliction, for he talks incessantly in a loud voice'. And the flies were 'awful'. At night, searchlights probed the sky for enemy Zeppelins. For six weeks there was little work to do. Graham Brown occupied himself drafting scientific papers and exploring Salonika and its surroundings with Stewart, his almost constant companion. They relaxed by bathing in the sea.

Salonika's streets were 'ramshackle'. The buildings, Roman, Byzantine and Turkish, were 'extraordinarily picturesque and interesting', as were the smells. The town's churches reawakened Graham Brown's interest in architecture and he detailed their features in his diary, noting the 'fine mosaics ... and faded frescoes' that decorated them. Succumbing to the gullibility of tourists, he was lured into curio shops where he was tempted into purchasing some Greek coins; in one he saw what he believed to be a Persian gold coin dating from the reign of Darius but did not have enough money to buy it. He worried that he had missed a bargain: 'thought a good deal about the Daric ... Feel I must buy it. If it is a fake it is a very good copy.' He returned to the shop but again baulked at the price and it required Stewart's skills at haggling to secure for him 'the Daric and a silver Greek coin for 100 drachmae'. A 'splendid lunch' could be obtained at the Hotel de Rom, as well as beer, cakes and ices at Floca's café. For entertainment there was cabaret featuring 'the famous belly dance', which Graham Brown observed with a mixture of amazement and prudery:

> A woman with a most magnificent figure did this and the movements of the pelvis back and abdomen are most extraordinary. I would not have believed it possible. The whole is rhythmic with the music and the abdominal muscles contract in such a manner as to move the anterior wall irregularly. The whole effect – while of great interest – was to me most horrible and quite devoid of that which it is supposed to have.

They climbed Mount Kotos[d] which was nine miles of rough walking from their camp and about 1,000 metres of ascent. Setting out in the predawn cool, they reached the summit four hours later:

---

d   Appears as Mount Chortiatis (1,219 metres) on modern maps.

The most striking thing about the summit is its aromatic smells ...
It smells balmy and almost exactly like the smell of an Italian church.
The coolness of the wind and the shade of the trees made it feel
like one.

They lay down to doze and 'all the time we could hear the slow firing of
heavy guns – but it sounded languid like the rest of life here – as if the day
was too drowsy for serious work'.

At the end of July he experienced the first of recurrent bouts of diarrhoea.
Despite feeling unwell he managed to work but was clearly dispirited:

Started *General Physiology of Nervous System* ... I wonder if it will
come to anything or if I shall live to finish it. I really do not think that
I would mind very much if I knew I should die here. But I want to
finish my work first.

And then, a few weeks later, on learning that he was to have general medical
duties, he vented his disappointment and frustration in his diary:

So goodbye to all ideas of neurology ... It makes me sick ... to feel
that I can't get the only work where I could be of any value. Any
freshly qualified man could do the work I am set to a hundred times
better ... yet nobody at all is doing the work which I want to do. It is
awful to have lived your life with one aim and to find all you have
done counts for nothing.

His first patients arrived at the end of August:

We are full up and the conditions are awful. There are nothing but
dysentery cases in our wards ... and they lie about on the floor and
dirty everything. Thousands of flies. Awful filth.

To add to his misery his colleagues were falling ill, leaving Graham Brown in
charge of eighty-four patients, but he 'managed to get the ward ship-shape
and fairly clean at last'. Necessary as this work was, Graham Brown wanted
a transfer and called on Lieutenant Colonel Purves-Stewart, consulting

physician to the British Salonika Force, to make his case. Purves-Stewart dissembled:

> He told me that neurological work was out of the question for me and that he himself scarcely saw one case a week (I judged this to be a lie). He wished he could have the benefit of my advice, etc, etc, etc, but as I was attached to the Serbian army he was not even allowed to take me to see a case. I got the impression that he could get me work if he liked but, for some reason or other, did not like. The whole interview was beastly for I felt that he was trying his hardest to placate me (in an oily sort of way) while keeping me out of his preserves.

Graham Brown's suspicions were further aroused when he attended a meeting of the Salonika Medical Society and discovered that 'the very cases I wish so much to examine are still coming in'. These suspicions were confirmed by the behaviour of Purves-Stewart who attempted to avoid eye contact by deliberately dropping his cane:

> I can only infer that the explanation of his conduct is that he does not wish me to see the cerebral cases – wishes to corner them for himself probably. Disgusting.

Graham Brown returned disconsolately to the wards and the mundane medical tasks of sanitary inspections, inoculations and examining the men for scabies.

During August, the Allies halted the Bulgarian advance and then went on the offensive; by the end of November they had made substantial territorial gains but, with growing casualties and the onset of winter, the offensive was closed down. Nevertheless, the British continued to mount a number of raids and on 30 November Graham Brown was ordered to proceed to the front that night and report to the 80th Field Ambulance which was situated about six miles behind the British front line in the Doiran sector. He travelled overnight by ambulance train with stretchers serving as beds in converted cattle trucks; all were filthy. The next morning, after little sleep, he looked out through the central door, which had been opened because of the smell, to see 'a bleak and desolate country'. From the railhead he went on horseback for several miles across the plain, which reminded him of Rannoch Moor; it was 'sopping wet'. On arrival, there was some firing close by. Graham Brown felt elated: 'It is like a picnic – or camping out in peacetime. There seems to be a spirit of adventure and manliness about.'

The next day he was sent further forward as temporary relief for the medical officer of 114th Brigade Field Artillery, positioned just three miles from the front. Out of curiosity and bravado, he accepted an invitation to go up to the front-line trenches. He borrowed a steel helmet and set out, reaching the trenches without incident, and went on to an observation post from where he had a 'very fine view of the country': steep ridges, deep ravines and hills dominated by one almost 600 metres high, known to the British as the Devil's Eye, from where the enemy maintained a constant watch. Graham Brown could plainly see the enemy's trenches and wire, and French corpses lying in no man's land being picked over by magpies. On his way back, he came under enemy artillery fire, two 'pip-squeaks' bursting less than fifty feet away. Shelling continued as he retired, tripping over wire and stumbling over shell holes. He recalled: 'I did not feel very uncomfortable tho' I wished to be out of it' and 'I made myself think of the central nervous system and walked quickly on.' On reaching the comparative safety of 'A' battery, he concluded that it had been 'one of the most interesting and exciting days I have ever spent'. After a brief spell as relief medical officer to 10th Battalion Black Watch, Graham Brown rejoined 80th Field Ambulance.

For most of December, a 'jolly' or 'stunt' had been brewing. The plan required an initial bombardment of the Bulgarian position, to break the barbed wire, followed by an attack by the British infantry, who were to blow up the remaining enemy defences before retiring. After repeated postponements the attack was eventually launched on 23 December. Graham Brown, with Stewart, went forward to witness it: 'I had a strange sense of excitement and enjoyment.' The next morning the wounded began to drift in. The injuries were generally slight and had been caused mainly by British shrapnel; the infantry had not properly synchronised their watches with the artillery and consequently advanced four minutes too soon, walking into their own barrage.

Following this raid, both the activity at the front and the work of the field ambulance slackened. Graham Brown commenced a study of shell shock, examining troops for 'nervousness' before and after occupying a 'hot trench', but his work attracted the disapproval of the army authorities whose view was that medical officers should concentrate on managing the sick and wounded rather than 'scientific investigation'. In particular, 'they did not look with favour on our examination of combatants for "nervous instability" [because] they thought it might give rise to malingering'.

At the beginning of February 1917, Graham Brown's temporary attachment to the field ambulance ended and he returned to the 38th General Hospital. Graham Brown and Stewart continued to press for the opportunity to look after neurological cases and lobbied General Whitehead, director of medical services, who agreed to their transfer to 36th and 37th General Hospitals serving the Royal Serbian Army, which was about to launch an attack. Inevitably there would be casualties, amongst whom there might be suitable cases for study. The hospitals were situated at Vertekop, about forty miles west of Salonika, on the road to Monastir, much closer to the enemy lines and 'constantly subject to bombing by enemy aircraft'. A few days before Graham Brown arrived at the 36th, two nurses had been killed in a raid and within a fortnight he was under aerial bombardment:

> I went to my own ward just as the alarm sounded and the first bombs
> began to fall. I got my cases out and those who could not be moved,
> down on to the floor and covered with mattresses … I must say that
> it was rather nervous work.

He took shelter in his dugout. Two or three bombs fell less than a hundred yards away: 'One was an enormous explosion and shook everything. I could feel the walls of the trench quiver and come together.'

In the early autumn of 1917, more than twelve months since arriving in Macedonia, Graham Brown's persistence at last resulted in a posting to a specialised neurological department established within the 48th General Hospital at Eurendjik, a few miles east of Salonika. Eventually the unit comprised eight officers and nineteen other ranks and in November 1918, with the war over, it was transferred to 43rd General Hospital with Graham Brown as officer in command. On Christmas Day he was promoted to acting major. In partnership with Stewart, he meticulously studied cases of spinal-cord injury and made a novel observation concerning changes in cutaneous sensation, which they termed 'heteraesthesia'.[e] They gathered data on the pattern of reflexes and, in a grim parallel with his experimental work on the spinal cat, Graham Brown observed rhythmic movements of the legs of a soldier whose spinal cord had been transected by a bayonet. Graham Brown also undertook a systematic study of over 200 cases of shell shock admitted to the neurological department. His approach was physiological rather than psychological. He looked for signs of an overactive thyroid gland; staring eyes – vividly recorded in the iconic photographs of shell-shocked soldiers – tremor and anxiety are features of hyperthyroidism. He recorded the state of the tendon reflexes and the results of tests of coordination and examined samples of the fluid that surrounds the brain and spinal cord. He classified forty-one per cent as suffering from 'concussion', a much larger proportion than the estimates of five to ten per cent reported by neurologists in other theatres of war. Graham Brown suggested that compared to the mud of Flanders and France, the ravines and rocky terrain of Macedonia favoured the development of blast injury.

In the spring of 1919 Graham Brown returned to England on leave. He was desperate to leave the army. He felt that the delay in being demobilised was harming his career prospects and his health was poor. Whilst recuperating in Cornwall, he applied for the chair of physiology at Bristol University. Sherrington, of course, did what he could behind the scenes and his Scottish chiefs gave their support. However, Professor Paton suspected that 'it is a chair that will be worked from London'.[13] Paton was right, and Graham Brown was not even invited for interview.[f]

In July 1919 he was posted in Captain's rank to Ashurst War Hospital, formerly the Oxford County Asylum, to manage soldiers with shell shock. At last, in November 1919, he was demobilised, categorised C3, which on re-enlistment would have meant that he was fit only for sedentary work in garrisons at home, and returned to his pre-war post in Manchester.

—❦

---

e   Their first case was an RAF observer who, while flying over enemy lines, had a miraculous escape from death when a live shell passed across his back tearing his jacket and causing extensive bruising but without breaking the skin.

f   Dr G.A. Buckmaster, the assistant professor of physiology at University College London was appointed. Given he was aged sixty, the appointment would appear to have been in recognition of long service, and competition from an energetic researcher, twenty years his junior, might have been awkward for the electors.

Torn between his sense of duty and wish to continue with his research, Graham Brown had been a reluctant volunteer for military service and characteristically determined to go to war on his own terms. It had, though, been a frustrating experience. Rightly, he had realised that the carnage on the Western Front afforded extraordinary opportunities for the study of cerebral and spinal cord injuries and he wanted to go to France. As well as enlisting Sherrington's backing he had canvassed for the support of others who might exert influence on his behalf, sending them bundles of reprints of his scientific papers as supporting evidence, but to no avail. Graham Brown may have run up against the vested interests of the London-based neurologists who provided much of the expert advice to the army. His father certainly thought so: 'That form of jealousy is quite characteristic of the London men', and he was not alone in suspecting that professional rivalry, with a view to enhancing future civilian private practice, was a factor in appointments.[g,14] Graham Brown's transfer to the British Salonika Force may have been to meet the exigencies of the medical services or was possibly the response of the military authorities exasperated by his importuning.

The nature of the war in Macedonia was very different to that waged in France. Morbidity and mortality from disease was vastly greater than that resulting from battle; the ratio of non-battle to battle casualties amongst the British Salonika Force was 20:1 and it was almost inevitable that Graham Brown had been initially placed in charge of a ward full of patients with dysentery. His eventual posting to the 48th General Hospital and neurological work had been the result of dogged persistence on his part; his energy and industry in difficult circumstances had been remarkable. But his studies on sensation were recondite and the methods complex and laborious; the results proved to be of little practical value and went largely unrecognised, partly due to his prolix writing style remaining unrestrained. His article describing the study on training and sensory localisation ran to over a hundred pages.

It was, in fact, his observations on shell shock that received most attention. Since the first cases of shell shock arrived in England from France at the end of 1914, there had been considerable public interest in the condition.

---

g   Sidelined in favour of his former colleague, Gordon Holmes, C.S. Myers, consultant psychologist to the army, who had played a key role in establishing services for victims of shell shock, wrote bitterly in his memoir, 'Colonel Holmes had previously told me that functional "nervous" disorders always formed a very large part of a civilian neurologist's practice. Naturally, therefore, he was little disposed to relinquish in army life what was so important a source of income in time of peace. Although he confessed that (like most "pure" neurologists) he took little interest in such cases.'

As the war dragged on the possibility that some soldiers who had been executed for cowardice may have been suffering from shell shock caused disquiet, leading to questions being raised in parliament. Two years after the Armistice 65,000 ex-servicemen were receiving pensions for war neuroses, 9,000 of whom were still receiving hospital treatment, placing a significant financial burden on the government. It was against this background of public and governmental concern that Lord Southborough proposed the committee of enquiry into shell shock, to which he was appointed chairman in 1920. The committee's remit was to ascertain the facts 'as to its origin, nature and remedial treatment' and to consider ways to prevent shell shock.[15] Graham Brown was one of fifty-nine witnesses, army staff officers, field commanders, regimental medical officers, neurologists and psychologists, who were interviewed by the committee. Their evidence was long on anecdote and opinion but short on facts and it is noteworthy that the only hard data published in the report were Graham Brown's systematic observations made in Salonika.

When the first cases of shell shock presented there had been doubt about its causation; in July 1915 the professor of medicine at Oxford wrote to a colleague: 'I cannot imagine what has got into the central nervous system of the men ... Hysterical dumbness, deafness, blindness, anaesthesia galore.'[16] However, twelve months later the view that it was principally the result of psychological trauma rather than brain injury due to concussion had been widely accepted, so it is surprising that the committee decided to re-examine the question. Sandwiched between the testimony of a major-general who referred back to his experience following defeat at the Battle of Maiwand in 1880, during the Second Afghan War, and that of Rivers who opined that shell shock was the result of an 'emotional wound', Graham Brown's evidence emphasised the debilitating role of physical illness, such as malaria, in predisposing a soldier to the development of shell shock. However, he agreed that purely psychological elements played a role and highlighted the power of suggestion in initiating and perpetuating symptoms, remarking that even a routine neurological examination could have a deleterious effect unless care was taken to avoid expressing surprise or undue interest in any abnormal findings.

Almost ten years after the end of the war he wrote an editorial calling for a critical review of the various treatments employed in managing shell shock, pointing out that sufficient time had elapsed to allow their long-term efficacy to be judged, and emphasised the importance of such a review, in case 'God forbid – we should again be faced with the problem'.[17] His call went largely unheeded.

At the end of the war, many of the experts in neurology and psychology who had given evidence to the Southborough committee were decorated and advanced to prestigious positions in universities and hospitals. Graham Brown received no such recognition for his service and he engaged in a protracted, and ultimately unsuccessful, dispute with the ministry about the value of his war pension, which he thought mean and unfair. He considered that 'the volunteer members of the profession ... did the whole of the actual medical and surgical work for the army' and from 1915 onwards had borne 'almost the whole of the personal risk'. Furthermore, promotion had been given rarely and when it had, younger men were favoured over the heads of their seniors in age and experience. In short, 'neither their professional ability nor the risks they ran received adequate recognition'.[18] The only official thanks that Graham Brown received arrived fifteen years after the end of the war in a brief letter from the curator and secretary of the Imperial War Museum, written on behalf of the director:

> Dear Sir,
> Lord Conway has handed to me your letter of the 20th April and has asked me to thank you for it and for the paper enclosed. As a matter of fact we had no example of this.
> Yours Truly

One can imagine Graham Brown enjoying a moment of mordant satisfaction as he annotated the letter: 'the paper referred to above was a specimen of the toilet paper which was issued to the British Salonika Force'.[19]

Chapter 5
Professor

Graham Brown's appointment to the chair of physiology at Cardiff in 1920 was greeted with relief by his father, who had suffered 'a good deal of anxiety' about his son's future, and congratulations from the rest of his family and supporters. Cathcart wrote with hortatory enthusiasm:

> You have got now to train good men for the future, drive into them some of that parching thirst for knowledge … It is a job well worth doing – your life is limited but you may kindle several good torches. Go ahead and prosper.

In a postscript he added that his wife had observed, 'now he can afford to get married' and, reflecting on his own connubial bliss, urged Graham Brown: 'Don't leave it off for too long.'[1] Graham Brown would disappoint Cathcart on both counts, educational and marital – he would remain a confirmed bachelor – and for the first time, we gain sight of the Graham Brown whose whole life would be mired in controversy.

The Department of Physiology had been established in 1893 as part of University College, Cardiff and as a first step in the development of a medical school in Wales. However, the First World War and a Royal Commission on university education in Wales delayed matters considerably. When the medical school opened in October 1921 there were several important issues, previously glossed over for expedience, which remained unresolved.[a] The Royal Commission's recommendation that the National School of Medicine should become an independent constituent college of the University of Wales had been opposed by University College, Cardiff, whose council

---

a   At the official opening, the Prince of Wales, the future King Edward VIII and chancellor of the university, passed through an arch of thigh bones held aloft by medical students and was photographed with the professor of anatomy and Graham Brown. According to his long-serving chief laboratory technician, Graham Brown subsequently and inexplicably had the professor of anatomy inked out and the photograph retaken.

considered it did not duly recognise the college's primacy and large financial stake in the foundation of the medical school and had mounted a vigorous campaign of opposition. In 1922 Whitehall re-opened the question of separation, ushering in a period of turmoil:

> [F]or nearly five years the future of the Welsh National School of Medicine was the subject of sharp controversy. This controversy involved the University of Wales, the University College of South Wales and Monmouthshire, Whitehall, the medical press and anyone else professing an interest in the future of medical education in Wales.[2]

Graham Brown, as professor of physiology and later dean of the faculty of medicine, was in the thick of it, gaining a reputation for being 'a formidable opponent' who 'did not always conceal his pleasure in the fight and victory'.[3]

There is nothing so dull as the forgotten departmental battles of the past and yet nothing at the same time quite so revealing of Graham Brown's character. As the pressure on University College to accept an independent medical school increased, its resolve to maintain control of the pre-clinical departments stiffened, placing Graham Brown at loggerheads with the college. The University of Wales sought expert opinion to support its view that the departments of anatomy and physiology should be incorporated within the new, independent medical school. On receiving the contradictory advice, the pro-chancellor concluded ruefully that the wrong men had been asked and appointed a different panel to deliver the right answer. However, in October 1927, the university authorities finally decided and agreed that the departments of anatomy and physiology would remain within the Cardiff College. Graham Brown remained stubbornly opposed to the arrangement and, undeterred by the waning enthusiasm for the struggle, carried on the campaign alone, even petitioning the Privy Council, but to no avail.

The affair irretrievably soured his relations with University College. When, in 1947, his reaching the retirement age of sixty-five prompted the college to invite his resignation, he accused it of acting *ultra vires* and argued in a style reminiscent of Sir Humphrey Appleby, that:

> [T]he power to remove given to the College by Statute 77 is limited
> by the exception in Article VII.4 of the Supplemental Charter of the
> College so far as appointments to the Departments of Anatomy and
> Physiology are concerned. If that is so the provision of Statute 77 as
> to the termination of my appointment at the age of 65 is also limited
> in the same way. My view therefore is that the College has no power
> to remove me or declare the Chair vacant.[4]

The university concluded wearily: 'It seems hardly possible that he
[Graham Brown] can have reached the conclusion that there is nowhere
in the University any executive authority to terminate his appointment.'[5]
Almost forty years later, recollections of Graham Brown's battle to retain
his post could still provoke 'quizzical smiles and shudders'.[6]

Whilst the wrangling over the constitution of the new medical school
continued, relations between University College and the Cardiff Royal
Infirmary were deteriorating. The infirmary was a traditional voluntary
hospital staffed by a closed hierarchy of honorary physicians and surgeons
and their assistants, whose advancement depended on death or retirement.
They received no remuneration for their hospital work, relying on private
practice for their income, and their sense of ownership of the hospital was
strong. Faced with the prospect of giving up control of some of their beds
to clinical professors appointed by the university, and the threat to their
incomes from additional clinicians, they required careful handling. However, in the rush to open the clinical school, University College had upset
the hospital staff and their discontent was the undercurrent to the row
that erupted between Graham Brown, dean of the faculty of medicine since
1922, and W. Mitchell Stevens, the infirmary's senior physician.

In May 1925 Stevens resigned his university appointment of clinical
teacher and publicly vented his frustration with University College,
Cardiff, the faculty of medicine and the professors of medicine and surgery
in a letter to the regional newspaper, *The Western Mail*. University College
responded by instigating an inquiry at which Stevens reiterated his griev-
ances and, getting personal, accused Graham Brown of neglecting his
duties, both as teacher and administrator:

> I don't think he has done any teaching for over eighteen months
> or so. He does very little work as dean. That is left to his clerk. Also I

know that he cannot be lecturing when I meet him in Queen Street during an hour at which, according to the timetable, he should be lecturing.[7]

He added damningly that when he asked his students about their knowledge of physiology they would 'simply howl with laughter' and said he had to teach them the elementary principles of physiology himself.

These allegations caused the senate to set up a committee to ascertain whether there were grounds for Graham Brown's dismissal. Graham Brown undoubtedly lacked enthusiasm for teaching. On his appointment as lecturer at Manchester he had cavilled about his teaching commitments. During conversations concerning his application for the chair at Bristol, he had been reported as saying openly that he 'disliked and despised teaching' and 'thought it a waste of time'.[8] Many years later, Professor Brocklehurst, physiologist and one-time climbing companion, recalled being told that Graham Brown had only accepted the chair at Cardiff 'on condition that he did no teaching'.[9] However, the question was: had Graham Brown neglected his duties? He had certainly delegated delivery of the great majority of lectures, practical classes and tutorials to his staff, but his principal responsibility was to ensure there was an effective and appropriate course of instruction in place, rather than specifically to teach it himself. The findings of the inquiry were inconclusive. Nevertheless, Graham Brown prudently relinquished the position of dean twelve months before his term expired.

Although enmired in university politics, Graham Brown still had a department to run. During his tenure he recruited a number of able scientists whose diverse research he enabled without direction or interference, and at least four progressed to professorial chairs. He grumbled that funding was inadequate: he and his staff had been obliged to purchase out of their own pockets apparatus, books and chairs; the technical staff had to make the cupboards, and equipment had been obtained on loan. Committees bored him and he would while away a meeting by composing doggerel lampooning his colleagues, which he scrawled on the back of the agenda.[b] He showed little interest in his students. 'The great man was too interested in monkeys

---

b   e.g. concerning Principal Trow: 'a flood   enow
                                      of blood   of Trow
                                      a spate   O well
                                      of hate   O hell'
                                      a ruck
                                      of muck

to have time for students,[10] declared one disgruntled student, and the professor had 'an unfortunate manner of attempting to treat one as a child'[11] complained another. Later generations of students were well aware of his priorities. A cartoon, published in their magazine *The Leech* and entitled 'Brown(ian) Movement', shows him escaping from the department in his climbing kit.

In 1927 Graham Brown was elected a Fellow of the Royal Society on the strength of his pre-war research. This distinction would surely have been a source of satisfaction to his exacting father but he had died two years before. Graham Brown had angled for election some years earlier when Sherrington had warned of the intense competition and advised on tactics, in particular the timing of his nomination because:

> [I]t is the 'third reading' which is the most propitious one on general grounds. If not arranged to have a good chance then a name is likely to lapse into backwater ... The thing to do now is ... to see what the waiting list now is like and to forecast whether this year or next is better.[12]

Graham Brown was proposed by Sir E. Sharpey-Schafer[c], professor of physiology at Edinburgh, and supported by a solidly Scottish faction that included the professors of pathology and pharmacology at Edinburgh and the professors of anatomy, physiology and pathology at Glasgow. Sherrington's name appears last in the list of nine supporters but, as the immediate past-president of the society, his influence was probably crucial. Some years later, Graham Brown would return the favour by marshalling support for Sherrington's nomination for the Nobel Prize that was awarded to him in 1932.

In spite of Graham Brown's election to the Royal Society, the truth was that his research had flagged. Although he published more articles between 1920 and 1927 than all his other Cardiff colleagues put together, half were a miscellany of case reports, commentaries and reviews and the remaining papers reported experiments consolidating his earlier work. In 1930 he submitted a series of four papers for publication in the *Proceedings of the Royal Society*. The editor, Henry Dale, a future Nobel laureate,

---

c   Schäfer had changed his name in 1918.

'did not feel at all convinced' that Graham Brown 'had found a profitable line of enquiry, or the best method of putting it forward', and three referees, 'men of wide and philosophical outlook in biology', agreed that the work did not merit publication.[13] This judgement of his peers must have been disheartening and thereafter his scientific publications dwindled and ceased.

In the late 1930s he returned to the problem of the control of locomotion. He devised an ingenious tilting treadmill[d] and, recalling Eadweard Muybridge's pioneering use of photography to settle the question of whether a galloping horse had all four hooves off the ground, he filmed his experiments.[e] He demonstrated that a cat in which the neural connections had been severed at the level of the midbrain was still able to perform coordinated movements by adjusting its gait (walking, trotting or galloping) according to the angle and speed of the treadmill. The implication of these observations was that the neuronal circuitry responsible for the coordination of locomotion was localised in a region of the midbrain below the level of transection and could function independently of signals from higher centres. However, as he did not publish any of his observations, Graham Brown's novel finding went unrecognised for twenty years. Subsequent research has revealed that a defined locomotor region is present in the midbrain of all vertebrates.

Graham Brown's professorial career did not fulfil its promise. The war years had been a frustrating prelude. The wrangling within the university that occupied so much of the early years of his tenure was a distraction from research and took its toll. It also brought out a display of obstinacy and implacability on his part that embittered relations within the university. However, if his ideas and the momentum of his research had faltered, something else had taken their place. From 1926 rock climbing and mountaineering ceased to be just a holiday pastime and became the obsession that during the 1930s would demand the majority of his focus and time.

---

d   The apparatus was assembled in his department's workshop, of which Graham Brown was justifiably proud. Its reputation for precision work was such that engine parts for Beaufighter bombers were manufactured there.

e   Born Edward Muggeridge in 1830, he died in 1904. Originally a bookseller, he took up professional photography and his pictures of Yosemite Valley made him famous. In 1874 he shot and killed his wife's lover, but was acquitted in a jury trial on the grounds of justifiable homicide.

Chapter 6
A New Direction

Graham Brown tells us that it was chance that led him into the mountains and in a preliminary draft of his climbing autobiography, *Brenva*, counselled the reader to 'distrust the stories of those who claim that mountains became their only ambition at an early age in life – when they first saw a hillock over the edge of the perambulator, or what not'.[1] His youthful interests certainly gave no hint of this later passion. As an adolescent and young man he fished; golfed, his father grudgingly paying the green fees; played fives and swam competitively for the university. However, in his twenties these pastimes had palled:

> Golf had soon lost its hold as a holiday occupation, and had sunk to the level of a Saturday's amusement. Fives remained what it has always been, one of the best ways of spending a vigorous hour. Fishing eventually lost its pride of place. Night poaching on Gladsmuir had been an exciting sport in more ways than one, and not without its anxieties; but that was a brief and disreputable phase.[2]

Years later he would nostalgically recall some factors which had 'turned his fancy as a boy to mountains': scrambling on the sea cliffs at Elie; reading G.M. Finn's 1892 novel *The Crystal Hunters*, which *The Spectator*'s reviewer considered 'the best Alpine book for boys we have seen yet'; and discovering in *Strand Magazine* an account of Mlle d'Angeville's ascent of Mont Blanc in 1838.[a,3] On reading that when she had reached the summit Mlle d'Angeville had insisted on being lifted up by her guides in order to say afterwards that she had been higher than Mont Blanc, Graham Brown went

---

a   Henriette d'Angeville (1794–1871) was the second woman to climb Mont Blanc. On the ascent she wore trousers in a loud check, a long coat, a huge feathered beret and a long black boa. According to the historian Claire Engel, d'Angeville displayed 'a virile courage' and 'hysterical tendencies'.

with his brothers to the top of Arthur's Seat where he persuaded them to raise him up on to their shoulders. When he boasted to his father that he had been higher than Arthur's Seat in Edinburgh he had – in line with his father's usual caustic attitude – been told off for being silly.

At Easter 1914 Graham Brown was camping in the Lake District at Mosedale, not far from the crags on Pillar, Gable and Scafell, the favoured haunts of rock climbers of the period. A chance meeting with Arnold Boyd resulted in a visit to Pillar Rock where they climbed *Slab & Notch*, nowadays used as the way down, and a few days later *Needle Ridge* and *Kern Knotts Chimney* on Gable.[b] At Whitsun he climbed some of the more difficult routes on the Napes and Scafell, including the intimidating *Keswick Brothers' Climb*. He was in the party that explored and made the first ascent of *Peregrine Gully* on Cam Spout Crag in Eskdale, a traditional gully climb involving loose rock, vegetation and surmounting a series of jammed boulders blocking the way, either by squirming behind, climbing over them with the aid of a shoulder or bypassing them by climbing the flanking wall. During these ten days he underwent a conversion. When, while a student in Strasbourg, he had first sampled rock climbing on the cliffs of the Karlsruher Grat in the Black Forest it had not appealed, and when, a few years later, he and his companions had borrowed a rope and again tried some climbing in the Lake District, he had concluded that it was 'mere gymnastics'. Now he was hooked. But two months later the First World War erupted and it was not until Easter 1920 that Graham Brown returned to rock climbing and the Lake District.

The war had depleted his small circle of climbing companions; of the eight with whom he had shared a rope before the war, two had been killed in action. Climbers were few in number and the crags uncrowded. The Lake District was quiet and secluded; motorcars were rare. Graham Brown's journey from Cardiff involved a train to Windermere; a bus to Chapel Stile, where he stayed the night, and a long walk up Langdale the following day, before heading over Esk Hause to Sty Head and finally down to Wasdale Head. He stayed at the Wastwater Hotel, an establishment redolent with history; photographs of rock-climbing pioneers covered the walls of the dining room; leather boots reeking of dubbin littered the hallway.[c] Climbing in the twenties was not strikingly different from the earliest days of the

---

b   A.W. Boyd (1885–1959), ornithologist and naturalist. The eponymous crack on Stanage Edge is named after him.

c   Full board: 12s/day. His bar bill for eight days at Easter 1926 was: eleven pints of beer: 7s 4d; two pints of shandy: 1s 8d; cider: 1s 3d and a gin and ginger beer: 2s.

sport at the end of the nineteenth century; clothes, equipment and techniques had not developed dramatically. Climbers wore discarded suits, old jackets and corduroy breeches and, when most men would have no more been seen bare-headed than they would without trousers, a woollen balaclava was a popular form of headgear. Nailed leather boots were the usual footwear, but for harder climbs plimsolls, known as 'rubbers' bought a size too small to give a tighter fit, were sometimes worn. Ropes were made of manilla hemp, which when wet became very heavy and almost unmanageable. Following an appalling accident on Scafell in 1903 when a falling leader dragged his three companions after him, the rope merely serving as a fatal bond, the use of the rope had been developed to provide rudimentary security; the second man attached himself to the rock and ran the rope over his shoulder whilst the leader advanced, looping the rope over flakes or spikes to add slender protection. Safe climbing was predicated on the dictum that the leader never falls. Graham Brown was usually second on the rope for he was not a naturally talented rock climber, achieving 'high competence' rather than displaying 'executant brilliance'.[4]

During a fortnight's holiday in August 1922 at Wasdale, Graham Brown met and climbed with Cecil Wood and Walter Petty. Wood and Petty were founder members of the Gritstone Club which had been formed a few months earlier by a group of friends from Bradford. These men were mainly professionals in the wool industry with the odd businessman, banker and lawyer. Graham Brown was invited to join their club. After a day's climbing and a good dinner, members enthusiastically discarded their middle class and, in some cases middle-aged, respectability. Graham Brown entered into the spirit:

> Brown, like the wise physician he is ... prescribed a flowing bowl
> of rum punch [and] we set to work at once with the praiseworthy
> object of lifting the roof.[5]

Singing was followed by horseplay. Climbing routes were rigged inside and outside the hotel, with balustrades used as belays, and they played at 'fox hunting'; one of the younger members served as the fox and the remainder formed the pack. There was also 'cork grabbing', an enigmatic and boisterous activity. What it entailed exactly has not been recorded but their antics resulted in the club being banned from holding its annual dinner at the

Flying Horseshoe in Clapham, North Yorkshire. Graham Brown was a popular member of the club, described as 'funny' and 'charming'; George Basterfield summed him up as 'a man possessed with the body of a respectable person and the soul of a vagabond'.[d,6]

Over the next three years Graham Brown regularly attended the club's meets in the Lake District at the traditional holiday periods of Christmas and New Year, Easter and Whitsun. Leslie Letts, almost twenty years his junior and a scion of the family of diary manufacturers, was a frequent companion and in 1924 would introduce him to the Alps. Inviting Graham Brown to stay at his family's home, Letts teased:

> My dear Tim, ... pack your patent expanding suitcase, gather together your golf-clubs not forgetting your best pair of silk pyjamas and your toothbrush. Also bring plenty of cash so that I may win it all from you at Bridge ... P.S. We usually dress Sat. evenings, so bring dinner jacket if possible.[e,7]

At Easter 1925 Graham Brown embarked on an exploration of Boat Howe Crag, situated on the northern flank of Kirkfell overlooking upper Ennerdale. He had noticed the crag on one of his pre-war walking tours and now wondered if it would provide good climbing. He persuaded Basterfield, who was climbing at the highest standard of the day, to join him. Snow still filled the gullies and the rock was wet but with the disregard for suboptimal conditions typical of the period, they made two new routes. Graham Brown was overjoyed. He wrote effusively to Letts and urged secrecy:

> G[eorge] B[asterfield] and I went round Kirkfell on Sunday for that crag which I thought I saw from Ennerdale. We hit it all right and it is a really big find. There are three large buttresses ... magnificent rock, hard and rough ... there was not a scratch on the rocks anywhere and no sign of anybody having been there before. It is rather a wonderful thing to think that these rocks may possibly be the finest climbing of all at Wasdale Head ... We are keeping the thing as dark as possible.[8]

---

d   G. Basterfield (1877–1949). A grocer by trade he was active in public life becoming a JP and mayor of Barrow-in-Furness. He was president of the Fell and Rock Climbing Club (FRCC) 1930–1931.

e   Graham Brown was known to his climbing companions as Tim or Timmy; in his late sixties, his young friends called him Graham.

But Basterfield leaked. 'Sorry I let our secret out,' he wrote apologetically, 'I will not tell anyone else about BHC, until we have cleaned the damned thing up from bottom to top.'[9] Graham Brown and Letts climbed two more new routes at Whitsun and the following year he unearthed four more routes, three of them in the Severe category, with J. de V. Hazard.[f] These climbs were respectable routes for the period but not at the cutting edge of difficulty. Graham Brown and his companions avoided the obvious challenge of the steep face of *The Prow* (all the features and climbs on the crag were given nautical names), which was eventually climbed in 1940 and still merits the grade of HVS. His hope that the crag would rival its neighbours for the quality of the climbing was unfulfilled; its aspect and altitude means that the rock is often dripping wet and covered in slimy moss.

Charles Warren provided a charming picture of Graham Brown in this new phase of his life:[g]

> I remember a gathering at the Wasdale Head Hotel in the old days at which G.B. was present and virtually presiding. He was telling about his pet crag in the Lake District, Boat How … The next day, young and old alike, we were all shepherded to Boat How. There seemed to be dozens of us because long before I got off the ground, as the last man on the rope, G.B. had finished the climb, had come down again, and was there to see us youngsters launched up the first pitch. That visit to Wasdale in the late 'twenties' stands out in my memory as a very pleasant episode in my life. I remember those days of the mantelpiece traverse in the old hotel sitting room and the other games we played there. And above all I remember as a very young man, the kindly presence and stimulating enthusiasm of Graham Brown.[10]

---

f   John de Vars Hazard was a member of the 1924 expedition to Mount Everest and was blamed, probably unfairly, for marooning four porters on the North Col.

g   C.B. Warren (1906–1999), physician, was a member of the expeditions to Everest in 1935, 1936 and 1938.

Chapter 7

To the Alps

By 1924 a semblance of normality had returned to the Alpine countries following the turmoil of the war. However, although the mountains were unchanged, national boundaries had been redrawn, sometimes with absurd consequences. The new Austro-Italian border ran through the middle of the Landshuter hut, situated 2,700 metres above the Brenner Pass; the Italians got the better portion of the hut but the water supply was on the Austrian side. In exchange for a supply of water, the Italians agreed to allow the passage of Austrian climbers across Italian territory to reach two passes leading to the Zillertal Alps, but insisted that each party be accompanied by a frontier guard and that a payment was made. Passports had become essential for Alpine travel and Italy restricted entry to certain points. A British party that had crossed into Italy via a high mountain pass was stopped by two armed border guards who demanded to see their passports. After some incomprehensible but seemingly good-natured banter, the party noticed that the guards were examining the passports upside down and so felt safe to go on its way, only to be brought promptly to a halt by the unmistakable sound of sliding breechblocks. The party was escorted down four miles and interviewed by an officer before being released.

The continental railway system had been restored but trains were often crowded, with standing room only, and passengers with the Paris-Lyon-Méditerranée railway company joked that PLM stood for Pour La Morgue. Travel by car was slow due to the unreliability of engines and the uneven quality of the roads; in 1922 it took three days to drive from Dieppe to La Grave in the Dauphiné Alps. Transport in and between Alpine valleys was being modernised though; horse-drawn diligences were gradually being replaced by motor buses: 'bright yellow, trailing a little yellow carrier behind for the mail, and driven by so solid, blue-eyed, and dependable a Swiss that we passed the steepest hairpins with hardly a tremor, and the three-note post-horn echoed musically from side to side of the rocky gorge.'[1]

The number of visitors to the Alps was increasing rapidly. In 1927 over 50,000 people visited the 105 huts run by the Swiss Alpine Club, an increase of more than fifty per cent in five years. Overcrowding was a frequent complaint. Generally the Swiss huts set the standard for comfort and cleanliness, but were considered expensive, and the best food was to be had in the Italian huts. *Plus ça change*. The menu at the 'heavenly' Vittoria Sella Hut included fresh chicken, zabaglione and, surprisingly, marmalade omelettes. This contrasted with the tepid, watery soup and goaty stew encountered elsewhere, although marmot ragout was apparently delicious. The Hotel Monte Rosa in Zermatt, the unofficial headquarters of the Alpine Club abroad, was 'as delightful as ever' even if the service was slow.

In May 1924 Letts invited Graham Brown to join him and Wood in a visit to the Alps that summer: 'I shall be very disappointed if you refuse – so please do your utmost to accept – we ought to be a cheery party'.[2] Their plan was to employ a guide for a week to develop their skills and then climb guideless for a week. Letts, with his experience of a single, short season in the Alps the previous year, undertook the organisation and outlined the costs:

> Journey 2nd class return, about £8; guide for 7 days at 30 francs per day, £8 10 shillings; food for guide and self same period say £5 (drinks incl); hotels and huts, say £3. Total to date £24-10s-0d. After this preliminary week the expenses of which I hope and believe I have overestimated, things would be much cheaper – we shall have little to spend on but food and drinks and hut fees for climbs – 10/- per day per person should easily cover it so another £7 to see the trip out. Grand total £31-10s-0d, say £35 for contingencies.[3]

He informed Graham Brown that all the climbing kit required was 'as for Lakes' plus dark glasses, puttees and an ice axe. He also advised on appropriate dress for Zermatt hotels. Before the war, 'it would have been unthinkable for an Englishman not to dress for dinner' recalled Arnold Lunn,[a] who remembered 'one miserable outcast' whose registered luggage did not arrive for a week:

---

a   Sir Arnold Lunn (1888–1974). Initially black-balled for the Alpine Club – exception was taken to his business connections and advocacy of ski-mountaineering – he was eventually elected an honorary member. He was knighted for his services to British skiing and Anglo-Swiss relations.

Everybody was kind to him, but he lost caste. He was slipping. He knew it. We knew it. The head waiter knew it. And then the cloud lifted. His luggage arrived. I shall never forget the expression on his face, when he appeared for the first time in evening dress. He looked like a man who had just been cleared by a court martial of a disgraceful charge.[4]

But standards had slipped. 'You should be a little more respectable than most of us are in the Lakes, but as far as I remember you were sufficiently "posh",' wrote Letts who recommended packing 'a decent lounge suit'.[5] Letts supplied the special equipment including a glacier lantern, flask for spirits, flask for tea, maps and a compass but he asked Graham Brown to provide a new rope, writing, 'It would perhaps be a fair division of expenses if you arrange about a rope … we ought not to have a frayed out affair – there may be some sudden jerks if we fall through crevasses!'[6]

On 11 July 1924, twenty-four hours after setting out from Victoria Station, Graham Brown and Letts arrived in Zermatt and checked in at the Monte Rosa Hotel. Graham Brown's first Alpine climb was on the Riffelhorn, a popular training peak reached easily and rapidly from the mountain railway to Gornergrat. Letts had engaged Gabriel Lochmatter as his guide and recommended Benoit Theytaz to Graham Brown saying, 'he is very steady and careful – not so dashing as my guide or so brilliant but I should judge on the whole safer'.[7]

Their guides permitted Graham Brown and Letts to lead them up the route, no doubt to enable them to assess their clients' abilities. Graham Brown found the climbing straightforward, no more than 'difficult' by Lakeland standards. The summit views were 'wonderful'. The vista is dominated by the hulks of the Breithorn, Lyskamm and Monte Rosa, which seem close enough to touch.

Graham Brown's next climb was the Wellenkuppe, his 'first snow mountain', and provided a trying and salutary experience for which his guide must be held responsible.[b] They had a lazy breakfast, were late leaving the Trift Hotel and as a result encountered soft snow on the glacier, which slowed progress. Thinking that their ice axes were an encumbrance in these conditions they left them on some rocks, only to find hard snow on the

b   The Wellenkuppe was first ascended in 1865 by Lord Francis Douglas who was killed two weeks later in the disaster on the Matterhorn. Douglas attended the Edinburgh Academy and was in the same class as Graham Brown's maternal uncle. Graham Brown claimed that Douglas was 'the earliest of all my Alpine heroes'. (NLS Acc 4338/205) summit ridge up which they had to kick steps laboriously. On the descent, while crossing a snowy couloir, Graham Brown's steps collapsed and he came on the rope swinging across the couloir and bumping into rocks on the far side, sustaining scrapes and bruises. They reached Zermatt late in the afternoon, well behind schedule for their rendezvous with Letts and Lochmatter, who were waiting and fretting at Riffelalp. Graham Brown and Theytaz arrived on the last train and were immediately and unceremoniously bundled by their companions into the descending train, as they were now too late to execute their plan of going up to the Bétamps Hut for an ascent of Monte Rosa.

Two days later the four of them reached the Dufourspitze on Monte Rosa via the Cresta Rey. First they ascended the Grenz Glacier which was riddled with hidden crevasses making for dangerous terrain and requiring great care but the surrounding ice and snow scenery was 'magnificent', and then climbed a steep ridge, on excellent rock, for 300 metres to the summit. Many years later Graham Brown recalled his feelings before setting out on this climb:

> I had slept fitfully and I awoke early … I lay on in a state of keen excitement and deep anxiety … for this was to be the day of my second alpine peak and my first 'big' expedition. My excitement needs no other explanation, but my anxiety does – although I think my state of mind was much the same as that of any climber who makes his first visit to the higher Alps after winning a firm background on British rocks with some experience of winter climbing at home. My ice axe in fact had already lost its original sheen and I had little anxiety about the rocks to be met on ordinary alpine routes. What did make me anxious was the length of these routes and the reputed effects of high altitude [sic]. I had done some mild training by running round deserted streets at night in heavy boots and I believed that I was physically fit, but (apart from long hill walks) I had never had a good test of stamina – was it good enough … and might I be one of those unfortunate men, who even when strong and fit, are prostrated by mountain sickness?[8]

He need not have worried. They made good time to the summit, at 4,634 metres the second highest in the Alps, and were back at the hut and snoozing on the nearby rocks by mid-afternoon. From Zermatt, Graham Brown,

Letts and their guides went over the Trifthorn to Zinal where they were joined by Cecil Wood. Theytaz was paid off; Letts and Graham Brown, Wood and Lochmatter formed two separate ropes for an ascent of Lo Besso.

From Zinal they made their way to Arolla in sleet and rain. Their final climb was the south-east ridge of the Petites Dents de Veisivi from the Col de Tsarmine, reached by a gruelling slog. The route follows a rocky ridge over a series of gendarmes. Graham Brown took the lead, keeping determinedly to the crest in spite of the protestations of Letts and Wood, who favoured the easier option of turning the pinnacles on their flanks. The awkward sections are now protected by bolts and pegs. This proved to be their last climb of the season. Bad weather set in and for four days they waited, passing the time working out boulder problems in between showers of snow and rain, but there was no sign of improvement and they decided to cut the holiday short – 'a great disappointment'.[9]

Letts prepared an ambitious itinerary for the following year. They planned to make a tour across the Bernese Oberland from Kandersteg to the Rhône valley and enter Italy via the Saastal and the Monte Moro Pass, returning to Zermatt over Monte Rosa. They were joined by a friend of Letts who was introduced to Graham Brown as 'a companion in dislike of ice and steep snow, for he crawls like a very worm on such occasions'.[10] At the beginning of their holiday heavy snowfall confined them in a hut for twenty-four hours and thereafter the weather remained poor. They had to modify their plans but managed to climb the Ebnefluh and Finsteraarhorn as well as making their second ascent of Dufourspitze on Monte Rosa, this time by the ordinary route, a tedious plod. Graham Brown, with guides Christian Almer III and Gabriel Lochmatter, ambitiously attempted the west-south-west ridge of the Täschhorn, known as the Teufelsgrat because of the difficulties posed by its great length (almost two kilometres) and loose rock, but they were turned back by stonefall. Relieved to escape unharmed, Lochmatter stopped at the little chapel at Täschalp to offer up a prayer of thanks. After just twelve days in the mountains, Graham Brown and Letts decamped to Baveno on Lake Maggiore for a week's bathing and boating.

Graham Brown's Alpine season in 1926 comprised two halves: the first was a guideless venture with fellow members of the Gritstone Club and met with limited success; the second gave him his first sight of the Brenva Face of Mont Blanc, breathing life into a long-held dream. At the beginning of July, Letts and Graham Brown met Wood and Leonard Wade at the

Gare de Lyon after a taxi ride across Paris, notorious for its excitement if not actual danger. They were on their way to the Graian Alps, a region popular at that time with parties making their first independent expeditions as the climbs are generally of moderate difficulty. As before, Letts was responsible for the 'staff-work'. He sent Graham Brown a list of kit, remarking 'I don't think I shall worry about soap, toothbrush, shaving tackle etc. for hut purposes. We never used them last year', and his last-minute instructions included a necessary injunction to Graham Brown to bring his passport.[11] They travelled by rail to Bourg St Maurice and then by taxi to Cogne, eighty miles away via the Little St Bernard Pass.

Their first climb was the Punta Nera, a subsidiary peak of the Grivola. The approach lay through a royal hunting reserve, where they encountered herds of ibex. They spent a cold night at the King's Camp *rifugio* where two gamekeepers provided them with wood for the stove and a blanket each. The route up Punta Nera is straightforward but they were early in the season and low-lying snow, often knee deep, turned it into an arduous expedition. Next they made the season's first ascent of the Gran Paradiso, the highest mountain in the region (4,061 metres). Dogged by poor weather and the conditions in the mountains, they retreated to the valley and took solace in ice creams in Aosta and bathing at Bellagio on Lake Como.

Prior to setting out for the Alps, Graham Brown had accepted an invitation to continue the season with R.J. Brocklehurst and his companion, Edwin Herbert.[c] Having returned to England in the interval, Graham Brown flew from Croydon to Basle, via Paris, to join them in Grindelwald on 12 August.[d] They climbed the Wetterhorn, Schreckhorn and Jungfrau by their ordinary routes but not without incident. On the descent from the Wetterhorn Herbert fell, pulling Graham Brown after him. Luckily they both slithered to a halt unharmed. Their itinerary now led to Mont Blanc. On the way they climbed the Grand Combin when the accident-prone Herbert dislodged a huge rock, which narrowly missed Graham Brown. From the Great St Bernard Pass they travelled by bus to Courmayeur, Graham Brown eagerly anticipating his first sight of the south side of Mont Blanc, which he glimpsed in the moonlight. Almost twenty years later, he refined his impressions for the readers of his book, *Brenva*:

c   R.J. Brocklehurst (1899-1995). Professor of physiology at Bristol University 1930-1965. F.S. Herbert (1899-1973). Solicitor. Created a life peer (Baron Tangley) in 1963 for public service. President of the Alpine Club 1953-1956.

d   Imperial Airways had commenced a passenger service on this route in June 1924, fare £8.

Its greatness was beyond expectation, its coldness something new
... The grand mountain seemed to be challenging yet forbidding,
inviting yet defying conquest, a prize offered but withheld ... The
greatness of Mont Blanc was compelling, and the moonlit peak was
urgent to be seen from all its sides, to be known in all its moods,
and to be climbed by all its ways.[12]

Two days later Graham Brown and his companions left Courmayeur to
climb Mont Blanc. They walked up Val Veni, which skirts the southern flank
of the mountain, and after a mile or two reached Plan Ponquet where there
was a clearing in the trees through which the Brenva Face of Mont Blanc
could be seen. Although limited, the view was sufficient to give substance
to his 'old daydream' of making a route up the face that 'had eased many
wearisome days during the Great War'.[13] Graham Brown always maintained
that an erroneous interpretation of Baedeker's map combined with reading A.E.W. Mason's *Running Water*, a romantic adventure published in 1907
in which the climax occurs on Mont Blanc's Brenva Ridge, had led him to
conjure up 'a mountain paradise', which he climbed in his dreams.[e] This was
the inspiration for his routes on the Brenva Face.

Graham Brown was elected to membership of the Alpine Club in December 1926. Professor George Gask[f] proposed him and he was seconded
by Letts, who had been elected twelve months earlier. Graham Brown's
qualifications for membership were unexceptional. His tally included a
dozen major peaks and a number of lesser summits, almost all climbed by
their ordinary routes in the company of a guide. Later he recalled that he
had been doubtful about the adequacy of his qualifications which he
bolstered with a list of rock climbs in the Lake District. Subsequently,
he learned that his list had been judged to be creditable for a man of his
age – he was forty-four – who had only recently commenced climbing in
the Alps. As for his mountain craft at this stage, some of his companions,
writing years later and tendentiously, recalled that he was slow – speed
being a mark of competence – and 'frankly unhappy on snow and ice'.[14]
Herbert, writing forty years later, put it more bluntly: 'neither in 1926 or 1927
was Graham Brown in my opinion fitted to lead a serious expedition'.[15]

---

e   A.E.W. Mason (1865–1948), a successful novelist, probably best known for his novel *The Four Feathers*,
     was a member of the Alpine Club and Graham Brown wrote his obituary for the *Alpine Journal*.

f   G.E. Gask (1875–1951), professor of surgery in London University.

Given Graham Brown's modest experience, his rising ambition to climb a new route on the Brenva Face, which accomplished alpinists had not yet dared to attempt, was somewhat presumptuous. However, many routes are first climbed in an armchair and he could scheme and dream. During the winter he pored over a photograph of the face and discerned a possible line of ascent. Now he needed a companion for the enterprise. Letts, whom Graham Brown might have hoped to join him, had already begun to make arrangements for the forthcoming season with three other friends and although his intention had been to include Graham Brown as a fifth member of the party, he realised the number was impractical and wrote, 'with much regret and some trepidation', asking to be released from his engagement, 'tacit or otherwise', to climb with Graham Brown.[16] When they next met Letts remarked on Graham Brown's coolness towards him; Graham Brown responded uncompromisingly that Letts had let him down. They never climbed together again. Instead, Graham Brown approached Herbert and proposed a grandiose expedition involving an ascent of Mont Blanc by the Brouillard Ridge and descent by the Peuterey Ridge, followed by his new route on the Brenva Face. At first Herbert ridiculed the idea: singly, any one of the routes was a challenge but to link three in a 'southern zigzag' was fanciful. But Graham Brown was irrepressible, and Herbert, who had been jilted recently and consequently was 'not averse to risk', was eventually persuaded to make climbing on the south side of Mont Blanc the goal for the season.

As they crossed the Col du Chardonnet from Champex to Chamonix with their guides on 31 July 1927, 'the morning glow on the Aiguille d'Argentière was the finest any of us had seen. The whole E. Face glowed pink.'[17] Before taking the train to Montenvers, crampons were sharpened and adjusted and tobacco was purchased. The next day they traversed the Aiguille des Petits Charmoz and Aiguille de l'M, a short training route on rock. That evening F.S. Smythe arrived at the hotel and Herbert fatefully introduced him to Graham Brown. On 3 August Graham Brown, Herbert and their guides went up to the Requin Hut, which was crowded and noisy. The next day they set out to climb the Dent du Requin. Herbert struggled with the difficulties and eventually abandoned the climb while Graham Brown and his guide pressed on, followed by two Swiss climbers. Suddenly, Graham Brown heard a cry and saw one of them 'falling like a log'. Coolly, he climbed down to examine the victim, who was pulseless and lay with his 'head smashed in'. The guides brought down the survivor. Herbert was badly shaken by the episode, his resolve and climbing technique deserting him, and was clearly in no state to accompany Graham Brown on a major expedition on the south side of Mont Blanc.

Bad weather forced them to 'loaf' at Montenvers. Graham Brown read, played dominoes and talked with Smythe, who impressed him with accounts of his climbs earlier in the season: the second ascent of the east ridge of the Aiguille du Plan, an ascent of the Brenva Ridge of Mont Blanc and an epic retreat from the Peuterey Ridge, all guideless. In comparison, Graham Brown's achievements had been pedestrian. Fresh snow covered the veranda of the hotel, an attempt on Mont Blanc by any route was out of the question and Herbert returned home, leaving a note for the slumbering Graham Brown asking him to send on his washing. Smythe, whose companions had also retreated to England, joined Graham Brown for a low-level walking tour while they waited for the weather to improve. A few days earlier, on 19 August, Graham Brown had noted in his diary without comment, that, at dinner, 'H[erbert] told S[mythe] about new Brenva route'.[18] He could have had no idea of its importance. Recorded here, in Graham Brown's minuscule hand, is the moment that would result in two magnificent new routes up Mont Blanc and a twenty-year feud.

Chapter 8
Climbs with F.S. Smythe

In 1927 Smythe, almost twenty years younger than Graham Brown, was already an accomplished mountaineer. Largely self-taught – he never climbed with guides – he had inevitably experienced a number of scrapes due to carelessness or foolhardiness, but the climbs he had made at the beginning of the season in 1927 demonstrated that his Alpine apprenticeship was over. His leadership on the descent from the Col du Peuterey over the Rochers Gruber in appalling conditions was, according to his grateful companion Graham Macphee, mountaineering of the highest order, and Winthrop Young, a future president of the Alpine Club, wrote in a gush of hyperbole, 'No greater mountaineering feat has been recorded than his [Smythe's] guideless descent in a snowstorm of the unclimbed Peuteret precipices on Mont Blanc.'[a,1]

Smythe, however, was without a career and still financially dependent on his mother, who worried that he seemed more interested in climbing than earning a living. After Berkhamsted School, where he played cricket for the 1st XI but was academically undistinguished, he had trained as an electrical engineer for which he had little enthusiasm or aptitude. In 1925 he accepted a post with the River Plate Telephone Company, which he quit within weeks of arriving in Argentina. Next, he joined the Royal Air Force as a trainee pilot and was sent to flying school in Egypt but was invalided out of the service within twelve months. Temperamentally, he was a loner and awkward. Raymond Greene, who knew him well, considered that these early experiences induced in Smythe an inferiority complex, which 'rendered him sometimes irritable, tactless and easily offended.'[b,2] – an impression not dispelled by Tony Smythe in his biography of his father – and perhaps

---

a   Graham Macphee (1898–1963) was reputedly the most expensive dentist in the North of England. An enthusiastic and able rock climber, he partnered some of the leading climbers of the inter-war period, gaining a reputation as the 'greatest second'.

b   Raymond Greene (1901–1982), brother of Graham, the novelist, was at school with Smythe and climbed with him on Kamet and Everest.

explains his tendency to embellish the truth, a trait that would have a profound influence on his relationship with Graham Brown, who prized accuracy and abhorred pretence.

Smythe and Graham Brown set out on their attempt to climb the Brenva Face on 30 August 1927. Leaving the Montenvers Hotel, they trudged up the Mer de Glace to the Requin Hut where fleas and restless neighbours disturbed their night. The next day they picked their way around and over crevasses and through the séracs that form the Géant icefall to reach the glacier above, and then crossed the Vallée Blanche to the Torino Hut, where they spent the rest of the day studying their objective. The Brenva Face is two miles from the hut as the crow flies but even at this distance the vast sweep of snow and rock, 1,400 metres high, presents a staggeringly impressive sight. Seen from the hut, the summit of Mont Blanc lies at the right-hand end of the skyline ridge; a great Y-shaped couloir descends from the summit and divides the face unequally. The left bank of the couloir is bounded by a rib of rock and snow, alternately; on the right, a twisting rib of rock divides the upper part of the couloir into two branches. The entire face is topped by a wall of menacing ice cliffs.

Graham Brown wanted to attempt the rib on the left side of the great couloir that he had seen the year before and set his heart on climbing. If Smythe had a plan it was inchoate. They scrutinised the face with the aid of a coin-in-the-slot telescope at the hut, changing a five-lira note into twenty-centesimi pieces to feed it. Smythe could not be persuaded that there was a way through the ice cliffs above the final buttress and emphatically rejected Graham Brown's proposition saying, 'it won't go, and you can put that in your [note]book.'[3] They searched for an alternative. Farther left the face looked impossible, but to the right the twisting rib that divides the great couloir seemed to offer a possible route. They studied the shadows on the face and noted when the sun left it, their careful assessment of the conditions turning a potentially hazardous enterprise into a reasonable undertaking.

When they left the hut before dawn the next day they were still uncertain of the approach to the foot of the Brenva Face as the lower third is invisible from the hut. They climbed to a vantage point to reconnoitre and from the summit of the Tour Ronde were able to discern a way. They descended to the Brenva Glacier, crossed a snowy bay and climbed up to a small col at the lower end of the Brenva Ridge. Here they halted for several hours during the afternoon to allow the sun to move off their route and the snow to harden. Then they cramponed across a series of gullies of snow and ice to reach a conspicuous buttress of red rock, which they named the Red Sentinel, situated some way up the face and offering a safe place to bivouac. They prepared for the night, which proved long and bitterly cold, huddling together, draped in a bivouac sac. To avoid suffocation, they had to raise the base of the sac at intervals, allowing a blast of cold air to enter, and through-out the night condensed moisture dripped disagreeably down the backs of their necks. Alarmingly, a sérac perched high above collapsed and chunks of ice swept noisily down the gullies on either side of the Red Sentinel, passing within a few yards of them. Sleep was impossible. The next morning they fumbled with frozen crampons, the metal sticking to their fingers, and even-tually quit their bivouac at 5.30 a.m. Some years later, Graham Brown recalled his feeling as they set out:

> It cannot be described in words save as a sort of expectancy of the unknown. On some occasions during the War I came near to it – once when lying flat on the snow in no man's land in dead silence, once at the Deepcut Ravine when I rode unwittingly into near view of enemy trenches … perhaps more particularly when daily duties included two walks across no man's land in full sight of the enemy but out of rifle-shot and too insignificant a target for the field guns. Take the apprehension out of these experiences and what remains is very nearly what I felt.[4]

In short, he was gripped. They went up and over the rock ridge that forms the lower border of the right-hand branch of the Y-shaped couloir and climbed as fast as they could to the foot of the twisting rib. Once on the rib they were safe from the risk of falling stones and ice. They continued up the rocks, bypassing difficulties on snow and ice, and climbed a very steep ice slope which necessitated a prolonged bout of laborious step cutting by Smythe. They were now beneath the wall of séracs that crowns the route. Smythe described the scene: 'a veil of ice javelins hung from the upper edge and beneath the wall was sheared away as though cut by the knife of a workman'.[5] A traverse leftwards led to a rib of ice that breached the barrier. The final obstacle was a small cornice which Smythe broke through and they stepped on to the summit slopes of Mont Blanc. At last the steepness relented and, 'with inexpressible relief', they shook hands and turned for a final view of their route. Graham Brown considered it to have been 'continuously sensational', observing that 'the Brenva glacier can be seen between your heels almost the whole way'.[6] Slowly, they went up the last hundred or so metres to the summit which was reached eleven hours after setting out from their bivouac. Smythe had led throughout. Graham Brown wrote frankly of himself, 'I'm too much of a rabbit at the game' and praised Smythe, as 'a great man'.[7] They spent the night at the Vallot Hut and descended to the valley the following day. Back at Montenvers, they celebrated their success with vintage wine and champagne in sufficient quantity that Graham Brown could not remember all the details of the latter part of the evening.

During the week of poor weather that followed, they managed to climb the Aiguille des Grands Charmoz, spending over an hour on the summit mulling over the philosophy of climbing and estimating the steepness of their route on the Brenva Face. They were on the brink of returning home when the weather improved and they set off for their last climb of the season, making the first ascent of Les Courtes from the Glacier de Talèfre. Their route ascended a long rib of rock, 600 metres from the glacier to the summit, and provided some rock climbing of interest but rather more nondescript scrambling. The next day it was snowing and they left for England together, stopping in Paris for two nights to go sightseeing and take in the cabarets at L'Olympia and the Moulin Rouge.

Back in England, Captain J.P. Farrar, a former president of the Alpine Club and now its Grand Old Man, applauded their ascent, saying that the route was 'the finest made up the finest face in the Alps'.[8] Smythe was invited to read a paper to the Alpine Club. Usually the paper formed the substance of a full-length article for the journal but Graham Brown argued that the article should be written jointly, citing as precedent the practice of joint authorship of papers by collaborators in scientific experiments, although his own record in this respect was hardly exemplary.[c] Smythe was unenthusiastic: their styles were incompatible, his own, 'flamboyant' and 'quite unorthodox', contrasting with Graham Brown's 'academic' style. He grumbled that 'one might as well get Noel Coward and G[eorge] B[ernard] S[haw] to turn out a play between them'.[9] Graham Brown continued to press for joint authorship. Exasperated, Smythe responded that 'it doesn't seem

---

c   Of his ninety-odd scientific papers, a dozen were co-authored. Single authorship was much more common in the past but, nevertheless, the statistic suggests that Graham Brown was not a collaborator by nature.

worthwhile worrying more about the matter. After all we climb for fun not to write papers.'[10] In the meantime he submitted a brief, factual account of the climb, based on Graham Brown's detailed notes, for publication in the November edition of the journal and included a picture of the Brenva Face on which a dotted line had been superimposed and labelled 'Mr Smythe's route'. Unsurprisingly, Graham Brown was piqued. He complained to his friend, Professor Gask, that the planning of the route was at least as much his as Smythe's and said he intended to take up the matter with the editor of the *Alpine Journal*, Colonel E.L. Strutt. Gask replied that although Graham Brown had a point, only 'small-minded people might be inclined to make a fuss'.[11] Graham Brown ignored the hint. Smythe delivered his paper at the Alpine Club in February 1928 and acknowledged Graham Brown's contribution to the preparation of his article for the journal but the gesture failed to mollify Graham Brown, who considered that the collaboration had been notional.

Despite their disagreements, Smythe and Graham Brown maintained friendly relations and they began to make plans for climbing together in 1928, though Smythe's light-hearted signing-off to a letter reveals the undercurrent of feelings: 'Looking forward to our next scrap. My turn to draw blood next time.'[12] Smythe, with an eye to journalistic opportunities, proposed an attempt on Mount Kenya to coincide with the visit of the Prince of Wales to the region, or alternatively and fantastically, going to the Rockies where 'the shooting – grizzly, caribou etc is first rate' and 'there is also the very remote chance of GOLD!'[13] Surprisingly, Graham Brown expressed enthusiasm for the trip to Kenya and went as far as establishing the possibility of free passages to Mombassa aboard a coal ship. But when Smythe cried off, unable to obtain financial support for the venture, and suggested that Graham Brown might want to go with somebody else, Graham Brown replied that he would much prefer to climb with him in the Alps than go to Kenya without him. Their thoughts returned to the unclimbed buttress on the left side of the great couloir on the Brenva Face. Although, publicly, Smythe expressed confidence in Graham Brown's mountaineering competence, writing:

> Personally the thought of a slip on the part of Graham Brown never entered my head, and I like to think that he felt the same. Mutual confidence in such a situation is the finest asset a climbing party can possess.[14]

privately, he had doubts and proposed that Ogier Ward and Graham Macphee, who had accompanied him on an ascent of the Brenva Ridge the previous year, join them to strengthen the party.[d]

At Easter 1928, Graham Brown and Smythe were amongst the party gathered by Winthrop Young at Pen-y-Pass, at the foot of Snowdon. These gatherings at Easter and Christmas, initiated by Young before the First World War, had developed into a tradition. Attendance was by invitation and many of the guests at this period were undergraduates who frequented the Youngs' home in Cambridge on Sunday evenings 'to sit at Geoffrey's feet and meet interesting people'.[15] The routine at Pen-y-Pass was an energetic day in the hills – walking or climbing – orchestrated by Young to ensure that everyone was catered for, followed by communal baths: 'endless discussions of details of climbs from bath tub to bath tub' and 'abstract argument through the steam'.[16] Then there was dinner, singing and indoor gymnastics. Graham Brown scribbled some notes concerning his climbs during the ten days but left no impressions of the antics at Pen-y-Pass, though he had formed the view that Young was a poseur, describing him as 'precious' and 'a bad influence on young Cambridge climbers'. [e,17] Young, in turn, disliked Graham Brown and, twenty years later, their mutual antipathy would erupt in a major row.

After a few days spent climbing some of the established routes on Lliwedd, the Mecca for rock climbers of the period, the Milestone Buttress of Tryfan and the Idwal slabs, Smythe and Graham Brown joined Jack Longland and Cuthbert Wakefield, alumni of the renascent and flourishing Cambridge University Mountaineering Club, in exploring the massive and imposing cliffs of Clogwyn Du'r Arddu.[f] The East Buttress is formed by a great wall split by cracks and had been climbed for the first time the year before; the West Buttress differs in character, comprising a series of overlapping slabs, and was their objective. Smythe's account of the exploration and eventual ascent of *Longland's Climb* provides the detail of Graham Brown's

---

d   In fact, Macphee had had to turn back, having broken his ice axe, and the resulting delay proved lifesaving for the rest of the party. If they had not stopped they would have been caught by an enormous avalanche that swept over the route ahead of them a few minutes later.

e   His collection of forty-two waistcoats, found in his wardrobe by his new wife, certainly suggests an excessive interest in his appearance.

f   Sir Jack Longland (1905–1993), president of the Alpine Club 1974–1977. According to Jim Perrin, Longland claimed to have been sexually involved with both Winthrop Young and his wife, Len [Eleanora]. During his lifetime, Longland bound Perrin to a vow of secrecy but intimated that after his death the story should be widely circulated. (*The Climbing Essays* p. 152) involvement for, oddly, Longland's own account fails to mention him.

The principal feature and challenge of the route is a narrow slab about seventy-five metres high which, on its left-hand side, overhangs another slab giving a sensation of great exposure; on the right, it is bounded by a steep wall and in the angle between the wall and the slab there is a chimney crack. The base of the slab was reached by a narrow chimney, which gave steep and damp climbing, followed by a gully and traverse past a large bollard. The slab itself appeared smooth and was dotted with unstable clods of turf. Longland led and was followed by Smythe, Graham Brown and Wakefield in that order. Whilst Longland and Smythe excavated and climbed the slab, Graham Brown remained at its base; Wakefield was farther behind at the bollard. After about ten metres, Longland reached a constricted stance in the crack. Smythe came up and past, pushing out the route another twenty metres to a small cave and flake belay. Drizzle turned to rain and it was getting cold; Graham Brown sustained a direct hit from a falling stone. The climb was abandoned. A few days later Smythe suggested that he and Graham Brown make another attempt but Graham Brown thought a party of two was inadequate and refused. It seems that their disagreement became heated because subsequently Smythe wrote to apologise. In a later annotation to this letter, Graham Brown states that Smythe had called him a coward. At Whitsun, they returned with Ogier Ward, but gales and rain precluded another attempt and Graham Brown and Ward went home. Smythe stayed on and joined Longland once again to make the successful first ascent with Fred Pigott and his party. This climb, together with Pigott's route on the East Buttress, ushered in the modern era of rock climbing in Wales but Graham Brown had been no more than a bystander.

At the beginning of July, Graham Brown and Smythe arrived in Kandersteg, in the Bernese Oberland, to get fit for their Mont Blanc climb later in the season. At the railway station they bumped into Ivan Waller, whom they had met at Pen-y-Pass; recently down from Cambridge, he was intending to climb some easy mountains on his own. Graham Brown and Smythe, increasingly uneasy in each other's company, immediately invited him to join them. They climbed the Altels from a delightful bivouac around a campfire and then transferred to Chamonix where Waller, the Alpine tyro, led them on the classic traverse of the Aiguille du Grépon. Waller, a talented rock climber on a par with his near contemporary, Longland, recalled that both Smythe and Graham Brown required some 'major haulage operations' on the difficult pitches. Smythe, tired and irritable, adopted a patronising tone with Waller, saying, 'you needn't call me Frank – call me Smythe (or Mr Smythe)'. Waller retorted by calling him a 'silly c**t'.[18] Years later, Graham Brown would amuse himself by writing a ludicrous parody of the climb in which he cast Smythe as an Irishman, who told tall tales, and Ivan Waller as a Russian, called Boris.[g]

While Graham Brown and Smythe awaited the arrival of Ward and Tom Blakeney, whom Smythe had decided to invite instead of Macphee for the attempt on the Brenva Face, they ascended the Moine Ridge on the Aiguille Verte.[h] Smythe forgot the electric lantern and took the wrong line; Graham Brown did not pay out the rope quickly enough and was always wasting time stopping to make notes. They squabbled. The route proved delicate and difficult. They were slow and did not reach the summit until late afternoon. On the descent they followed a trail of bits of newspaper, which they had laid on the way up, but darkness fell before they reached their cache of equipment and they were forced to bivouac without. This incompetent performance probably rekindled Smythe's doubts about the wisdom of venturing again on to the Brenva Face with Graham Brown who, in turn, sensed that Smythe's resolve was weakening and was surprised by Smythe's apparent satisfaction with their achievements to date: they had climbed just three routes during seventeen days of good weather, which seemed 'out of harmony with his professions of vigorous and adventurous climbing'.[19]

When Ward failed to join them as planned, Smythe dithered, postponing an attempt on the face because he had formed an erroneously pessimistic view of the conditions, which he considered dangerously icy. At last, on 27 July, Smythe, Graham Brown and Blakeney, accompanied by two porters, toiled up from Courmayeur to the Brenva bivouac, situated on an island of rock in the Brenva Glacier and used on the first ascent of the Brenva Ridge in 1865, with the intention of pressing on the next day to another bivouac below the Red Sentinel, before trying the great buttress. But that night they were overtaken by a violent thunderstorm, which Smythe described luridly:

> Long bloody fingers of light poured rays upon spectral cloud pennons writhing upwards on the wings of an unsuspected hurricane

---

g   Graham Brown believed, incorrectly, that Smythe had Irish antecedents.

h   T.S. Blakeney (1903–1976). The year before he had spent ten days with Smythe in Chamonix. The weather was 'continuously foul' and they achieved nothing.

... Weird beads of faint greenish light, like the watch-fires of goblins, danced and trembled on the spires of the Dames Anglaises ... A curtain of mauve fire descended; a crooked sword of intense light stabbed the crest of the Aiguille Noire de Pétéret; a tearing crack of thunder was flung from precipice to precipice ... Shaken by lightning, hail and rain, the Aiguille Blanche de Pétéret poured forth its avalanches of rocks, and through the darkness we saw torrents of fire streaming down its cliffs as the rocks ground and crashed together.[20]

An overhanging rock sheltered them from hailstones the size of small marbles, but they remained in significant danger from lightning strike, Graham Brown calmly observing and recording the frequency of the flashes. The storm passed. They were unscathed but they abandoned the climb. Blakeney, who was unwell, withdrew from any further attempts on the Brenva Face, and Smythe and Graham Brown scoured Chamonix for replacements without success. Again, they found themselves dependent on each other and in differing moods that would prove a toxic combination. Smythe, who fancied that he had psychic powers, had a premonition of death and was apprehensive and highly strung; Graham Brown was coolly and obsessively determined to climb the route of his dreams.[i]

On 6 and 7 August 1928 they climbed their second new route on the Brenva Face, following the mixed buttress on the left of the great couloir. Establishing exactly what happened is difficult, since it was precisely these details that would become the subject of their feud, and each man made claims and counter-claims to support their version of events. However, just two days after the ascent, Graham Brown wrote a detailed letter to Gask, giving an account of the climb based on his notes made during it, which has the advantage of immediacy, antedating any public discord, and provides the most reliable source.

The approach to the bivouac site beneath the Red Sentinel proved more difficult than the previous year. A deep couloir, its nearside overhanging, blocked their way. Graham Brown lowered Smythe into the base of the couloir where he cut some steps across and up the other side. Graham Brown was now faced with a discomforting prospect: although Smythe could

---

[i] According to his son and biographer, Smythe obtained the help of a spiritualist to cure a digestive disorder and communicated directly with her source, a seventeenth-century Sindh poet, and his psychic powers averted a catastrophe in a Bradford foundry in 1920.

provide the safety of a rope from above, he had to launch himself over the overhang and risk a frightening swing. Anxiously, he lowered himself over the edge and then dropped about two metres, dangling on the rope until he could cut a step. Graham Brown described the episode as 'one of the worst ordeals of my life'.[21] Their bivouac, however, was much more comfortable compared to the year before. They had sleeping bags, a cooker and generous provisions: tins of tongue and sardines, salami, two kilograms of bread, jam, chocolate, cocoa and tea.

They left the bivouac at just before 5.00 a.m. and made a rising traverse to the edge of the great couloir, the crossing of which was a committing and dangerous step. The couloir is a natural funnel for any ice falling from the séracs above and, whilst the risk is reduced during the hours before dawn and before the sun strikes the ice cliffs, later in the day it is a potential death trap. At their crossing point, the couloir was about sixty metres wide. Smythe led. Wearing crampons, they did not need to cut steps and were across in less than ten minutes but a continuous stream of powder snow, which buried their boots, flowed down the couloir, an insistent reminder of the potential hazard from the cliffs above. Once on the buttress, they climbed over rocks and a series of snow and ice arêtes which became progressively steeper. The third arête was 'exceedingly narrow with a crest of pure ice so thin that sunlight showed through it'.[22] The ascent of the final arête required much step cutting and the glutinous quality of the ice made for arduous work. Smythe was in the lead and Graham Brown followed, cutting intermediate steps to accommodate his shorter stride. For long stretches they moved one at a time and progress was slow.

They reached the foot of the final rock buttress beneath the wall of séracs at 1.40 p.m. The key to climbing the buttress appeared to be a short corner, about four metres high, formed between the leaning base of the buttress and a rib of rock. Below the corner a steep ice slope fell away merging with the rocks forming the left wall of the great couloir. They jammed their ice axes between the ice and rock to provide a rudimentary belay and Smythe attempted to climb the corner but was unsuccessful. Graham Brown tried and failed. With a rising sense of desperation they both tried again. Graham Brown offered his shoulder to Smythe who was still unable to get up and he came down heavily on Graham Brown, ripping his jacket with his crampons. Smythe suggested retreating down their line of ascent or trying to escape by crossing the great couloir to reach the upper part of their route of the previous year, which would expose them to the risk of being swept away by falling ice from the séracs above. Given the impasse and the uncertainties of what lay ahead, retreat may have seemed to be the only reasonable option though it would have been lengthy and dangerous, but Smythe had extricated himself from difficulties on big mountains before. That Smythe, faced with Graham Brown's obstinacy and probably shaken after his uncontrolled slither from the corner, argued vehemently – even hysterically as Graham Brown alleged – for retreat is credible. The only alternative was to descend the steep ice slope and attempt to turn the rock rib in the hope of finding a way up the buttress above. Graham Brown climbed down, cutting steps to the toe of the rib, and then led around its base and up the far side, running out the full length of their rope. The ice was steep, the exposure great and the belay precarious. This passage was committing and decisive. Smythe followed. The route above appeared to be by a rocky gully but steep rocks barred the way to it and they had to climb a difficult five-metre chimney, which proved very strenuous. Smythe started up still carrying his rucksack but, drained by his step cutting, the strength in his arms ran out and he had to descend. Graham Brown left his sack with Smythe and, unencumbered, managed to swarm up the chimney. A subsequent party considered this pitch to be the crux of the route. As they prospected the route to the top of the buttress, the lead changed hands, Smythe finding the way through the séracs, which fortunately proved relatively straightforward.

Arriving on the summit slopes they were buffeted by a strong wind and sought shelter in a crevasse to rest and eat. It was late and they were tired. They abandoned their original plan to descend the Miage Face to the Sella Hut but, instead of going directly over Mont Blanc to the Vallot Hut, they first turned south to visit the top of Mont Blanc de Courmayeur. The powerful wind caused both men to stagger and Graham Brown slipped, falling a few feet. They finally arrived at the summit of Mont Blanc at 8.20 p.m., fifteen hours after setting out from their bivouac. On their return to Montenvers the next day, they toasted their success with a bottle of sparkling wine each but their celebration masked the fact that their relations had reached breaking point. Within a few weeks they were barely on speaking terms.

Smythe returned to England leaving more cause for discord in his wake. Although he had dropped Macphee from the original party to attempt the Brenva climb, Smythe had arranged to meet him in Courmayeur on 9 August, when he and Graham Brown were still at Montenvers, recuperating from their Mont Blanc climb. Finding himself abandoned, Macphee sent a post-card to Smythe to remind him of their arrangement. Smythe, however, was set on going home, apparently in order to take his mother on holiday, and left Graham Brown to manage the situation. In the interval, Graham Brown, whose enthusiasm and ambition were unquenched, had engaged a guide for an ascent of Mont Blanc by the Brouillard Ridge, one of the great ridges on the Italian side of the mountain, first ascended in 1911 and climbed rarely since. He declined to alter his plans. He considered that Macphee was not up to participating in a major expedition so soon in his holiday and that his predicament was Smythe's responsibility. A disgruntled Macphee summed up the sorry episode as the result of 'carelessness and thoughtlessness on the part of Smythe and downright selfishness on the part of the professor.'[23]

Back in England, Smythe seized the opportunity for some publicity, writing an article for *The Times* of 18 August, in which he deliberately omitted naming Graham Brown, referring to him anonymously as 'a friend'. He also gave an interview to *The Western Mail*, Cardiff's and Graham Brown's local paper, which appeared under the dramatic headline: 'Perilous New Route – A Thirty Hours Task'. The article concluded with a reference to Smythe having been invalided out of the RAF – his doctors advising him to be careful about climbing stairs – and yet, ten months later, he had climbed Mont Blanc. This construct disturbed Graham Brown who was beginning to suspect that Smythe had a tendency to embroider the truth. His suspicion was confirmed when he discovered later that Smythe's medical discharge had been due to the mundane conditions of inflammation of the eyelids and the effects of glare.[j]

On his return to Cardiff, Graham Brown wrote to Smythe saying that he had prepared an account of their climb for publication in the *Alpine Journal* and that he had placed their names in alphabetical order, which he hoped Smythe would agree was fair. In the meantime Smythe had sent an angry letter to Graham Brown criticising him for failing to partner Macphee. Graham Brown responded temperately but remarked sanctimoniously that in order not to disrupt arrangements with Smythe for their holiday, he had declined the honour of presenting Sir Thomas Lewis, an eminent physician, to the Prince of Wales, who was the university's chancellor. In this, he was

---

j   In 1932 Graham Brown was serving on a committee with Sir David Munro, the former director of the RAF Medical Service, who seemingly had no qualms about breaching patient confidentiality and made Smythe's medical report available to Graham Brown.

being disingenuous; the invitation to make the presentation had arrived after he had left for the Alps and the Prince of Wales did not turn up to the ceremony. Smythe followed up this salvo with a letter, inflammatory in content and vitriolic in tone, denigrating Graham Brown's contribution to their successful climb, accusing him of telling lies and objecting strongly to the alphabetical order of their names:

> I am sorry you missed the honour you suggested, but you have at least had the honour of being taken up two of the greatest climbs in the Alps – an honour which would not have occurred had you not met me … in addition [Macphee] has told me certain lies you have spread about me … one of which is that I wanted to turn back on the climb, but that you by your example and leadership saved the situation [and] I need hardly point out that … the invariable custom is to place the leader's name first. I have therefore written to Strutt … asking him to amend [the] order of names.[24]

and added that his arrangements for climbing the following year did not include him. But Graham Brown had already decided not to climb with Smythe again and never replied to this letter.

Chapter 9
Fallout

The ascents of the *Sentinelle Rouge* and *Route Major*, as the 1928 climb would become known, were remarkable achievements. The climbs had required sound mountaineering skills, nice judgement of the conditions to minimise the risks, and daring. That both Smythe and Graham Brown should want to enjoy the credit for these climbs is understandable but their jockeying for priority caused dismay within the Alpine Club.

A month after their ascent of *Route Major*, Smythe wrote to Strutt, offering his notes on the climb for publication in the *Alpine Journal*:

> Graham Brown informs me that he has sent you the notes. Do you want mine? I have gone to some trouble in preparing them. Graham Brown tells me that he would like his name placed first. As however I did 95% of the climb perhaps the usual procedure of placing the leader's name first would save misunderstanding, particularly among Continentals ... my reason for wishing to include these remarks and particulars as to the actual portions of the climb led by Graham Brown are because of his abominable behaviour to my friend Macphee and because of gross lies he has been spreading about for his own benefit and glorification.

With rising indignation and a hint of paranoia, he continued:

> I consider Graham Brown's behaviour the act of an absolute cad and I don't mind who knows it ... he spread lies about me – one of them being that I wanted to turn back on the climb, but that he – Graham Brown – by his magnificent leadership and example saved the situation ... the things Graham Brown has been spreading about me

behind my back are unbelievable … after what he has been saying about me I have no hesitation in defending myself with interest!'[1]

Graham Brown invited Gask and Strutt to lunch with a view to them arbitrating on the matter of the order of names. Gask declined, saying, 'I do not pretend to be able to adjudicate in this little difficulty, and after all it seems to me a small one.' And, probably in common with most disinterested parties, added, 'I never thought in my mind whether you led or Smythe. Anyway it was a jolly good climb and there is lots of credit for both.'[2] Strutt was aghast: 'It is unheard of that two companions on a climb should struggle for precedence on paper when that same credit is attached to both.'[3]

In November 1928 Graham Brown's factual account of the *Route Major* was published in the journal's section, New Expeditions, with Smythe's name appearing first. Graham Brown did not let the matter rest and Strutt was obliged to explain that he had 'unconsciously' and 'without a thought of anyone thereby being offended'[4] placed Smythe's name first, that alphabetical order had never occurred to him and anyway, 'no one ever notices which name comes first'.[5] Inadvertently, however, he had given Graham Brown an additional cause to hold a grievance, for, at Smythe's instigation, he had appended an editorial note to Graham Brown's account:

> The possibility of this ascent was first pointed out to Mr Smythe by Mr T.B. [sic] Blakeney in 1926, who specifically indicated the great buttress by which this climb was accomplished.'[6]

Smythe repeated the assertion in an article for *Blackwood's Magazine* and his book, *Climbs and Ski Runs*.[a] Graham Brown was shocked and mortified; after all, for years he had imagined a climb on the Brenva Face and had identified the line of *Route Major* in 1926, proposing it the following year to Smythe who had rejected it. Smythe's statement seemed calculated to erode Graham Brown's claim on priority for the discovery of the routes and it fuelled their feud. Did Smythe deliberately inflate Blakeney's contribution? Graham Brown certainly thought so, for if Blakeney's proposal was the basis of a plan for climbing the Brenva Face, why had Smythe not mentioned it before? He was sure that Smythe had not done so and sought

---

a   The margins of Graham Brown's copy of Smythe's book are crammed with comments such as 'inaccurate', 'absurd' and 'pure rot'.

corroboration from Herbert, asking him to recall their conversations with Smythe at Montenvers in August 1927. Herbert responded that his recollections were very hazy. Graham Brown pressed him further and lured him to dinner at the Athenaeum where he made notes of their conversation. He recorded that Herbert 'would swear ... in a court of law' that he had no memory of Smythe mentioning a route on the Brenva Face and got Herbert to authenticate the statement with his initials.[7] Graham Brown interrogated Blakeney and concluded that he had seen the possibility, but no more than that, of a route on the Brenva Face and Blakeney admitted it had been just a 'germ of an idea'.[8] Graham Brown's suspicions that Smythe's assertion had been intended to discredit him and worse, that he had manipulated the truth for his own advantage, were confirmed. Deprived due recognition for his contribution to the inception and climbing of the routes on the Brenva Face, Graham Brown's rancour was not propitiated by apologies from Smythe who wrote regretting that there had been a row and asked to restore amicable relations. He grovelled:

> I should like to express my deep regret for the pain that I must have caused you, and I sincerely trust that you will forgive me ... Your very kind and generous review of 'Climbs and Ski Runs' was much appreciated and served to heap coals of fire on my head ... Yours regretfully and apologetically[9]

Graham Brown persisted in exhuming the past. He suspected Smythe of deceit regarding the arrangements for submitting a joint article describing their ascent of the Sentinelle Rouge. He asked Sydney Spencer, honorary secretary of the Alpine Club, and Strutt for their recollections and admonished them not to discuss the matter between themselves. Spencer, who pleaded that his memories were rather vague, was puzzled by Graham Brown's motives and advised him 'to commit the whole thing to oblivion'.[10]

At the end of August 1932, Graham Brown and Strutt returned to England together from Chamonix, where they had attended the International Alpine Congress as representatives of the Alpine Club. On the journey Strutt told Graham Brown that Smythe had recounted a story that Graham Brown had fallen on the Route Major and that Smythe had saved his life. Flabbergasted, Graham Brown immediately made notes, rendered almost illegible by the motion of the train. Back in England he pressed Strutt for detail. Strutt told him, 'I do remember S[mythe] saying you fell off and both of you fell 100ft before the rope hitched' and added disdainfully, 'S[mythe] told me such a lot of b[a]lls that I was bored to death and paid little attention.'[11] It seems Strutt kept the tale to himself and Smythe did not circulate it widely, although within a few months of their ascent of *Route Major* he had written to Geoffrey Winthrop Young to counter Graham Brown's 'poisonous lies' and give his version of what had occurred on the ridge leading to the summit of Mont Blanc de Courmayeur:

> [W]hen 10ft up, he came off, fell past me and flew off down the hard ice slope on the Quintino Sella side. I had no belay at all, and it was only a miracle that saved us. I managed to take in the rope as he slid down the rocks and somehow got it round a knob as big as my thumb. The fall was so bad that a wisp of rope was left on the knob but the rope (a Beale) held. For this I got not a word of thanks ... though I flatter myself that it was the quickest bit of work I've ever done in my life as the fall above was quite 10ft and the strain came on the rope when he was on the ice slope only 5ft below me. All he said was that he thought he would have stopped himself – and this on hard <u>polished</u> ice! The fact that it took a quarter of an hour to untie his rope at the end of the day is a slight testimony as to what <u>did</u> stop him.[12]

The veracity of the story remains in doubt. Graham Brown flatly denied it, dismissing it as complete fabrication, and the fact that Smythe did not mention the episode in any of his published accounts suggests some uneasiness about its accuracy.

The discovery that this story had been circulating, without his knowledge, amongst some members of the Alpine Club for several years and that Smythe was still referring to a quarrel between them incensed Graham Brown who could no longer contain his anger. Choosing his moment, he wrote to Smythe, maliciously antedating his letter to 24 December and arranging for it to be posted on Christmas Eve. The content was distinctly lacking in seasonal cheer.

Dear Mr Smythe

… You cannot have forgotten the scene you made at the ice-run on our 1928 Brenva ascent, and how you screamed as I lowered you down on the rope. You cannot have forgotten how you screamed in the corner when we tried to climb by that route, and then fell on me in crampons; nor how you behaved after that, and wished to give up the climb. You cannot have forgotten many other incidents.[13]

Smythe replied:

Dear Professor Graham Brown,

… Your letter contains statements about me which are untrue and which are merely intended to wound. It takes two to make a quarrel, but I am perfectly prepared to admit that my original letter began it.

He went on to reiterate his version of events, including the disputed fall, in sensational detail. But recognising that he and Graham Brown were going to serve together on the committee of the Alpine Club, proffered another olive branch, saying that he was prepared to meet 'on the friendliest possible footing'.[14] Graham Brown was implacable. He wrote back to Smythe saying that his letter was full of invention and that, incredibly, Smythe had come to believe in his 'fantasies'. He signed off, saying, 'I wish to have as little to do with you as I can' and 'I do not wish to receive any reply to this letter.'[15] The breakdown in their relations was complete.

Chapter 10
Alpine Heyday

At the tail end of the 1928 season, after Smythe had returned to England to take his mother on holiday, Graham Brown climbed the Grandes Jorasses by the ordinary route from Italy and traversed the Weisshorn up the classic north ridge and down the Schaligrat – the first time these ridges had been so combined. He was guided by Alexander Graven from Zermatt, who, aged thirty, had made over 120 ascents on peaks around Zermatt but, in common with the majority of guides, had very little experience of mountains outside his local district. Graham Brown engaged him for the following year's season and gave notice of his ambition in a letter asking Graven whether he had given further thought to attempting the as yet unclimbed North Face of the Matterhorn. Graven replied guardedly that it was still plastered in snow.

They met in Zermatt on 15 July. Graham Brown spent almost six weeks in the Alps during which at least a week's climbing was lost to bad weather, but he completed some fine expeditions. His list included the classic traverses of the Täschhorn and Dom, the Nadelgrat and an airy expedition from the Triftjoch to the Schalijoch, climbing all the intervening summits, completed over two separate days. They made one foray to the south side of Mont Blanc and climbed Pic Moore, an insignificant peak situated at the foot of the Brenva Ridge, but from its top there is an uninterrupted view of the Brenva Face which allowed Graham Brown to examine closely the approaches to a possible route up the pear-shaped buttress to the left of *Route Major*. At the Torino Hut he encountered Smythe, who had made an unsuccessful attempt on a new route on the south-east face of Mont Maudit. Graham Brown noted that Smythe had turned back on the same day that an Italian party had successfully made a route up the face, further evidence, in his view, that Smythe lacked drive. Graham Brown's 1929 season consolidated his alpine technique on traditional routes and established his partnership with Graven that would prove so fruitful.

In 1930 his goal was to climb the Peuterey Ridge of Mont Blanc, the most difficult ridge on the mountain. He asked Alfred Zürcher, a wealthy and flamboyant Swiss businessman, to join him. They had become friendly following their first meeting at Montenvers in August 1928, when Zürcher introduced Graven to Graham Brown. Zürcher responded with a different proposition, the north-east face of Piz Roseg, and they agreed to meet in Pontresina at the beginning of August. Beforehand, Graham Brown and Graven embarked on a round of peak-bagging from Zermatt. The weather was mixed; they encountered hail or falling snow on over half of their expeditions but the sun shone more often than not. A sanguine Graham Brown observed, 'such weather has this advantage that the effects of cloud and mist and sun add a beauty to the mountains not seen on cloudless days'.[1]

They climbed six peaks of more than 4,000 metres and a number of lesser summits before recording a tour de force, traversing from the Margherita Hut on Monte Rosa's Signalkuppe to the Breuiljoch and down to Zermatt in sixteen hours and fifty minutes, over Lyskamm, Castor, Pollux and the Breithorn, adding six more summits of more than 4,000 metres to their tally. This high-altitude traverse is over twelve miles long and Graham Brown's achievement is testimony to his endurance.

Geoffrey Winthrop Young, who had a reputation for speed and extraordinary stamina, had attempted a similar feat before the war. In his book, *On High Hills*, he states that he started from Riffelberg, thus adding the ascent of Monte Rosa to the expedition, but on reaching the summit of Castor with the afternoon still ahead, his guide refused to go on, claiming that he had sprained his wrist. Later Young wrote disdainfully that 'the vapour of funk' had 'condensed into a concrete symptom'.[2] To make his displeasure clear, he insisted on retracing their steps back over the summit of Lyskamm rather than descending directly, adding several hours of exertion to their expedition. In 1937 Graham Brown heard at second-hand an account of the expedition as told by Young's guide, Heinrich Pollinger. They started out from the Bétamps Hut, not Riffelberg, reducing the length of the expedition by several hours, and turned back on the west peak of Lyskamm, not Castor, because they met a party who warned of icy conditions ahead. Of course, Pollinger may have had his own agenda but the story reinforced Graham Brown's growing suspicion that Young tended to be economical with the truth.

Graham Brown travelled to Pontresina by train and noted ironically that the so-called Glacier Express took ten-and-a-half hours for the journey

(165 miles), and was remarkable, even by Swiss standards, for the extremely high fare. Graham Brown and Graven teamed up with Zürcher and Josef Knubel who combined on a separate rope, and climbed three major snow and ice routes: the north face of Piz Scerscen via the ice nose, the north-east face of Piz Roseg, and the west face of Piz Bernina – a first ascent. The ice nose on Piz Scerscen presented a wall of about sixty metres and Graham Brown estimated its steepness as approaching eighty degrees. Graven gave an exemplary display of contemporary ice craft, single-handedly cutting handholds and steps all the way, which drew plaudits from the rest of the party, and then lowered two ropes knotted together to protect and assist the others. The problem of the north-east face of Piz Roseg was to negotiate a safe way through the barrier of monstrous, overhanging ice cliffs at mid-height when the only feasible route was itself threatened by a glacier suspended – seemingly miraculously defying gravity – 600 metres above. The solution was a careful assessment of conditions and speed through the danger zone. Graham Brown and the guides devoted a day to ascending the mountain by one of its ridges and venturing on to the face to inspect it. On their successful ascent it took just one hour and twenty minutes, climbing and cutting steps faster than they had ever done before, to ascend 300 metres and reach the shelf above the ice walls at mid-height, where they were no longer exposed to the risk of falling ice. Oddly, they donned crampons only after this passage, perhaps because lower down there were some rocky sections which they preferred to tackle in nailed boots. The challenges of the west face of Piz Bernina were similar to those on Piz Roseg but a relatively short (100–120 metres), steep rock wall beneath the summit posed an additional obstacle. All but Graham Brown had doubts about the feasibility of breaking through the rocks and hesitated about making the attempt. However, his certainty was rewarded with an uncomplicated ascent in six hours from the hut, the rocks proving to be furnished with plentiful holds. Graham Brown and Graven returned to Zermatt with Zürcher and Knubel and capped these successes by adding the Teufelsgrat on the Täschhorn, from which he had turned back in 1925 and 1929, and the Younggrat on the Breithorn – the third ascent, Knubel having made the first, twenty-four years before – to his already impressive haul of climbs.

Graham Brown had good reason to be pleased with his season: seven of the fourteen alpine expeditions judged by Strutt as being worthy of noticing in the *Alpine Journal* were his. He summed up his feelings:

I therefore ended the 1930 season in a feeling of confidence and satisfaction. There could be little doubt that the climbs I had done would
give me a 'reputation' independent of the climbs I had done with
Smythe. For my feeling that I was regarded merely as one of Smythe's
companions could now be discarded, and with that my feeling of
injustice about an untrue inferiority.[3]

That did not stop him brooding over Smythe's calumny. He concluded that
Smythe's outburst over Macphee's treatment in 1928 had been a ruse to
manufacture a quarrel that would serve as an explanation for the severance
of their partnership and deflect attention from the real reason, namely that
Graham Brown had witnessed a breakdown and had chosen not to climb
with Smythe again. He began to assemble a dossier of Smythe's failings and
solicited the opinions of Smythe's companions, who were generally reluctant to abet him. Waller, no friend of Smythe, wrote, 'I will answer your
questions since you ask me so nicely, but it seems a bit like writing dirty
stories, to which I object!'[4] And Graham Brown did not shrink from putting
words into their mouths. Summarising Ward's opinion of Smythe's climbing
proficiency, obtained at dinner at the Athenaeum, he wrote, 'You did not
consider Smythe good on difficult ice.'[5] Ward corrected him, saying that
Graham Brown must have misunderstood him because he had never seen
Smythe on difficult ice and that 'he appeared to me to be a good goer on
snow.'[6] Graham Brown asked Basil Goodfellow to recall their day's climbing
with Smythe on Lliwedd during the gathering at Pen-y-Pass in 1928 and
suggested that Smythe had been feeble.[a] Goodfellow replied that he had
a clear memory of events and did not 'remember any exhibition of terror,
but merely a display of unfitness'.[7]

At the beginning of July 1931 Goodfellow, to whom Graham Brown had
confided his hope of making a third new route on the Brenva Face, joined
Graham Brown and Graven at Montenvers. Josef Knubel was engaged as an
extra guide. On 6 July they traversed the Aiguille des Grands Charmoz.
As they passed over the summit, unbeknown to them, Willo Welzenbach
and Willy Merkl were a few hundred metres below, making an attempt on
the north face that would turn into 'a supreme epic of endurance, willpower
and skill pushed to the limit'.[8] A series of storms pinned the Germans down

---

a   B.R. Goodfellow (1902–1972). Ivan Waller's contemporary at Cambridge. He became a vice-president of
     the Alpine Club (1959–1960).

on the face for three days. The story of their climb and eventual escape received wide publicity and set the scene for the dramas of the attempts on the unclimbed Nordwands during the 1930s, against which Strutt fulminated in the pages of the *Alpine Journal*. This coincidence could be seen as symbolic of the divergence in styles of alpinism that occurred between the wars: Welzenbach representing the innovative and daring modern school, for whom the prize would outweigh the risk, and Graham Brown traditional alpinism, which he would take to its highest standards, rooted in the view that no climb was worth a man's life.

Back at the Montenvers Hotel it was snowing hard and the next day Graham Brown's party slogged up to the Requin Hut from where Graham Brown was introduced to skiing. The unsettled weather and copious fresh snow rendered climbing on the Brenva Face unsafe. Instead, he determined to try the Brenva Ridge. With his guides he planned a timetable that would see them past the difficulties before noon and reduce the risk of being caught in a storm. They made a swift ascent, reaching the summit of Mont Blanc in just seven-and-a-half hours from the Torino Hut. The notorious ice arête, which the pioneers had climbed by sitting astride it *à cheval* and shuffling upwards, 'was very narrowed and corniched ... but a rapid piece of step-cutting took us along it, to my surprise, in nine minutes only'.[9]

Preparations for the 1932 season were overshadowed by a dispute with Zürcher who Graham Brown considered had played a 'very dirty trick' by poaching the services of Graven for the month of August. 'Zürcher seems to have gone to Graven and offered him better terms,' he complained; his action was 'incredible' and a 'great surprise' because their relationship had 'always been a most pleasant one, entirely free of any dispute whatsoever'.[10] On top of his difficulty regarding Graven's services, Graham Brown failed to find an amateur to accompany him: Goodfellow was unavailable, travelling around the world on business and Longland declined his invitation, giving the unfavourable rates of currency exchange and the state of his bank balance as an excuse. In the end, he climbed with Graven and Knubel during July and met Strutt in August for some 'mild guideless walks', wandering over the low-lying cols and peaks of the Chablais Alps, returning to their hotel in time to dress and join Mrs Strutt for champagne and lobster at dinner.

When Graham Brown met his guides at Montenvers at the beginning of July, his priority was to make a third new route on the Brenva Face. He had identified an almost direct line from the Brenva Glacier to the summit of Mont Blanc de Courmayeur taking a rocky rib to a buttress, shaped like a hanging pear and about 275 metres high. Above the buttress was another rocky outcrop capped by the wall of ice cliffs that extends across the Brenva Face. But the weather was 'most wretched' and he altered his plans. On 12 July, they went up to the Gamba Hut, situated in the Innominata basin on the south side of Mont Blanc, and he swore to himself that he would remain there until he could leave by the Peuterey Ridge. It would prove to be third time lucky.

On the first attempt they climbed in hail and mist to the summit of the Aiguille Blanche, from where the colossal scale of the ridge briefly revealed itself. Graham Brown wrote:

> [W]hen you have climbed some 5000ft and have reached a fine and difficult summit, you usually think that the day's work is over. As you come towards this summit, the view in front is largely hidden. When you reach it, you see the great hog's-back of the 'Eckpfeiler' rising across the valley formed by Col de Pétéret to a height of perhaps 1000ft above the col. And that itself is only a step on the way to Mont Blanc de Courmayeur, which soars up to the left another 1500ft or so above the 'Eckpfeiler'. Your fantastic feeling of accomplishment disappears. What you have done becomes merely a measure of what is still to do, and you realise, for the first time in its fullness, the magnificence of the ridge you have set out to climb.[11]

The mist closed in again and the poor visibility obliged them to abandon the climb and make the hazardous descent from the Col de Peuterey. Fortunately, the weather was not as severe as that encountered by Smythe in 1927 and they had the benefit of Knubel's knowledge of the lower section. They avoided the Rochers Gruber by risking steep ice and rockfall in the couloir lying between them and the rock buttress leading to the north summit of the Aiguille Blanche. A week later they turned back in a snowstorm and a further week elapsed before Graham Brown could record, 'got the damned thing at last. It was well worth it.'[12] Their climb from the Gamba Hut to the summit of Mont Blanc and descent to the Grand Mulets Hut took seventeen and a half hours, a highly respectable time: even today, only very fast parties complete the route in a day and most spend a night en route at the Dames Anglaises bivouac hut.

Graham Brown had spent eighteen nights at the Gamba Hut. In between attempts, he had occupied himself making detailed notes of entries in the hut book and subsisted on a diet of bread, cheese and salami. His guides, who required spiritual sustenance as well, descended to Courmayeur each Sunday to attend Mass. Although his stubbornness was rewarded with success, the prolonged stay induced frustration and, eventually, argument. Graham Brown recorded that there was 'a most extraordinary row' between Knubel and Graven carried out in Schweizer-Deutsch. The gist of it, according to Graham Brown's understanding and Graven's later explanation, was that Knubel felt his skill and judgement were being ignored. Knubel, whose exploits had earned him a place in the front rank of guides, resented being always placed in the middle of the rope, which certainly could be viewed as insulting.[b] He thought Graven – almost twenty years his junior – was rash, that Graham Brown knew nothing of mountain conditions and declared the route of *The Pear* 'suicidal'. Graham Brown, sensing criticism, was quick to see it as a manifestation of weakness and, although amity was restored superficially and they continued together for the remainder of his season, Graham Brown had marked Knubel down as a 'funk'. At Christmas he sent a belated cheque to him to settle his account for the summer's guiding, and wrote disingenuously:

> I shall not be climbing with you again next summer, but I would like you to know how much I enjoyed climbing with you the last two years … it is with very much regret that I must terminate our brief companionship. Your kindness of heart and your pleasant companionship, and the way you looked after my comfort, will always be as happy memories as that of the brilliance of your climbing.[13]

In his diary, he wrote, 'Knubel is a nice man, a natural gentleman' but added, 'I do wish he had more "guts".'[14] This was not the first occasion that Graham Brown had fallen out with his guide: Brocklehurst recalled that in 1926, Graham Brown had been 'laying down the law interminably to their guide' who 'lost all patience and said, "Herr Professor, you may be a Herr Professor, but you talk like a little girl."'[15] Nor would it be the last.

---

b   Josef Knubel (1881–1961). His career as a guide spanned half a century. He was a cautious and safe mountaineer. At the close of his career, 'few would have disputed his claim to be considered the most famous of living guides'. (AJ 67: 206)

Chapter 11
The Alpine Club

The Alpine Club was an altogether more modest establishment than Graham Brown's other London club, the Athenaeum, the exclusive haunt of men of distinction in the arts and science, to which he had been elected with Sherrington's support. Situated on Pall Mall, with its Doric portico, bas-relief frieze copied from the Parthenon, and mounting-block erected for the assistance of the first Duke of Wellington, a founder member, the Athenaeum was a world away from the Alpine Club's humbler premises at 23 Savile Row. The latter club's membership still included some who had climbed during the 'silver age' of alpinism, in the second half of the nine- teenth century; in 1920 there were thirty members of fifty years' standing or more. Its traditions were 'piously handed down from generation to gener- ation'[1] leading to a view that the club was getting out of touch, 'browsing in a comfortable old age.'[2] Presidents came and went every three years and in the period between the wars the club's ethos was embodied in Sydney Spencer, honorary secretary for a record eleven years (1923–1934), and Edward Strutt, editor of the *Alpine Journal* for ten (1927–1937). Strutt, through the medium of the journal, prescribed what was proper mountain- eering practice and castigated the deviants: those who wore crampons, used pitons, took unjustifiable risks, and Germans, who were guilty on all three counts. Spencer guarded the social traditions. A new member of the club recalled Spencer explaining to him that 'in addition to being the oldest mountaineering body in the world, the Alpine Club is a unique one – a club for gentlemen who also climb.'[3]

Graham Brown made his debut as a lecturer at the Alpine Club on 6 Nov- ember 1928; the president, Sir George Morse, was in the chair.[a] Graham Brown's dispute regarding the notes published in the *Alpine Journal* was

---

a   G.H. Morse (1857–1931): chairman of a Norfolk brewery and Lord Mayor of Norwich. He was an early practitioner of guideless climbing. He traversed the Matterhorn in his sixty-fifth year.

still fresh; he felt 'quite shy' of Strutt and Spencer and worried that they had formed the opinion that he 'was a very pushing sort of man, and out for personal "credit".[4] He wanted to make a favourable impression and prior to the meeting took the precaution of inquiring about dress code and was advised that a dinner jacket was acceptable, although some speakers still favoured full evening dress. He illustrated his talks with his own slides, which were highly praised. He was an enthusiastic and accomplished photographer; during his ascent of the Peuterey Ridge, he took over eighty photographs, which must have added an hour or two to the time taken for the climb.[b]

The preparation of his articles for publication in the *Alpine Journal* generated an extensive correspondence with Strutt, their shared concern for topographical and historical accuracy forming a basis for a growing friendship. Graham Brown had not curbed his prolix style; even after Strutt had wielded his editorial blue pencil, his article describing his season in 1930 ran to thirty pages. Nor had he overcome his tardiness; Strutt had to pester him to return the proofs so that the journal could go to press on time.

Graham Brown developed a serious interest in Alpine history, which he cultivated through avid book collecting. At Spencer's invitation he contributed a historical chapter to the volume on mountaineering in the Lonsdale Library.[c] In it he expounded his views on the attractions of the sport which place him squarely in the 'heroic' rather than the 'aesthetic' school of mountaineering:[d]

> Mountaineering, as practised today in Europe, is really an acquired taste ... Whilst the scenery of the valleys appeals to many tastes, like any sweet wine, the taste for high scenery has to be acquired, like a palate for great vintages. Much of the pleasure is intellectual rather than aesthetic – the recognition of old friends from new aspects, the sight of mountains (with our very eyes) which we have long known

b Between 1925 and 1954 Graham Brown took over 10,000 photographs which he catalogued by hand, giving the date and time, place, subject, exposure time and aperture for each.

c The Lonsdale Library of Sports, Games and Pastimes was conceived as a series of authoritative, instructional books. The volume on cricket was edited by Douglas Jardine who led the 'bodyline' tour to Australia in 1932-1933. HRH the Duke of Gloucester was co-editor of the volume on big game hunting – 'the best and most comprehensive book on African shooting yet published'.

d In his history of British climbing Simon Thompson discerned two strands in the motivation of climbers. Aesthetes emphasise the beauty and spiritual appeal of mountains; the heroic school is more concerned with personal courage and the pursuit of freedom and self-fulfilment. The aesthetic school is contemplative, the heroic is competitive.

by history and repute. The intimate views which we gain during an ascent are beautiful, but the summit view rarely is; save for recognitions which we may make, it is often an incoherent jumble of peaks. The possibility of actual exploration (with all its strong incentive) has almost passed; no virgin summits remain in the Alps, and few yet untried ways to old peaks. Nevertheless mountaineering is as attractive as it ever was. This attraction is in part due to the physical and intellectual pleasure of the exercise of its technique – comparable to that given by a good stroke at tennis, played correctly and placed with accuracy. But, in part, the attraction is historical and social. There is an indescribable pleasure in repeating a great mountain ascent the history of which is well known to you, and overcoming with your own judgement and limbs the difficulties which you have long known from books.

There is a different pleasure, but as great, in discussing your ascents with friends, who have accomplished them on other occasions, or perhaps have shared your own experiences. These are but a few of the pleasures of the modern mountaineer.[5]

In 1932 Graham Brown represented the Alpine Club at the International Congress of Alpinism at Chamonix, where he delivered a paper reviewing the club's achievements during the preceding decade and aired his own views on mountaineering during this period, which were more measured and sympathetic than Strutt's strictures. Crampons were permissible – he used them himself – pitons, too, but not on British rock. He admired the spirit of the younger generation and although he thought its members sometimes displayed 'an insobriety of judgement', he dismissed the view that certain routes were totally unjustifiable. 'What is unjustifiable, however,' he believed, 'is criticism that a certain route is itself unjustifiable under any conditions – for it is possible that any route however dangerous it seems to be, is a safe one (as far as objective danger is concerned) under some special conditions of weather and mountain', and he counselled: 'two things must be allied in attempts upon the few unsolved problems of the Alps – sobriety of judgement and intoxication of courage ('daring' if you will.)'.[6] These were the attributes that had underpinned his own successes on the Brenva Face. He also recognised the importance of rock climbing in the contemporary British climbing scene and the high standards attained. He had the temerity to suggest to Strutt that descriptions of 'first-class British rock-climbs' should be included in the journal, arguing that the accounts would show 'foreign rock-climbers that first-class rock-climbing has been done in Great Britain' and 'it would knit our home rock climbers to the Club.'[7] The suggestion was ignored; after all, it was the *Alpine Journal*.

Graham Brown considered that he did 'not set much store on "reputation"',[8] but was undoubtedly gratified by a remark made by Eustace Thomas: 'You know, people did not give you much of the credit for the Brenva climbs, but now they are beginning to think that you have been unfairly treated.'[e,9] In 1932 he was offered a seat on the club's committee, which he was 'honoured and flattered' to accept.[10] Whilst Graham Brown's prestige within the club was increasing, Smythe was the subject of muttered disapproval. His self-publicity and moneymaking from lecturing and writing about mountaineering rankled with some members, whom he provoked further with an after-dinner speech in which he likened the Alpine Club to a yak, a creature with a reputation for stupidity and stubbornness. Graham Brown thought it was in poor taste; Strutt considered it 'the most vulgar that he had heard'; even the kindly Sherrington, who was Graham Brown's guest, apparently commented, 'Your friend can climb but he can't speak.'[11] The timing of the speech – in reply to the toast 'The Alpine Club' at its annual dinner – was tactless, but Smythe was articulating a view held by some younger members of the club, namely that the establishment was out of touch. With Douglas Busk, he enlisted like-minded members into a group calling itself the 'Young Shavers', whose aim was to modernise the outlook of the club.[f,g]

In 1931 Smythe led a successful expedition to Kamet in the Garwhal Himalaya. He and his companions were the first climbers to reach a summit of 25,000 feet (7,620 metres), although greater altitudes had been reached on Everest. Graham Brown was unimpressed. In an article for the *Alpine Journal*, he dismissed the ascent as 'a mere record', implying that there had been no significant mountaineering challenge, which upset both the earlier explorers of the mountain and members of the successful expedition.[12] C.F. Meade, who had made several unsuccessful attempts, protested to the

---

e   Eustace Thomas (1869–1960) was the first Englishman to climb all the summits over 4,000 metres in the Alps.

f   D.L. Busk (1906–1990), diplomat. He was also a member of what Graham Brown considered to be a cabal of Old Etonians that plotted to have him removed from the editorship of the *Alpine Journal*.

g   Busk recalled that one morning he received a phone call from Smythe who said, 'All my best ideas come to me in my bath and I've just had one. Let us call ourselves the "Young Shavers"' to distinguish themselves from the traditionalists within the club, some of whom wore beards. (*Mountain*, 54: 40–45)

editor of the journal that the ascent of Kamet posed a 'formidable' mountaineering problem. E.B. Beauman, one of Smythe's team, wrote to Spencer
complaining on behalf of the expedition and demanded that his letter
should be placed before the committee of the Alpine Club. Spencer pleaded
with Graham Brown to write, 'a short letter saying that you had no intention
of belittling the performance of the Kamet Expedition' adding, 'I should
take it as a personal favour if you would.'[13] But, of course, depreciating the
performance of Smythe's expedition was exactly his intention and Graham
Brown was intransigent.

Towards the end of 1932 the possibility of an expedition to Everest in the
following year became known and a team needed to be selected. Graham
Brown was tantalised; a younger man with a record in the Alps similar to his
would have been a strong contender for a place, but he was now fifty years
old and, realising that his age was against him, did not apply. So, he was flattered to learn that he had been seriously considered as a candidate but any
pleasure he had from this recognition was counterbalanced by the fact that
Smythe had been chosen. He wrote to Goodfellow:

> I don't know whether to be glad or sorry that he [Smythe] is in the
> party – for I cannot help feeling that the expedition will show him in
> his true colours … I suppose this is a bit mean of me; I really feel that
> he, by being taken, is keeping out some better man than himself.[14]

He set out to discredit Smythe, giving his version of events on the *Route
Major* to Spencer and Strutt, who, according to Graham Brown, concluded
'that Ruttledge [the appointed leader of the expedition] should be told of
Smythe's weakness and the possibility of his cowardice'. He noted smugly:

> I must say that the fact that the leader of the Everest expedition has
> been properly warned of the possible danger which Smythe may be
> to the expedition is a great relief to me. I have always been afraid for
> my own conscience should there be a disaster; and now feel acquit-
> ted of any personal responsibility.[15]

1   John Graham Brown (centre) with his children (clockwise from top left): TGB, Thor, Alex and Janey, *c.*1896. *Photo by courtesy of Francis Graham-Brown.*
2   Professor Charles Sherrington *c.*1905. *Photo by courtesy of the Wellcome Collection.*
3   TGB at foot of Y Boulder in Mosedale, June 1914. *Reproduced with permission of the National Library of Scotland.*
4   TGB climbing Y Boulder. *Reproduced with permission of the National Library of Scotland.*

5 Gritstone Club at Langdale, Easter 1923. TGB second left. *Photo by courtesy of the Gritstone Club.*

6 Dufourspitze, Monte Rosa, 1925. Standing: (L–R) Letts and Christian Almer; sitting (L–R) TGB and Gabriel Lochmatter. *Reproduced with permission of the National Library of Scotland.*

7 TGB, Lake Como, 1926. *Photo by H.C. Wood, reproduced with permission of the National Library of Scotland.*

8 The fateful meeting at Montenvers, 1927. (L–R) E.S. Herbert, TGB, F.S. Smythe. *Photo by G. Macphee, Alpine Club Photo Library, London.*

9 TGB making notes at the bivouac hut on Col d'Estelette, en route to the Aiguille de Tré la Tête, August 1927. His companion, Herbert, who took the photo, annotated it: 'authentic contemporary portrait of Diogenes'. *Reproduced with permission of the National Library of Scotland.*

10 The Brenva Face seen from the Rochefort Ridge. *Photo by Peter Foster.*

11 The Brenva Face of Mont Blanc showing (L–R) the lines of *Via della Pera* ●, *Route Major* ●, *Sentinelle Rouge* ● and the *Brenva Spur* ●. *Reproduced with permission of the National Library of Scotland.*

12 Smythe on easier ground at the top of the *Sentinelle Rouge. September 1927. Photo by TGB, reproduced with permission of the National Library of Scotland.*

13 Professor Graham Brown, FRS, c.1929. *Reproduced with permission of the National Library of Scotland.*

14 Summit of Aiguille des Grands Charmoz, 1931. (L–R) Graven, Knubel, TGB. *Photo by B. Goodfellow, reproduced with permission of the National Library of Scotland.*

15 TGB roping down. Chamonix Aiguilles, 1931. *Photo by B. Goodfellow, reproduced with permission of the National Library of Scotland.*

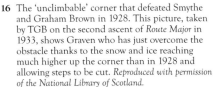

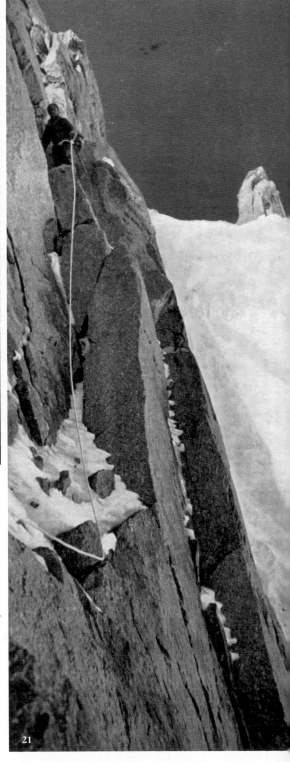

16 The 'unclimbable' corner that defeated Smythe and Graham Brown in 1928. This picture, taken by TGB on the second ascent of *Route Major* in 1933, shows Graven who has just overcome the obstacle thanks to the snow and ice reaching much higher up the corner than in 1928 and allowing steps to be cut. *Reproduced with permission of the National Library of Scotland.*

17 Aufdenblatten at the top of the 'unclimbable' corner in 1933. Beneath him is the rock tongue. In 1928 TGB descended steep snow and ice behind it, turning at its base, and then ascended the steep snow/ice in the foreground. *Photo by TGB, reproduced with permission of the National Library of Scotland.*

18 Annus Mirabilis, 1933. TGB at the Promontoire Hut. *Alpine Club Photo Library, London.*

19 Frank Smythe, Everest 1933. © *Royal Geographical Society (with IBG).*

20 Aufdenblatten on the *Pear Buttress*, 1933. *Photo by TGB, reproduced with permission of the National Library of Scotland.*

21 Graven nearing the top of the *Pear Buttress*, 1933. *Photo by TGB, reproduced with permission of the National Library of Scotland.*

22 Mount Foraker, 1932 (aerial view from about 3,000 metres). *Photo by Henry Hall jnr., by courtesy of the NLS.*

23 The Foraker party. (L–R) Storey, Oscar Houston, Waterston, Charlie Houston, TGB. *Reproduced with permission of the National Library of Scotland.*

24 Mount Foraker from Spy-Glass Hill, 1934: 'That view ... must be one of the greatest mountain views in the world' (*Alpine Journal*, 47: 26). The highest point on the skyline is the north-east summit, about ten miles away as the crow flies. *Photo by C.S. Houston, reproduced with permission of the National Library of Scotland.*

25 North-east summit of Mount Foraker. (L–R) Waterston, TGB, Houston. 'The cheap thermometer ... indicated a temperature of -4°F (-20°C) ... the wind exaggerated the coldness.' (*Alpine Journal*, 47: 21). *Reproduced with permission of the National Library of Scotland.*

26 The summiteers. (L–R) TGB, Houston, Waterston. TGB and Houston are wearing tailor-made, windproof suits of Grenfell cloth, designed by Houston and costing $25. All three are wearing Barker boots. *Reproduced with permission of the National Library of Scotland.*

27 A snowy Easter 1936. TGB belaying on Arrowhead Ridge on the Napes. *Photo by Geoffrey Barratt, reproduced with permission of the National Library of Scotland.*

28 Nanda Devi 'seen from entry on the meadows of the inner basin'. *Photo by C.S. Houston, reproduced with permission of the National Library of Scotland.*

29 TGB, Nanda Devi expedition, 1936. *Photo by Adams Carter, reproduced with permission of the National Library of Scotland.*

30 Charlie Houston. Nanda Devi expedition, 1936. *Photo by Adams Carter, reproduced with permission of the National Library of Scotland.*

31 South Ridge of Nanda Devi. 'Bird's eye view of the ridge walking down from Camp II.' *Photo by C.S. Houston, reproduced with permission of the National Library of Scotland.*

32 South Ridge of Nanda Devi. The route of ascent follows the rocky ridge in the middle of the picture (from R–L) that merges with a less prominent snow arête (just below the left-hand skyline) which was followed to the mixed ground and summit above. *Reproduced with permission of the National Library of Scotland.*

33

A

34

33 Masherbrum from the south. Seen from Masherbrum Glacier. *Photo by TGB, RGS Collection by courtesy of John Russell.*

34 Masherbrum showing the highest point reached (A). *Photo by TGB, RGS Collection by courtesy of John Russell.*

35 Dak bungalow at Zoji La. Front to back: TGB, Harrison and Waller. Note the skis propped against the wall. *Photo by Robin Hodgkin, courtesy of Adam Hodgkin.*

36 Masherbrum seen from Hushe Valley. *Photo by Robin Hodgkin, courtesy of Adam Hodgkin.*

37 Scaly Alley. A party of porters can be seen halfway up the slope on the right. *Photo by Robin Hodgkin, courtesy of Adam Hodgkin.*

38 TGB (R) in conversation with Swiss mountaineer André Roch at Kleine Scheidegg, 1948. Goodfellow, who took the photo, recorded that the subject of their animated conversation was 'Brenva'. *Alpine Club Photo Library, London.*

39 Glencoe, 1950. (L–R) Colin Pibworth, TGB and Gordon Parish. *Reproduced with permission of the National Library of Scotland.*

40 TGB, Glencoe, 1950. *Photo by D. Bird, reproduced with permission of the National Library of Scotland.*

41 Alpine Club Centenary Reception, December 1957. TGB presenting a copy of *The First Ascent of Mont Blanc* to HRH Prince Philip. *Alpine Club Photo Library, London.*
42 *Thekla* in Bergen, 1959. *Reproduced with permission of the National Library of Scotland.*
43 TGB at sea. *Reproduced with permission of the National Library of Scotland.*

When, to his dismay, he learned that the message may not have been delivered, possibly due to a diplomatic oversight on the part of Spencer and Strutt, Graham Brown took matters into his own hands and invited Ruttledge to lunch with him at the Athenaeum. Still smarting from his recent discovery that the tale of Smythe saving his life on *Route Major* had been circulating in the Alpine Club, Graham Brown was in no mood to be delicate and told Ruttledge that he:

> regarded Smythe as a fraud ... I said he funked ... I said he would probably have no 'guts' at high elevation ... I told him that Smythe told lies.[16]

Smythe and members of his team on Kamet formed the core of the expedition to Everest in 1933 and Smythe played a prominent role. He overcame the technical crux of the route, the steep and in places overhanging twelve-metre ice wall, which blocked the way to the North Col and later, when his companion Eric Shipton turned back from their summit attempt, he pressed on alone reaching an altitude of 8,595 metres. These achievements were proof of Smythe's skill and determination and made nonsense of Graham Brown's slanderous attack.

The expedition's failure to reach the summit led to questions being asked about its leadership and the effectiveness of the Mount Everest Committee, which was responsible for its planning. Again, Graham Brown, who was still serving on the committee of the Alpine Club, was sucked into controversy. The re-appointment of Hugh Ruttledge as leader for the 1936 expedition was a messy business and polarised opinions. Ruttledge was challenged for the leadership by Colin Crawford, who had been a member of the expeditions in 1922 and 1933.[h] On both occasions Crawford had been slow to acclimatise but in 1933 had worked hard in support of the expedition, making half a dozen trips to resupply Camp IV at 6,950 metres, seventy metres or so below the crest of the North Col. His challenge had the backing of a number of members of the 1933 expedition, who considered Ruttledge's leadership had been weak. But Sir Percy Cox, chairman of the MEC, pushed Ruttledge's appointment through using his casting vote and exacerbated matters by demanding Crawford's resignation from the committee. Cox went to the

---

h   C.G. Crawford (1890–1959). He died in his seventieth year, reputedly with a smile on his face, having just hit a ball for six out of his local cricket ground.

Alpine Club to explain his reasons and following his presentation, C.F. Meade, the vice president, and Graham Brown proposed the motion that Crawford should resign from the MEC, which was duly passed. But when they learned that Cox's statement may have been economical with the truth, Meade and Graham Brown became uneasy about their action and advised Crawford to refrain from resigning whilst they tried to unravel Cox's chicanery. For a fortnight, he and Meade corresponded almost daily and when, for the first time in a week, there was no letter from Meade, Graham Brown quipped, 'my life is empty'.[17] They concluded that Crawford had been treated unfairly and at the next meeting of the Alpine Club's committee sought endorsement for their advice to Crawford not to resign, but their motion was defeated and they both resigned. Graham Brown considered they had mishandled the affair and wrote to Meade, 'This just shows that I don't think quite quickly enough during a debate [but] on the other hand, I think that both of us have the knack of getting down to essentials when we think at leisure.'[18] Their challenge was the first of several attempts to re-align the relationship between the Alpine Club and the MEC and modernise the approach to climbing Everest.

The MEC's procedure for selecting the members of the Everest expeditions was a particular concern. There was still a suspicion that being a good chap counted for more than being a good climber. The selection of J.M. Gavin for the 1936 expedition was a case in point. Aged twenty-four, educated at public school and Cambridge, he was a lieutenant in the Royal Engineers and had spent two brief seasons in the Alps before joining Smythe in Zermatt in 1935, where they climbed a number of classic routes. On the basis of this experience, Smythe recommended him for selection, subject to a satisfactory medical report, and proposed him for membership of the Alpine Club. According to the club's procedure his application was first considered by the committee, which included Graham Brown, and it would have been surprising if a nominee of Smythe's did not receive special scrutiny by him. The majority view was that Gavin's qualifications were insufficient for membership and he was advised to defer his application for another year. In the meantime Gavin had performed extremely well in the physical examination supervised by the RAF and had been invited officially to join the Everest expedition.[i] Thus there arose the incongruous situation that the MEC, strongly influenced by Smythe, had selected someone to attempt Everest whose mountaineering experience was judged inadequate for membership of the Alpine Club. The Alpine Club committee was asked to reconsider. To avoid embarrassment all round, the committee, which no longer included Meade and Graham Brown, accepted Gavin's qualifications and his name went forward for balloting by the membership. Graham Brown sensed there had been 'a wangle' and wrote to Meade, who, in turn, protested to the club's secretary. When the secretary responded, Meade replied, summing up the issue at stake:

> According to your letter the Everest Committee has selected an inexperienced mountaineer on the strength of a medical report, and apparently the AC committee approve the wisdom of this action. I agree that the man in question was, as you say, on the borderline, but my point is that he was unfortunately on the wrong side of it.[19]

Graham Brown talked of blackballing him, and probably did, but Gavin was duly elected. Smythe, who was already on his way to Everest, 'heard with considerable amusement the idiotic goings on at the AC' and wrote to his friend, Greene:

> Had Gavin been blackballed the whole expedition would have resigned en bloc. As it is I've come to the conclusion that a club that includes such as Finch and Graham Brown is not worth belonging to … So I shall probably save my next year's sub, and do a damn good dinner on it.[20]

The campaign to reform the Everest Committee grumbled on for several years with Graham Brown sniping from the wings.

---

i   Great importance was attached to the results of a test that involved blowing through a tube to raise and sustain a column of mercury, even though its value as a predictor of performance at high altitude was unproven. A poor result was the downfall of a number of aspirants (including John Hunt). Gavin's result was exceptional. Graham Brown wondered whether he had cheated and wrote to Sir David Munro, asking whether the test could be manipulated. Munro thought it would be impossible to falsify the result.

Chapter 12
Annus Mirabilis

Graham Brown's Alpine season in 1933 was remarkable. During an extraordinary fortnight, he climbed Mont Blanc six times, making three new
routes, two of which were at the highest standard of difficulty for the period.
In addition he made half a dozen first ascents on peaks above Zermatt and
in the Dauphiné. Strutt, who was not prone to flattery, wrote, 'Your season
was truly miraculous, I don't think anyone has quite equalled it, not even
G.W.Y. in 1911.'[1]

Uncharacteristically, Graham Brown commenced preparations for his
season well in advance. He endeavoured to smooth over his dispute with
Zürcher about Graven's services. He was sure that Zürcher 'must have been
acting under some sort of mistaken idea', that he had only to state his
'position clearly' for Zürcher to agree that Graven should guide Graham
Brown in July and August, and concluded, 'Now do be a good fellow and
drop this business about Graven.'[2] Zürcher's response was silent acquies-
cence. Graven expressed reservations about tackling major new expeditions,
on which the difficulties were completely unknown, with just an amateur
client in tow, even allowing for Graham Brown's undoubted competence,
so Graham Brown agreed to employ an additional guide. He engaged Alfred
Aufdenblatten, recommended to him by Richard Kay, a fellow member of
the Alpine Club, who wrote, 'He is in apple pie condition, and is a really first-
class fellow both on rock and ice.' He could personally vouch for his steadi-
ness and strength because Aufdenblatten had saved his life. Whilst climbing
the Dent Blanche, Kay's leading guide was struck and killed by a rock
dislodged by a party above; as he fell, he pulled Kay after him but 'Alfred's
presence of mind at the critical second and his wonderful agility and
strength' prevented Kay being dragged to his death.[3] Nevertheless, Kay
warned that Aufdenblatten was unwilling to attempt routes such as the
North Face of the Grandes Jorasses or the South Face of the Täschhorn

because he considered them too dangerous for a man with a wife and two children dependent on him. Graham Brown replied:

Aufdenblatten seems to me a most attractive proposition [and] I am glad that he takes climbing seriously enough to decline to tackle the N face of the Grandes Jorasses or the S face of the Täschhorn – at any rate without very grave consideration.[4]

However, when Aufdenblatten's prudence later frustrated Graham Brown's ambition, understanding was replaced by the accusation of cowardice.

Graham Brown also wanted to recruit another amateur to the party, for if Graven had made a case for a second guide, Graham Brown considered that the ideal team comprised a party of four, climbing as two separate ropes, enabling each pair to climb independently but allowing for mutual support in the face of major difficulties. He approached A.E. Foot, a schoolmaster at Eton, who had made a guided ascent of the Peuterey Ridge in 1930 and whose name he had spotted in the Gamba Hut book during his lengthy sojourn there the previous season. In his letter to him, Graham Brown outlined his objectives:

I like to be climbing all the time, and hate being down in the valley more than is absolutely necessary. I want to complete the great ridges of Mt. Blanc. I want to go out for new ways of any sort – but particularly for the big ones; and these are rare and fairly difficult. If I thought that there was a sound way up the Grandes Jorasses, where the party would not be in danger, I would go for it like a shot.[5]

Foot replied self-deprecatingly that he was no 'fire-eater' and that his instinct was 'always to go up the mountain by the railway if the cogs on which it runs look sound'.[6] Graham Brown responded to his teasing saying, 'I am not naturally gifted with very long legs, and the doctor says that pulling them is bad for them'.[7] Foot was unable to join Graham Brown and instead put him in touch with his companion on the Peuterey Ridge, J.M. Vyvyan, whom he described as 'the sort of fellow who dreams of the North Face of the Grandes Jorasses'.[8] Vyvyan, a diplomat attached to the British Embassy in Moscow, was due some leave and agreed to climb with Graham Brown but dropped out after just one route because he was unfit. Consequently,

Graham Brown spent the season climbing with Graven and Aufdenblatten until Goodfellow joined him for the last two weeks. Graham Brown had lobbied Goodfellow's employers to obtain additional leave for him so they could attempt the *Pear Buttress* together, but to his chagrin, Goodfellow, unaware of the favour, chose to spend the extra fortnight climbing guideless in the Valais, before meeting Graham Brown in the Dauphiné.

Graham Brown arrived in Zermatt on Sunday 9 July having slipped through French and Swiss customs with two pounds of contraband tobacco secreted in his luggage, and after just three hours' sleep, set out for the north face of the Wellenkuppe. He shunned the usual practice of getting fit and acclimatising to altitude on smaller, 'training' peaks, and instead would attempt a big peak at the beginning of every Alpine holiday, saying in justi-fication, 'While this practice may have the appearance of intensifying the initial purgatory, it actually shortens the painful training that one always dreads.'[9] Adhering to this policy, he chose for his next climb the Matterhorn via the Zmutt Ridge, a classic testpiece. He and his guides went up to the Hörnli Hut the following day but a storm prevented them setting foot on the route. Just five days after arriving in the Alps from England, Graham Brown made a new route on Monte Rosa, climbing the Weisstor (north-north-west) face of Nordend, another example of his astute judgement of conditions and potentially dangerous terrain. This face is high and com-prises an almost continuous wall of compact rock, capped by ice cliffs formed by the edge of the glacier which flows north-west from Nordend. The climbing was sometimes difficult and was very exposed throughout. The crux was a ninety-metre traverse on steep ice below the ice cliffs to reach a gap. Graven cut steps with one hand while maintaining balance with the other, using handholds he had nicked in the ice. Graham Brown noted that this 'exceptional passage occupied nearly an hour.'[10]

On 20 July Graham Brown set out for the Italian side of Mont Blanc. He travelled by bus to Courmayeur, via Martigny and the Great St Bernard Pass. Sitting next to the driver, he indulged his habit of note-taking, recording the changing speed of the bus and the gears employed. As they approached the Italian customs post, he stuffed his pipe tobacco into his pockets and tried to 'look innocent'. Asked if he had any chocolate or cigarettes he was able to reply truthfully that he did not. Fortunately his luggage, which contained a camera and twenty rolls of film, was not searched. Had they been discov-ered they would have been confiscated; in Mussolini's Italy, a foreigner with a camera was a potential spy.

In Courmayeur, 'a hot and stuffy place', he stayed at the Savoy Hotel, which he described to Whymper's daughter, who had asked him to recommend some accommodation, as 'a very simple and a not too clean place and I don't think it would do for you at all'.[11] The good hotels were rather too 'dressy' for his taste.

Just before 1.00 a.m. on 26 July Graham Brown and his guides left the Torino Hut by lantern light to attempt *The Pear*, the missing panel from his 'triptych' on the Brenva Face of Mont Blanc. They followed the now familiar route to Col Moore from where, instead of climbing up and across to the Red Sentinel, they traversed horizontally over broken rocks and a series of snow- and ice-filled couloirs to reach the edge of a large snow slope which separated them from the rocks that led to the foot of the *Pear Buttress*, about 150 metres away. Here in the dim light they paused to examine the proposed line. In his sanitised account, Graham Brown wrote that 'the dominance of *The Pear* had a strong psychological effect which forbade the attempt to the party' and that 'it was the end of a dream'.[12] His diary makes it clear that Aufdenblatten refused to go on because he considered that the route was too dangerous – almost all of it is exposed to the risk of avalanche and falling stones or ice. Graham Brown wrote, 'Aufdenblatten's cowardice [scratched out and replaced with faint heart] had ruined my hopes. ... I could have hated Aufdenblatten at that moment'.[13] Thwarted, Graham Brown reacted by directing his guides to *Route Major*, which still awaited a second ascent.

By 6.30 a.m. they had crossed the great couloir and were safely established on the rib where they removed their crampons and enjoyed a halt in the sun. Graham Brown relished the prospect of reassessing objectively the difficulties and quality of the route, for he recognised that the uncertainties surrounding a first ascent may have distorted his impressions. With Graven and Aufdenblatten sharing the lead, Graham Brown was able to record and photograph the climb in painstaking detail. The character of the climb differed from 1928 in two important respects. First, snow reached much higher up the 'unclimbable' corner, enabling Graven to ascend it directly without much difficulty and avoid the need to cut steps down and around the rock tongue, as Graham Brown had done on the first ascent. Secondly, during the five years that had elapsed, the summit ice had advanced and the final buttress was capped by a formidable ice cliff, mainly overhanging and more than ten metres high at its lowest point. Graven produced another fine display of ice craft to overcome the obstacle. Graham Brown followed and was forced to straddle the flake of ice *à cheval* to progress. At every stage on the climb, Graham Brown anxiously asked Graven for his assessment of the difficulties. As far as the final buttress, Graven rated the route as '*Ganz gut*' – quite good – for guideless climbers. But after overcoming the final buttress and the séracs above, his opinion was more respectful: '*Ich congratuliere sie, Herr Brown.*'[14]

On reaching the col between the summits of Mont Blanc, Graham Brown resurrected the idea of making the first crossing by going down the south-west Miage Face. After descending for forty-five minutes they met dangerously soft snow and were forced to retrace their steps and locate the rocky rib of the Tournette Spur that flanks the face and provides a safer way down. The time spent on this detour proved critical. Night fell before they reached the Sella Hut and, at 10.40 p.m., twenty-one-and-a-half hours after leaving the Torino Hut, they were forced to bivouac. They passed a miserably cold and sleepless night, which seemed interminable. When, at last, dawn broke, they roused themselves 'not from sleep, but from a sort of numb lethargy'.[15] Still in the shadow of Mont Blanc there was no sun to warm them and in an attempt to thaw their frozen boots they were reduced to burning pieces of paper inside them.

Over the next two days they made their way westward in easy stages to the Durier Hut, perched on the Col de Miage. Refreshed, Graham Brown now decided on another lengthy expedition, returning to Courmayeur over the summits of Aiguille de Bionnassay, Mont Blanc, Mont Maudit and Mont Blanc du Tacul. On their descent, late in the day, they toiled in dreadful heat through soft, deep snow from the Col du Midi to the Col du Géant. Graham Brown confessed that he had been driven on by the prospect of a record. The journey took nineteen hours and forty minutes. After a day's rest they went up to the Gamba Hut and the next day climbed Mont Blanc by the Brouillard Arête, another long and tiring ascent. They battled against a strong and chilling wind 'which seemed to be a mad and vicious thing bent on stupefying us' and still fatigued from their previous climbs, just kept 'slogging along'.[16]

Graham Brown resolved to make another attempt on *The Pear*. 'Would I pluck it or would it fall to some robber?' he wondered, but he was determined: 'I felt that the fruit must be mine, for I would have the whole Brenva face to myself.'[17] Aufdenblatten remained unwilling, Graham Brown noting in his diary that 'G[raven] says that Alfred will not go as he is frightened',[18] but a few days later, he capitulated. On the way up to the Torino Hut they met Miss Whymper coming down from an ascent of the Dent du Géant. The following day was spent resting and recuperating in the hut because Graham Brown had slept badly the previous night due to the rowdiness of some English undergraduates staying in his hotel: 'O & C men. Strange clothes ... Gramophone. Few gentlemen.'[19] With Graven he drew up a timetable for the next day's climbing that would minimise their exposure to the risk of falling ice and agreed a plan of retreat if they were 'hopelessly stopped'. Their talk engendered some apprehension. Graham Brown's chance meeting with Whymper's daughter caused him to reflect that 'like Whymper and the Matterhorn this *Pear* had grown on me and obsessed me for several years.'[20]

At 4.15 a.m. on 5 August, they reached the point where they had turned back ten days earlier and set out at once to traverse the snow and ice slope to gain the rocks that lead to the foot of *The Pear*:

> [T]he silence gripped me. Far below on our left was the surface of the glacier, across which rose in deep shadow the mass of the Eck-pfeiler and the Pétéret Arête, its crest brooding under the thin milk-iness of the moonlight sky. In front was the great face, incredibly magnificent in the faint light, rising abruptly in dim majesty. All was in darkness, so that vague shape alone could be seen, and the differ-ence between snow and rock scarcely showed in the reflected light from the moon-bathed slopes on the right and high above us. We went ever deeper into shadow until distance and size were no more, and we seemed to be penetrating the very essence of a grandeur which knew no measure and had no form. The night was still black.[21]

The spikes of their crampons were blunt from heavy use and Graven had to nick steps in the ice, which he did so rapidly that Graham Brown could hardly keep pace and he slipped, stopping his slide using his axe and grazing his knuckles in the process. They went on as quickly as possible until they reached the relative safety of the rock rib up which they continued, arriving at the base of *The Pear* at the same time as the first rays of sunshine. The crux of the route lay above. Telescopic inspection of the rocks had suggested they might be unclimbable, but, although steep, the granite was sound and amply provided with holds and they progressed rapidly up a succession of little walls and steep chimneys. At 6.00 a.m. they halted on a ledge. Lost in the immensity of the Brenva Face, their situation was 'magnificent' and the view looking out and towards Mont Maudit was a 'wonderful scene'.[22] On the left, close at hand, was 'a great precipice of red rock, nearly vertical' and beyond it the 'white silhouette' of the Brenva Ridge. Farther round 'the wild and incredible' ridge of the Aiguilles du Diable dominated the view and the distant skyline comprised the summits of the peaks that form the monstrous southern wall above the Argentière Glacier.

They went on, weaving their way upwards by a series of ledges, the difficulties never sufficient to hold them up but always demanding concentration, to reach a point just below a prominent snow ledge, about three-quarters of the way up the buttress. From this point there was a choice of routes to the top of the buttress. The left hand lay over broken rocks but was exposed to the risk of falling ice; the right hand looked much steeper and more difficult, but was considerably safer. Prudently, they took the latter.[a] The climbing was very exposed: Graham Brown observed matter-of-factly that a falling object would not come to a halt until it reached the surface of the glacier almost a thousand metres below. Their route followed the only line of weakness: 'The climbing had given the very strong impression that there was no choice of route and that twelve feet or less of smooth rock if met anywhere on the way would stop us for good.'[23] They were committed. The tension rose. At one point Graven wavered, saying, 'This is the end of *The Pear*' but with Graham Brown's encouragement pressed on.[24] Eventually they emerged on to easier ground and saw that no insuperable difficulties lay ahead. Graham Brown described 'this moment of deliverance':

> Below are the dark, doubtful approach and the splendid buttress, where all the difficulties of the route are pressed into less than a thousand feet of suspense – the action deliberate and grave, the line of ascent like a thread which might snap. Above are to come interest, variety and rare beauty, but complete assurance and wide freedom – the climbing buoyant and light-hearted.[25]

---

a   The party that made the second ascent and took the alternative line was almost overwhelmed by falling ice.

They climbed up snow and rock to the summit of a prominent gendarme. Looking up, the view was dominated by a massive ice cliff, its sheer face, about 150 metres high, etched with a geometric design of undulating striations formed over the years by successive layers of ice and snow. The final section of the route lay up steep snow and passed through a barrier of séracs which, except for one part, posed no problems. Thirteen hours after leaving the Torino Hut, they arrived on the summit of Mont Blanc de Courmayeur. Their ascent had been watched through the coin-in-the-slot telescope at the Torino Hut, where, according to Miss Whymper, 'there was much demand for small change that day!'[26]

Their intention was to descend by the Peuterey Ridge, since this was potentially the quickest way down to Courmayeur and Graham Brown's guides were anxious to attend Mass the following day. Aufdenblatten started down 'very gingerly'; Graven became impatient. There was an altercation and Graven was 'rude and contemptuous'. Clearly descent by this route in the icy conditions would have been very slow so they turned back and made the long descent to the Dôme Hut, which they reached at 7.30 p.m. They rested, drank hot coffee and ate supper before setting off again for Courmayeur in twilight. As night fell the moon rose and they made their way down the rubble-strewn Miage Glacier by its light. At just after midnight, as they trudged down Val Veni, they were stopped by two Italian soldiers who demanded to see their papers. A torch was shone into Graham Brown's face and the resulting stupid grin convinced the guards that the party was harmless. They arrived in Courmayeur at 2.00 a.m. on Sunday morning, almost twenty-six hours since setting out from the Torino Hut.

They rested. Graham Brown immediately set to writing a detailed letter to Professor Gask, twelve sides of close handwriting, describing his ascent of *Route Major* and *The Pear*. He was sensitive to possible criticism that their ascent of *The Pear* had been reckless; after all, Knubel had thought it suicidal, Aufdenblatten had initially refused to attempt it, and another respected guide described the ascent as 'the first and last'.[27] In his letter, he rehearsed his defence:

> People will say, of course, that it is risky – perhaps unjustifiable. If they do, it is all rot. The route certainly <u>may</u> be dangerous; but if proper precautions are taken – the state of the séracs verified and the foot of the ridge reached early in the day, the route is no more

dangerous than the ordinary route to the Grépon. In justification of our judgement – no ice fell whilst we were on the face. In justification of my own sobriety, I abandoned all thought of the route last year, when the séracs looked dangerous.'[b,28]

He was also anxious to establish the quality and difficulty of *The Pear* and discussed the matter repeatedly with Graven who said that *The Pear* and *Route Major* were 'in a class by themselves'. However, Graham Brown's joy in his success must be imagined for it only surfaces in his writing with the 1944 publication of his book, *Brenva*, in which Arnold Lunn, mountaineer and critic, discerned:

> It is with a mind wholly engrossed with the pride of a great achieve-ment that Graham Brown turns for the last time in the Val Veni to see the moonlight sleeping on that great Alpine face which will be associated with his name so long as mountain literature is read. To quote Genesis with due alteration, 'And Brown saw every route that he had made, and, behold it was very good.'[29]

Graham Brown's next expedition was an ascent of the Innominata Face of Mont Blanc. A discontinuous rib of three great steps, each formed by a striking buttress or tower of rock, provides the line. The first ascent had been made in 1919 by S.L. Courtauld, E.G. Oliver and their guides who included Adolf Aufdenblatten, Alfred's brother, but the difficulties had forced them to take a line to the left of the rib, avoiding the upper rock buttresses. On the second ascent, the rib was followed almost to the base of the final tower before once again escaping to the left. Graham Brown's intention was to find a more direct way up the face.

On 7 August his party went up to the Gamba Hut where Zürcher was also staying prior to an attempt on the Peuterey Ridge. Lying on their bunks they chatted and the question of who had first claim on Graven's services re-emerged. Neither man would accept that the other had priority and their mutual resentment grew. After a day of rest, Graham Brown and his guides set out, following the route taken by the previous parties until they reached the foot of the second step, where they traversed right. As they crossed two

---

b   The approach to the Grépon via the Nantillons Glacier is exposed briefly to the risk of falling séracs.

snow gullies a chunk of falling ice struck Graham Brown on the arm, which was badly bruised, and another dislodged Aufdenblatten's ice axe from his grasp. They climbed up snow, ice and rocks to the foot of a steep buttress of red rock, the south pillar of Frêney, where they were level with the base of the third step on the Innominata Ridge, at an altitude of about 4,300 metres. The technically most difficult section of the climb started at this point. They climbed steep chimneys and cracks; ledges were small and their stances insecure: they carried no pitons or karabiners. The views were 'of surpassing grandeur … perhaps the greatest spectacles of rock scenery I have ever had',[30] and the exposure was dramatic: 'Our position was an extraordinary one and delightful … I do not think I have ever before experienced so "wide" a feeling of exposure: it was almost as if I was floating in the air.'[31] After two hours' climbing they reached easier ground. It was unbearably hot and they halted to melt snow and make lemonade. They continued slowly over the summits of Mont Blanc to the Vallot Hut where Graven, who had once had an ambition to be a chef, conjured up 'an excellent meal' of hot soup, bread, cheese, salami and lumps of sugar. Given the limitations of the ingredients, a ravenous and uncritical appetite rather than Graven's culinary skill was probably the basis of Graham Brown's appreciation.

Graham Brown wanted to return to Courmayeur over the summit of Mont Blanc by the north-west face, a route that Graven dismissed as pointless, prompting Graham Brown to note privately that Graven was 'getting uppish!' The north-west face offers an obvious, direct approach to the summit from the Grand Plateau but it is a wide, crevassed snow slope, exposed to falling séracs in its lower part, and the established routes ascended its safer, flanking ridges. Graham Brown admitted that the route was 'rather a joke' but he had a pressing motive: he wanted 'to have a new way to Mont Blanc entirely to myself', for he was still in competition with Smythe and resolved to lead the route himself.[32] Graven acquiesced, saying that he would tie on to the middle of the rope and be a 'tourist' for the day. Graham Brown picked a way through the crevasses and cut steps up some steep snow. The crux was a short wall of snow which he overcame with the help of a shove from Graven's ice axe. That evening, back at the Torino Hut, he relaxed in the company of his guides, drinking tea and *vin chaud*, and 'because of the wine perhaps, or because of the mental and bodily satisfaction of the splendid climbing of the past two days … took to boasting'.[33] Graham Brown had climbed Mont Blanc six times within a fortnight, making three new routes and bringing his total number of ascents of Mont Blanc to eleven.

The next day they went down to the Leschaux Hut, situated below the North Face of the Grandes Jorasses. During 1931 and 1932 the North Face of the Jorasses had become regarded as one of the last great challenges in the Alps and was the object of international competition, sometimes lethal. German, Italian and French teams, guided and guideless, made a number of assaults but none had reached higher than the party led by the French guide Armand Charlet, which had managed to climb the first 180 metres up the Walker Spur in 1928. Welzenbach had made a reconnaissance just three weeks before Graham Brown arrived at the hut on 11 August, but poor weather had limited it to a routine approach to the foot of the face and the Italians, Giusto Gervasutti and Piero Zanetti[c], were still at the hut, having spent the past few days observing and reconnoitring the face. The purpose of Graham Brown's visit is unclear. In 1932 he had paid a solitary visit to the hut from where he carefully examined the face and sketched possible lines of ascent in his notebook but, given Aufdenblatten's earlier and categorical refusal to venture on to the face, it seems unlikely that he was intending to make an attempt. They had a cold supper as they had run out of fuel. Two nights before at the Vallot Hut, Graven, anticipating Zürcher's arrival from the Peuterey Ridge, had used extra fuel to brew a hot drink, which Zürcher had ungraciously declined. Graham Brown went to bed, 'cold inside and regretting the waste of "meta" on Zürcher and resentful of his treatment of Graven'. The next morning's cold breakfast was 'horrible' and Graham Brown lamented, 'O Zürcher!'[34]

Graham Brown's last major expedition from Courmayeur that year was a traverse of the Col du Dolent, from Italy to France. This was only the second traverse from south to north since Whymper's original passage in 1865. Whymper had described it as 'the *beau-ideal* of a pass'. The French side is a very steep slope of snow and ice down which Whymper's guide, Michel Croz, had cut steps, but Graham Brown's party descended by the rocks at the side, sliding down the rope in a series of seven rappels. On reaching the Glacier d'Argentière, their plan was to cross into Switzerland over the Col d'Argentière but it was not immediately obvious which of the several branch glaciers led to the col. As neither guide was familiar with the area,

---

c   A few days later they attempted the Croz Spur, reaching the first tower before being forced back by rockfall and storm.

there was some discussion about the route to be taken. Graham Brown's view prevailed and proved correct causing him to reflect on 'the weakness of even good guides when in little-known "country"'. In his journal he disparaged Aufdenblatten, writing, 'A[ufdenblatten]'s mistakes did not matter, for, despite his reputation, he is little more than a good porter.' As for Graven, Graham Brown saw 'very clearly the limitations even of one of the greatest guides. There is no imaginative or intellectual side to their nature in this respect.' He continued:

> They cannot even interpret from a map the 'lie' ... Perhaps all this seems to be asking far too much of a mere peasant, but Graven is so much above all the other guides whom I have met in intellectual equipment.[35]

On 20 August Goodfellow joined Graham Brown in Courmayeur and they drove to La Bérarde in the Dauphiné. Their plans included the classic traverse of the Meije and new routes on the challenging north faces of Le Rateau and Ailefroide. Graven and Aufdenblatten, unfamiliar with the region and probably enervated by their exertions on Mont Blanc, were more circumspect. They proposed an itinerary of standard routes approached from a hotel in the valley. The indefatigable Graham Brown was 'astounded'; the idea of climbing from a hotel was 'preposterous'; Graven seemed 'to have the fear of the unknown and to have lost his enterprise.'[36] Aufdenblatten pleaded ill health, claiming that he had a fever. Graham Brown examined him, noting that his skin was cold and pulse rate normal, and concluded that 'there was nothing further amiss than that his stomach might be out of order (I am sure that he was suffering from loss of "guts" but in any case he had been over-eating).'[37] Confiding in his journal, he added contemptuously that he:

> felt revolted with him in the same sort of queer way in which I had been revolted by Smythe's breakdown and cowardice ... in both cases ... there is a thing which I cannot stand and that is pretense [sic]. Both of them talked large and pretended an adventurousness and courage which they had not got.[38]

Aufdenblatten insisted that he was too ill to climb and returned to Zermatt.

A local guide, Casimir Rodier, was engaged in his place. 'Once Rodier joined the party our whole outlook was changed,' observed Goodfellow:

> Our sick guide had been nervous on Le Rateau, for in some circles in Zermatt, the Dauphiné peaks, la Meije in particular, seem to be credited with almost supernatural difficulties. Rodier's absolute confidence reacted on Graven, and he gave then the very best of his superb powers in gay challenge, as it were, to a charming and brilliant foreigner.[39]

In just over a week they traversed the Meije, Les Écrins and the Ailfroide and made a new route up the north face of Les Bans. In contrast to his climbs on Mont Blanc, these routes were predominantly rock climbs. The rock was often rotten, especially on the Ailfroide; tottering gendarmes wobbled alarmingly as they climbed over them, and the technical difficulties were of a high standard for the period. Goodfellow considered that their route on Les Bans, where fortunately the quality of the rock was 'flawless', was comparable in difficulty to the harder routes on Gimmer Crag with pitches of Severe and some of Very Severe standard. Graham Brown had unashamedly accepted a pull from the rope on these sections.

On reaching La Bérarde after the final climb of the season, Graham Brown 'slunk into the hotel by the back way as my clothes were much torn.'[40] The state of his clothing and equipment bore testimony to the season's rigour. Almost everything was worn out: breeches, hat, boots, crampons – so often sharpened that the spikes were too short – and the shaft of his axe was cracked and bound with copper wire. In just under eight weeks in the Alps, Graham Brown had had only five days of rest: three were enforced by bad weather and two were spent in travelling between regions. The remainder of his holiday had been spent on foot, either going from the valley to a hut – mechanical uplift being limited to the cog-railways serving popular belvederes such as Gornergrat and Montenvers – or on expeditions in the high mountains.

He travelled back to England in Goodfellow's Alvis, carefully documenting their progress: the 752-mile journey from Grenoble to London was completed at an average speed of 34.4 mph. Once home, he set about confirming the topographical details of his new routes and agreeing names for the features. As editor of the *Alpine Journal*, Strutt's approval was crucial.

Regarding his ascent of *Route Major* and descent of the Miage Face of Mont Blanc, Graham Brown pleaded, 'Do give me the pass if you can, and let me call it Col Major – it is one of my ambitions.'[41] He also asked Strutt to try to persuade the Italian authorities to triangulate the small gendarme above *The Pear*, which he named prettily, Aiguille de la Belle Étoile. He was particular about the name for his new route on the Brenva Face, insisting that it should be called the *Via della Pera* and not *Route de la Poire* because he had been told that the French had a double meaning and could be construed as 'the route of the bloody fool'. Preoccupied with these niceties, Graham Brown inconsiderately neglected to deal with the mundane matter of settling his guides' accounts. The unfortunate Aufdenblatten, who had bills to pay, was obliged to remind Graham Brown and trying to make light of the matter, wrote, 'I don't know where to steal the necessary.'[42] Two months later and just a few days before Christmas, Graham Brown sent him a cheque and returned his *führerbuch*, in which clients recorded comments on their guide. Damning with faint praise, Graham Brown had written, 'He is extremely cautious and safe in his judgements, and may be relied upon with confidence not to allow any party of which he is the leader to get into difficulties.'[43]

Graham Brown's partnership with Graven had developed to be comparable to the famous pairings of amateur and guide such as Mummery and Burgener, Ryan and the Lochmatters, and Young and Knubel. His and Graven's achievements in 1933 represented the apogee of a long tradition in which ambitious and determined amateurs combined with strong and technically expert guides to make new and difficult ascents. As the essayist Jim Perrin observed, mountaineering in the mid-1930s was at the moment when 'the balance between romance, risk and achievement was so perfectly held.'[44] Graham Brown and Graven had pushed the unsophisticated, traditional style of climbing, unchanged for thirty years, to its limit. The rise in standards of difficulty that followed would depend on new equipment – pitons for rock and ice to provide protection and aid progress, crampons with front points to reduce the need for cutting steps and so increase speed on steep snow and ice – and rope techniques being pioneered in the Eastern Alps.

During the 1930s guideless climbing had been on the increase, especially amongst the younger generation who could not afford the expense of employing a guide, and the view that guideless climbing was intrinsically more meritorious began to prevail. But, as Graham Brown observed with justification, 'much so-called guideless climbing consists merely in the ascent of ordinary routes by well marked tracks'.[45] He might have added that it was also often incompetent, for as one practitioner observed, 'one never knew whether one would reach the top of one's mountain, and sometimes not even if it was the right peak', claiming that 'in consequence the joy of success was far keener'.[46] Longland, chosen for Everest in 1933, spoke for many when he remarked that 'the urge to reach sufficient competence just to repeat some of Geoffrey Winthrop Young's great routes and traverses was enough to keep me happy for a number of seasons'.[47] Indeed, none of the members of the 1933 Everest expedition who represented the cream of British mountaineers – notwithstanding the idiosyncrasies of the Mount Everest Committee – could match Graham Brown's list of successes in the Alps. Nine years after his first visit to the Alps, Graham Brown, aged fifty-one, was the foremost alpinist in Britain.

Chapter 13
C.S. Houston and Mount Foraker

Charles Houston, who died in 2009 aged ninety-six, achieved distinction as a mountaineer and in the study of high-altitude medicine, as well as pursuing a varied career as a general practitioner, director of the Peace Corps in India and professor of community medicine at the University of Vermont. His was not just a distinguished career, but a long one. In 1938 he led a reconnaissance expedition to K2, reaching 7,925 metres. Fifteen years later he led another expedition to the mountain and the week-long 'Homeric retreat' of his party has been acclaimed as 'the finest moment in the history of American mountaineering'.[1] Between 1968 and 1979 he directed physiological research at the high-altitude laboratory (5,300 metres) on Mount Logan in Yukon territory. His book, *Going Higher: the story of man and altitude*, first published in 1980, ran to five editions. His longevity allowed him to reminisce in interviews, lectures and articles, about events that had occurred sixty years earlier, but sometimes his reminiscences were at variance with his diaries and letters. His biographer remarked that he would never let truth get in the way of a good story.

Houston was born in New York City and enjoyed a privileged east-coast upbringing. He was educated expensively at an exclusive private school and Harvard University. His father, Oscar, a successful and wealthy lawyer, believed in the educational value of foreign travel and in 1925 had taken his family to Europe. After visiting Paris, Charlie and his parents spent a week walking from the southern shore of Lake Geneva to Chamonix, crossing the Col du Brévant where they had sight of Mont Blanc a few miles away and their guide produced a bottle of Asti Spumante to celebrate. At the Montenvers Hotel, Oscar had hired a guide and porter to take his twelve-year-old son up the nearby Aiguille de l'M, Charlie's first Alpine summit. Six years later, Houston returned to Europe with his father and together they spent a week in the Austrian Tyrol, trekking from hut to hut. Oscar, sensing Charlie's growing enthusiasm for mountaineering, which he was pleased to encourage, arranged for him to go to Chamonix the following year and climb with Alfred Couttet (dubbed 'Champion'), one of the leading Chamoniard guides. On 4 August 1932, the nineteen-year-old Houston was in between climbs and alone at Montenvers Hotel, where Graham Brown was also staying. Passing by Graham Brown's table, Houston heard him say, 'I believe we speak the same language' and they struck up a conversation.[2] Later that evening he noted admiringly in his diary:

> Met T. Graham Brown of England – He's just done the Pétéret Ridge also a first crossing of Col Maudit. Fine fellow takes notes during all his climbs. He's made two new ascensions up from the Brenva glacier to Mt. Blanc both guideless – a real climber and also lover of mountains.[3]

Graham Brown was matter-of-fact: 'Had dinner. Thereafter chatted with a nice American.'[4] A few days later they made an excursion together, ascending the Mer de Glace to the Leschaux glacier where they inspected the surrounding peaks and discussed possible routes up the North Face of the Grandes Jorasses. Houston suggested that they form a team to attempt the face:

> Finally I asked him if he'd try it with me and Couttet? He said he'd like to but had already discussed it too deeply with his guide Gravan [sic]. Make plans for next year. Will try it then. Couttet and I and Brown and Gravan in two combinable ropes.[5]

Houston's suggestion was as presumptuous as it was ambitious. Graham Brown found Houston's naive enthusiasm attractive: 'he is a great lad and the sort with whom one might go to look at the North Face of the Grandes Jorasses',[6] but it is unlikely that he took the proposal seriously and he was probably surprised to receive, six months later, an invitation from Houston to join him in another ambitious project:

> Dear Dr Brown, I don't know whether or not you will remember me the writer, at all events one day last August on the glacier de Leschaux we made some tentative climbing plans for this coming summer.

Another opportunity has arisen, however, and it is concerning this that I am writing to you.

My father and I, together with Andrew Taylor and a fourth man, are planning a trip in Alaska next July to attempt the ascent of Mt. Foraker, 17,000 feet high, the highest unclimbed peak of North America, and we would like very much to have you join us if possible. The climb, naturally, is one of the best, the country completely unknown in that region, and we feel the adventure should be very interesting. We plan to leave New York around the fifteenth of June, returning late in August. Taylor has spent much time climbing in Alaska and is well experienced in outfitting such an expedition. The expense, I think, could be arranged satisfactorily.

If you are interested I wish you would let me know as soon as possible and I will give you the details of our plans. I hope very much you will be able to come as we are very anxious to have you.[7]

Following a second letter urging him to cable his decision, Graham Brown replied that he could not spare the time, giving university examinations as an excuse. The expedition was subsequently postponed due to Oscar's commitments and Charlie joined fellow members of the Harvard Mountaineering Club on an expedition to attempt Mount Crillon in Alaska, while Graham Brown triumphed in the Alps.

The expedition to Foraker in 1934 was a Houston family venture. Oscar, who was no climber but had an interest in mountain exploration[a], underwrote the expenses. Charlie, now with recent experience of mountaineering in Alaska, was responsible for organising the food and equipment and recruiting the climbers. Gathering a team proved problematical. There seems to have been a reluctance to enlist in a father-and-son enterprise, with the twenty-year-old Charlie at its head. None of his companions on the expedition to Crillon joined the party for Foraker. Eventually, Houston managed to recruit Chychele Waterston and Charles (Bunny) Storey. Waterston, a school teacher in Andover, some thirty miles from Harvard, was originally from Scotland and had some experience of ordinary routes in the European Alps, but he had done no climbing in the last five years due to a shoulder injury. Storey, a freshman at Harvard, was a mountaineering

---

a   Oscar Houston (1883–1969). In 1950, his enterprise resulted in permission for the first visit by westerners to the Nepali side of Mount Everest.

novice and had never seen a glacier. The expedition lacked experience of serious mountaineering and Houston continued to press Graham Brown to join. His presence would be invaluable.

After his success in the Alps the previous year, which would have been diffi-cult to equal, Graham Brown was tempted by the novelty of climbing in Alaska with its special character, combining mountaineering with aspects of polar travel. If he had any misgivings that his brief acquaintance with Houston was a slender basis for a three-month expedition together they were over-ridden by the opportunity presented and he agreed to join the expedition, providing he could obtain leave. Oscar used his connections and the princi-pal of the University College of South Wales soon received a letter from the Alaskan delegate to the United States Congress, Anthony J. Dimond, an early champion of Alaskan statehood, announcing that there was 'attention beyond the ordinary centring on the expedition' and he hoped that 'Professor Brown may obtain leave of absence so that he may participate in this endeavour'.[8]

Meanwhile Charlie pressed on with the preparations. He asked Graham Brown to experiment with Huntley & Palmers' 'hardtack' – Graham Brown noted: 'avoid this!' – and Bovril Pemmican: 'Saves trouble. Makes rather greasy soup. Better raw.'[9] Drawing on his experience of provisioning the Crillon expedition, Houston organised the rations in bags, which he and Storey packed in the basement of his hall of residence at Harvard. 'Ordin-ary' bags, weighing 28lb each, contained rations for six men for two days and 'high camp' bags (23lb) held sufficient for three men for three days. Graham Brown thought this 'an excellent arrangement' but Bill Tilman[b], who encountered the system on one of Houston's later expeditions, wryly described it as an 'Ordeal by Planning or the Scientific Martyrdom of Man': the victim being told not only what to eat but in what amount and when.[10]

Graham Brown made his personal preparations, ordering hand-knitted sweaters and underwear from Shetland and purchasing for ten guineas a sleeping bag, based on the Everest design but with extra down. He submit-ted himself to a precautionary medical examination by Dr Claude Wilson, a physician in Tunbridge Wells and past president of the Alpine Club, and was relieved to learn that he was 'fit enough to tackle the sort of thing I still wish to climb'.[11] In a more sombre vein, he wrote to Sydney Spencer informing

---

b   H.W. Tilman (1898–1977). Renowned for his austerity in the mountains, he shared the view of his equally famous companion, Eric Shipton, that 'the most important thing about expedition food is that there is some'.

him of his wish that in the event of his death, the Alpine Club should receive his book collection, notebooks and journals. With just a few days left before he was due to sail at the beginning of June, Graham Brown discovered that his passport had expired and that he had lost Houston's address.

Despite the last-minute hitches, Graham Brown arrived in New York on 8 June and was met by Charlie's parents. Oscar immediately whisked him off to lunch at his club before putting him on the train to Great Neck, Long Island[c], where Oscar's butler met him. Graham Brown was captivated by New York, the Houstons and their friends. He went sightseeing, ascending a sixty-storey skyscraper in an elevator for a view of the city, noting: 'came up 800 feet in 40 seconds (ear pressure effects)'.[12] He ate hamburgers and apple pie and ice cream; he sampled different cocktails appreciatively, recording their recipes meticulously. Every other day there was a party, which usually involved swimming with 'much ducking and ragging' sometimes till after midnight. For months afterwards, Graham Brown's antics were still being referred to, in letters and cards, by Charlie's young friends. The contrast with the staid atmosphere of the Athenaeum and Alpine clubs where he customarily sought his company was enticing and refreshing.

On 17 June, Graham Brown, Oscar and Charles Houston left New York from Pennsylvania station and reached Montreal the next day where they met Waterston and Storey. The party continued across Canada by rail:

> The 'colonist car' in which we are travelling is a sort of 'steerage' class. And I find it not only interesting and jolly, but also very comfortable – and that because we are sleeping in our own sleeping bags on our own air-mattresses. We have our own food with us and it is all a glorious picnic, because we practically have the car to ourselves ... The party has already shaken together and is a very happy one.[13]

On their arrival in Seattle they were entangled in a dockers' strike. Shipping bound for Alaska, which could only be reached by sea, was still being worked, but the employers attempted to load some ships for other destinations using strike-breakers, whom they protected with machine guns. According to Graham Brown, 'there was a sort of battle' which 'was all in

---

c   Great Neck on the north shore of Long Island was the model for Scott Fitzgerald's fictional West Egg where Gatsby's mansion was situated and where Scott Fitzgerald and his wife rented a house for 'eighteen drunken months in 1922–1923'. Gatsby's glittering parties were based on entertainments thrown by various Great Neck millionaires.

the game, but the machine guns were considered unsporting by the strikers who thereupon revoked the treaty about Alaska ships'.[14] They were stranded. But they learned that a ship bound for Alaska was sailing from Vancouver in eight hours' time and managed to transfer their 700lb of kit on to a bus and cover the 148 miles from Seattle with two hours to spare.

The ten-day voyage to the Alaskan port of Seward was a 'beautiful journey' with landward views of wooded islands, snow peaks and glaciers calving into the sea. From Seward they travelled north by rail for 350 miles to McKinley Park station where the party transferred to motorcars. They drove for sixty miles along a made-up road then through a stretch of rough country – where one of the cars was nearly stranded in a glacier torrent – to Copper Mountain, which they reached on 3 July. Here they met their horse-train and Carl Anderson, an Alaskan hunting-guide, whom Oscar had engaged for the expedition. After a four-day ride over about seventy-five miles of untracked tundra – 'a rolling moorland of moss and bog-holes dotted with innumerable lakes and pools'[15] – in a steady and soaking drizzle, they reached the junction of the streams from the East and West Foraker glaciers on the fringe of the spruce forest, where they established a base camp. 'The journey had its little adventures,' wrote Graham Brown, 'such as are incidental to pack animals in dense belts of forest or of dwarf trees, to steep banks and deep bog holes, to the fording of difficult rivers and to the general naughtiness of horses'.[16] Houston elaborated:

> We were all sadly out of condition … our equipment was dispersed in a score of cases that must each one be opened every night … and few of us had ever travelled with a pack-train before … We seemed invariably to pitch camp around midnight in the heaviest rain of the day, and to spend the entire morning (when it was not raining) in looking for the horses.[17]

The next day the sky cleared and the sun shone. They dried themselves out and busied themselves with chores: Storey cleaned the kitchen while Anderson helped Houston build a ladder to reach the cache that had been constructed to keep food out of reach of bears; Waterston repaired a flysheet and Oscar built a 'swell latrine'. But, according to Charlie, Graham Brown displayed 'absolutely no camping sense'.[18]

Foraker and its surroundings were unexplored. Their rough map showed 'nice blank spaces and some sketchy glaciers'[19] and the next five days were spent in reconnaissance. First, they scrambled for several hours to the top of a nearby hill of about 1,700 metres, from where they had a distant but impressive view: Mount McKinley to the left connected by a 'grandly proportioned' ridge to Mount Foraker on the right. Next, they advanced about eight miles up the West Foraker Glacier from where they obtained an almost complete view of the north face of Foraker, the summit rising up at the left-hand end of an almost horizontal crest that extends for about two miles. Several ribs of snow and ice run up this face: the left-hand rib climbs 3,300 metres directly from the glacier to the summit; the most rightward (north-west) lies at a gentler angle and was chosen as the route of ascent. Graham Brown considered the view 'to be not only the most beautiful which I have seen in the mountain world, but also the greatest'. The scale of the peaks astonished him: 'great as was the beauty of the face, it was not that which made the strongest impression, but the extraordinary appearance of "bigness"';[20] the colours in Alaska moved him: the 'ethereal blue tint' of the snow was 'a thing at which to wonder' and 'the grey granite varies this egg-shell blue with a deeper shade; the pink granite seems to be in complement with it. The whole is of an unbelievable delicacy'.[21]

Their next task was to transport equipment and food up the West Foraker Glacier, for about ten miles, to a site from which an attempt could be made to gain the north-west ridge. It required placing three intermediate camps, taking a week of back-breaking work. They carried loads using Yukon pack-boards consisting of laced canvas over a wooden frame, which Graham Brown ruefully observed had 'one practical disadvantage' namely, 'they enable much heavier loads to be taken than is at all fit and proper'. Charlie directed the back-packing, apportioning the weight to be carried according to the distance to be covered: 'when that was short, the packs were "heavy" (75lb upwards, excluding the weight of the board, which weighs between 7 and 8lb); when the distance was longer, the loads were "medium" (between 60 and 70lb)'.[22] Graham Brown had 'a good deal of misgiving' as to whether he would cope with the toil but after the expedition he wrote that his 'fears were unfounded and (for my personal satisfaction, and with pride) ... that Charlie Houston rates me as a good packer'.[23]

Camp III, situated by a little lake of clear green water, was so peaceful and comfortable they called it Tranquility. On 26 July they set out across the glacier and climbed up into a snow basin, picking their way between crevasses, until they were stopped by a wide crack, the far side of which reared up vertically and overhung in places. A traverse rightwards led to a narrowing of the crack and a snow-bridge, lying at an angle of at least fifty degrees, up which they cut steps and handholds to reach steep snow slopes above and, eventually, a site for Camp IV at 2,600 metres on the north-west ridge. The bridge was flimsy: when probed with an ice axe the shaft passed completely through and it was only remotely safe when frozen hard. They did not dare to carry loads across it and hauled their packs up and over the crack with ropes. From Camp IV they climbed a curving snow arête to gain the crest of the ridge which continued almost horizontally for 1,100 steps – Graham Brown counted them – past teetering ice blocks and around crevasses which criss-crossed the ridge, at the end of which they placed Camp V. Here Oscar, Storey and Anderson turned back, leaving Charlie, Graham Brown and Waterston with sufficient supplies to make an assault on the summit. Two more narrow snow arêtes, 'more sensational and steeper than the upper snow arêtes on *Route Major*'[24] led to Camp VI (3,450 metres). Snow and ice gave way to rocks for the next 600 metres. In parts the route was tricky and the climbing sufficiently delicate to necessitate removing their packs which had to be hauled. Back on snow, Camp VII, the highest, was established at 4,050 metres.

On 6 August, a month after arriving at base camp, they set out for the summit. The cold was intense and the risk of frostbite considerable. They wore their warmest clothes under windproof suits of Grenfell cloth, cut like engineers' overalls, with fur-lined hoods. Graham Brown had three pairs of gloves beneath his gauntlets and three pairs of socks inside his Barker boots.[d] One hundred and fifty metres of climbing led to the crest above the north face from where they looked down the other side to a flat glacier, about three miles in length, on the far side of which rose the south-west peak of Foraker 1,000 metres above. The higher north-east peak lay at the head of the glacier, about one and a half miles away. They descended to the glacier, planting willow wands every seventy-five paces to mark the route for their return. The final ascent of about 600 metres was up a ridge of broken rocks followed by a steep cone of ice. The view south-east from the summit revealed an unmapped area of hundreds of square miles, and because of Foraker's dominant height, probably as much as 2,000 metres above the mountains

---

d   'Barker boots' were made of rubber with crepe-rubber soles and leather leggings. Graham Brown had taken a pair of leather boots copied from one of the Everest models but found that they were too cold even at 3,000 metres.

stretching before them, it was 'an aeroplane view', 'like looking down on to a relief map', the peaks 'set like chains of islands in an ocean of snow'.[25]

Graham Brown, Charlie Houston and Waterston spent twenty-two days on the ridge. The interminable relaying of loads meant they had to climb almost the whole route as far as Camp VII four times over. It snowed in varying amounts during fourteen days. A blizzard confined them to Camp VII for two days after their ascent of the north-east peak and another storm stopped them in their tent for two days on the descent. Snow conditions were generally awful. 'The going was perfectly terrible for I sank over my knees in corn snow at every step' and 'kicking steps took an immense amount of energy' wrote Houston, who confided in his diary that 'several times I was ready to quit'.[26] Forty days after setting out, they returned to their base camp, having carried down all their equipment except for a single petrol tin. On 24 August Bill Alloway, the wrangler, arrived with horses for the journey out. It was Charlie's twenty-first birthday and they feasted on pot-roasted caribou, slaughtered illicitly, green peas and potatoes, followed by oranges and fudge, all washed down with whisky. Alloway maintained that he had been confident of the team succeeding: 'I told them you were a tough lot of guys and if you couldn't do it, it couldn't be done. They said the little Englishman was too old but I said he washed in snow on July 8 and he was the toughest of the lot'.[27]

Six days later, news of their success appeared on the front page of the *New York Times*. Their achievement was considerable and significant. The approach to the mountain, the lie of the glaciers and possible routes were unknown and they had not had the benefit of prior aerial reconnaissance, which was being gradually adopted in Alaskan exploration. Nor did they have the assistance of air supply, which was impracticable; once the horse-train turned back from below the first camp on the Foraker Glacier, all the load carrying was done by the team. Having gained the north-west ridge they did not place any fixed camps but took their tent and supplies with them, although this necessitated carrying more than once to some camps. The success of their 'capsule' style of ascent encouraged Houston and Graham Brown to believe that Himalayan peaks could be tackled in a similar way, an idea well in advance of the times. Reflecting on the climb, Graham Brown wrote, 'The humdrum narrative leaves me with a sense of disappointment that our adventures should have been so little in keeping with the theme'.[28] Apart from the weather and Waterston falling into a crevasse, disappearing from view 'like a condemned man', from which he was extricated without great difficulty, the climb was remarkably free of incident. But the stress of expedition life had led to some friction.

Graham Brown's critical eye focused on Waterston. In his diary he disparaged Waterston's mountaineering skills and accused him of lacking determination, a fault bound to attract Graham Brown's contempt. He criticised Waterston's attempt at map-making: 'the affair was incredibly wrong all over … almost comic … and showed an absence of topographical sense,'[29] and noted pettily that Waterston did not do his fair share of the washing-up. Waterston sensed Graham Brown's indignation and after the expedition wrote, 'there were several disputes and difficulties between us on the mountain, which have absolutely no importance I believe, and yet I keep wishing I could find some way of dispersing them.'[30] Graham Brown dismissed Waterston's regrets, saying that he had 'taken things far too seriously'.[31]

Charlie, on the other hand, 'had quite a tiff with Timmy and said some things I didn't mean to about his general uselessness around camp. He really is perfectly helpless.' He reflected, 'I don't know what it is that makes me continuously nasty to him … it is a form of relaxation of nervous tension for me to blow up at someone.'[32] After the expedition he wrote apologetically to Graham Brown, who had sent him a gift of a mounted piece of rock from the summit of Foraker, saying, 'I hate to think of the scene I made refusing the original piece! Whenever I think of my more BM[e] moments I wonder that we are still on speaking terms, and am very grateful for your broadmindedness for the fact that we are.'[33]

The outcome of the expedition was a growing friendship between Charlie and Graham Brown. When the time came to return to England, Graham Brown was reluctant to leave. He wrote to Charlie, 'What a fine send-off you gave me. I wasn't in very good form, because I was depressed to be leaving, and I was sorry to be going at all!'[34] And the Houstons and their friends, whom he had charmed, missed him. 'You've no idea how many hearts you won over here,' wrote Charlie's mother,

> I'm not pulling your leg – everybody talks about you and when you're coming back – which we all hope you will do – and what a good person you are. Really Timmy, you've a very important place in our lives – and I want you to feel so.[35]

---

e   Neither Houston nor Graham Brown is explicit about the abbreviation. In his letters, Houston refers to 'black moods' but 'bloody minded' usually fits the context.

Chapter 14
Himalayan Prospects

Three weeks after arriving back in Cardiff, Graham Brown wrote to Charlie to make plans for climbing in 1935: 'What about next year? I shall be very greatly disappointed if we don't manage to climb together – either in Alaska or the Alps.'[1] His letter crossed with one from Charlie in which he floated the possibility of them joining an expedition to climb Nanga Parbat (8,126 metres), situated at the extreme western end of the Himalaya. Ten days later, Graham Brown replied, 'The Nanga Parbat expedition interests me very greatly and I should love to go – but only if you are going yourself … I want to climb with you next summer – wherever we can settle to go.'[2] Although conditional on Charlie's participation, Graham Brown's otherwise unqualified enthusiasm is surprising, given that only three months earlier three Germans and six Sherpas had died in their attempt to climb the mountain. At the time, this disastrous loss of life, through exhaustion and exposure, was unparalleled in Himalayan mountaineering.

Houston had been talking to two men with experience of high-altitude mountaineering: Terris Moore, who had climbed the Chinese peak Minya Konka (7,556 metres), and Fritz Wiessner, a member of the German-American expedition to Nanga Parbat in 1932, and they had drawn up a provisional plan based on a climbing party of eight, recruited from Germany, America and England. They estimated the cost to individuals at $3,000. Graham Brown re-affirmed his wish to be included despite the expense, which was 'the devil', but finding other climbers with ability, time to spare and the requisite funds proved difficult. Moore wavered but Wiessner remained keen. Graham Brown and Houston, however, had reservations about Wiessner as a companion: he could be domineering, autocratic and wilful to the point of obstinacy. But after Houston had climbed with him, their doubts were dispelled. 'I am certain he is alright,' wrote Houston,

'I have every confidence in the world in him both as a climber and leader.'[a,3] Short of personnel, Houston concluded desperately that, in order to make up eight paying members, it would be necessary to invite Miss Knowlton, 'though none of us are too anxious to have a woman along.'[4] Elizabeth Knowlton had accompanied the German-American expedition to Nanga Parbat in 1932. She had looked after supplies, acted as the expedition's news-paper correspondent, filing articles for the *New York Times*, and reached 6,000 metres on the mountain. 'With regard to Elizabeth Knowlton,' Graham Brown replied:

> I was very much attracted by her book, and liked her attitude. My own feeling is, however, that women are out of place in such an expedition (as you know I feel). But I don't hold this feeling too strongly. It seems to me, all the same, that it would probably be much safer if she were not on the expedition. From what I have read of her book I am sure that her presence would not weaken the deter-mination of the party – as that of some women might do; but the presence of any woman is liable to bring in complicating factors ... If one woman goes, why not others; what about the wives of married members? There are all sorts of complications ... [5]

As they struggled to recruit a team, Graham Brown voiced concerns about the structure of the expedition. It was too large and he was worried about his proposed role as medical officer because:

> the last medical work I did was during the War when it consisted in the simple 'First Aid' work of a Field Ambulance. I do not think I could take more responsibility than that, and I know almost nothing about the proper sort of pills to give to ailing porters. I would of course do my best – but that would be very little.[6]

The prospect of the expedition ever setting out was receding. Charlie wrote, 'Fritz and I are getting pretty frantic now about the whole thing, for time is getting so darn short that even if we do get the permission, there is almost no time to get the planning done.' Graham Brown's characteristic

---

a   Nevertheless, Wiessner's expedition to K2, in 1939, on which one member and three Sherpas died, ended in recrimination and threats of litigation.

dilatoriness over correspondence was a factor. Houston complained, 'I have sent you five telegrams … and to date have gotten only one answer that said very little. I hate to have to be BM about it, Timmy, but if we really want to go on this damn trip we have to do something quickly.'[7]

One week before Christmas 1934, Houston cabled Graham Brown instructing him to apply to the India Office for permission, but the news on the grapevine was not encouraging. Strutt informed Graham Brown that there was little chance of their expedition being granted permission, and 'should there be any expedition allowed, it would be the Hun survivors of 1934'.[8] Their application was refused. Graham Brown wrote to Houston telling him that the trip was off – 'a bitter disappointment' – and suggested spending time together in the Alps instead. Houston hesitated, saying that he had been invited to join an expedition to attempt Mount Waddington in British Columbia and there were rumours of an expedition to K2 or Kangchenjunga, but, a few days later, agreed to join Graham Brown in the Alps that summer.

Although plans for climbing were the main subject of their correspondence, Houston's letters frequently contained news about himself. In his final year at Harvard, he was working hard and hoped to get on to the dean's list, but his exams had not gone well, he had had a car crash, ruining the car and breaking his nose, and he had woman trouble. In a 'foul black mood', he confided in Graham Brown:

> I don't know why I should be telling you my troubles with my loves, except that you are almost the best friend that I have. At least you know me better than anyone else, including my family perhaps, and you still show signs of liking me … Also you are one of the few people I feel that I can talk to or write to freely … [9]

He continued:

> I get these horrible fits of depression [but] I know damn well that I would rather be very high at times and very low at others than go along on the level all the time.[10]

Graham Brown responded with some banal counselling:

I know how beastly it is to be depressed, and it is awfully difficult to give advice because different things suit different people. Some people get over it by having a good sweat at a fast game, and other people do so by having an absorbing hobby ... I think depression very often comes from giving too high a value to things that do not really matter very much ... nothing really matters enough to worry about ... things almost always turn out quite simply and quite well in the long run.[11]

Houston would suffer recurrent bouts of depression throughout his life.

As their holiday in the Alps drew closer, Houston became more cheerful. He pressed Graham Brown to consider returning to America afterwards and his mother added her blandishments:

If you could have heard the shouts and cheers [when] Charles and I said we were going to try to get you to come back with him ... you wouldn't hesitate a minute and throw precaution and all other things to the winds – and come! ... The mint juleps have nothing to do with the cordiality of the invitation. It was given in cold sobriety in the presence of many enthusiastic seconders. Joking aside, we want most awfully to have you here again ... Please come.

In a more maternal vein, she continued:

Well Charlie is off for a good summer and is looking forward to it very keenly. Take good care of each other – I'm very fond of you both and don't want anything to go wrong. To make things sure I ... went down to the four-leaf clover patch where I found them last year (Remember how we sat down on the grass ... and I found you some clovers for luck?) Well here's another[b] ... [12]

Graham Brown was tempted by the invitation, saying that he 'would just love to go back' and he knew 'what a good time it would mean', but he considered that it would be too expensive. He signed off affectionately, 'Do give my love to everybody.'[13]

---

b   This archived letter contains a now perfectly pressed four-leaf clover.

Houston arrived in Cardiff on 6 July 1935. Graham Brown showed him around his laboratory. The next day they travelled up to London and went sightseeing. At Buckingham Palace they waited loyally to see the king and queen drive in. They dined at the Athenaeum and the following morning went to the Alpine Club before leaving by train for the Alps. On arriving in Zermatt, they obtained rooms in the annexe of the Monte Rosa Hotel. Walking through the town, Graham Brown sighted Smythe, who was assessing candidates for the following year's Everest expedition, and noted critically:

> we watched Smythe's party set out to walk up to the Bétamps Hut. But Smythe himself stayed behind to go up to Rotenboden by train, there to meet the others. There was some joking about Smythe carrying the 'heavy sack' but the incident seemed typical to me, and did not create a good impression (training for Everest!).[14]

Graham Brown had, as usual, engaged Graven who, despite Graham Brown's enthusiastic endorsement of Houston's skill and strength, was reluctant to guide two amateurs on difficult routes without support. Theodor Biner was hired as second guide and they climbed as two separate ropes: Graven and Graham Brown, Biner and Houston. Together they climbed some of the great peaks around Zermatt by established routes but in novel and challenging combinations, for example: a traverse of Dent Blanche by the *Ferpècle Arête* and *Viereselgrat* and the east face of the Nordend of Monte Rosa by the *Brioschi Route* descending by the *Cresta di Santa Caterina*. The latter involved multiple abseils and, on one of them, Houston was launched into the void. 'I went down, spinning free,' he recalled,

> but saw no place to stop, whereupon shouts from above advised me to climb back up again. My emotions will be appreciated only by him who has climbed the thin rappel rope. After some futile struggles I was hauled ignominiously up, kicking furiously, stiff, tired, and very unhappy.[15]

Assessing this expedition some years later, Graham Brown wrote, 'In its balance of climbing interest during ascent and descent, and in its extraordinary maintenance of that interest for so many hours, this traverse assuredly approaches very near to perfection.'[16] The traverse was, however, contrived, seeking out difficulty for difficulty's sake. Strutt, who had no time for complex rope manoeuvres, observed that there was an obvious and easier descent, and he considered it the 'gentlemanly' way down. Nevertheless, these climbs were examples of traditional alpinism at the highest level.

At the end of July, the guides were released and Graham Brown and Houston joined Charlie's fellow members of the Harvard Mountaineering Club, Dan Brown and Arthur Emmons, but bad weather prevailed and they achieved little. Houston and his friends decided to initiate Graham Brown as an honorary member of their club. According to Graham Brown's journal, the 'chief features' of the ceremony were 'blindfolding, an abseil from the top floor of the dependence, fireworks (which did not go off properly!) and a rock climb'.[17] Fifty years later, Houston recounted the episode thus:

> We blindfolded him and told him he had to be initiated. We roped him up and made him cut steps up the paths of the hotel gardens. Then we made him climb the stairs to the second storey of the annexe and rappel out of the window blindfolded. Then we made him climb a small boulder in the garden and belay while we tried to pull him off. We ended up by having him bivouac on a chair tied to one of the trees on the main street. We tied him in snugly and took off his blindfold. I don't think I'll ever forget his look of astonishment and horror when he looked around at the considerable crowd – fifty or a hundred people – who were watching all this and realised that some of the leading lights of the Alpine Club were there.[18]

Graham Brown recorded that it was all 'very amusing'.

His last climb of the season was an ascent by the ordinary route of Dufourspitze, on Monte Rosa, with Art Emmons, who had accompanied Terris Moore to Minya Konka in 1932 and suffered severe frostbite that cost him all his toes. They joked about making the first 'toe-less ascent' of Monte Rosa, but Emmons found descending slow and painful, needing frequent halts to rub his feet and restore the circulation. Following this climb they went together to Baveno for some relaxation and spent a languorous day boating and bathing on Lake Maggiore. 'We bought a watermelon, some yellow plums, some peaches and a bottle of Chianti [and] rowed up the lake towards the spit where Leslie Letts and I spent a similar day in 1925. We sunbathed ashore … it was delightfully lazy … my mind wandered …

we scarcely spoke ... then we had a delightful bathe in the calm almost oily water.' After dinner, they sat on the hotel's terrace by the lake, 'listening to the music and too lazy to talk'. They went to bed 'much sunburnt'.[19]

Graham Brown returned to England via Zürich where over dinner he gossiped with Hans Lauper,[c] dentist by profession and a talented amateur alpinist. Lauper thought that their mutual acquaintance, Zürcher, aspired to be 'a big noise' in mountaineering circles, but he was 'not a strong climber' and 'was apt to lose his head', and Dyhrenfurth, who had led the International Himalaya Expedition to Kangchenjunga in 1930 that had included Smythe in the party, was vain, conceited and unsporting, wanting to win 'by any means fair or foul' – to gain advantage in a tennis tournament, he had used a racquet of 'enormous size'.[20] Graham Brown told Lauper about the frailties exhibited by Knubel and Aufdenblatten during his attempts on the *Pear Buttress* and made sure to mention Graven's praise for his own efforts on the first ascent of *Route Major*.

On his return to America Houston wrote to thank Graham Brown for a 'really great summer', saying 'it could only have been better if I had been less bloody at times'.[21] Graham Brown reassured him: 'As for the BM ... I don't regret it on either side, because a bit of bad temper now and then doesn't make any real difference if no sting is left behind.'[22] A series of letters exchanged over the ensuing months illuminates the relationship that had developed between them. Houston wrote:

> I wish to hell I could figure a way to spend a year abroad working with you; it would be a grand year and an important one but I don't see how it can be done. Or I wish you would spend a year over here, anywhere near enough to talk to. You're one of the few, in fact the only one, I can talk to, and I feel I can confide in you more than in anyone else at all. But I suppose it is better we be half a world apart – so I'll confine myself to letters, and I hope to write more often though not so volubly ... And I would like to hear from you more often; if only you could just write a line or so when you feel like it without feeling bound to send a whole epistle. When you are down and out, tell me about it, and get it off your chest.[23]

---

c   Hans Lauper (1895–1936). A Swiss member of the Alpine Club, he made a number of important, difficult new routes in the Bernese Oberland, with and without guides, including the north-east face of the Eiger, with Zürcher, Graven and Knubel in 1933.

Graham Brown replied:

> I often think of the grand time we had last summer, and I do wish the
> Atlantic wasn't so wide. It would be fine to have you near, and we
> could get away to the hills now and then – but that's all a dream.[24]

Houston again:

> … last summer has grown on me a lot, and I realise what a swell trip
> we had, and I am anxious to go again with you. You certainly are the
> only person alive whom I can be completely honest and natural with
> and hence you are bound to be very best friend or bitterest enemy.[25]

Graham Brown responded:

> I am fixed to climb with you each year as long as you like, and I have
> never had a better friend or one I can trust more on a mountain or
> anywhere else.[26]

Houston told his biographer that he regretted the lack of a close relationship
with his father, whom he regarded as complex and hidden, and it is easy
to imagine that he saw Graham Brown as a role model and mentor, their
shared interest in mountaineering and science providing a bond. In one
of his earliest letters, Houston described an experiment he had been con-
ducting – 'testing a secret theory' – which had excited him, adding bashfully
that it 'probably means nothing to you, and interests you less, but it's my
first original work'.[27] At medical school, as he began to acquire some knowledge of physiology and neurology, he became 'very keenly interested' in
Graham Brown's research and asked 'to sit humbly at your feet while you
pore [sic] words of wisdom in my ears'.[28] Graham Brown, reminded of his
own difficulties with his father, saw his valued friendship with Sherrington
mirrored in his friendship with Houston, for whom he had developed a
warm affection.

At the beginning of December Houston wrote with 'some news which I
hope will blow you right out of your chair', saying, 'How would you like to
go to Kangchenjunga?' Elaborating on the ambitious scheme which had
been drawn up by Emmons, with Adams Carter and Bill (Farney) Loomis,

all in their twenties and affiliated to the Harvard Mountaineering Club, he continued: it was to be a 'small-scale party in equipment and porters, running on the Alaskan plan ... there would be none of this 300 porters business' and importantly, 'there is no appointed leader ... we do not wish to follow the German military regime. In preparations committees will be as efficient and in climbing the most experienced will rule.'[29] Looking back years later, Houston reflected, 'it's hard to believe how naïve and presumptuous we were.'[30]

Kangchenjunga (8,586 metres), the third highest mountain in the world, had already repulsed three large-scale expeditions. Recognising their lack of Himalayan experience, Houston asked Graham Brown to recruit 'several additional top class climbers to make it a going party.'[31] In a follow-up letter, a few days later, Emmons emphasised the need for 'at least two of your young First Rate climbers of past high-altitude Himalayan experience',[32] adding that they were counting on Graham Brown's 'shrewdness and sagacity' and hoped that he would act as the expedition's representative in England. Graham Brown turned for advice to Eric Shipton, who had been to Everest in 1933 and had just returned from leading another expedition to the mountain. They drew up a longlist of a dozen candidates from amongst those who had been considered and rejected by the Everest Committee for the forthcoming attempt in 1936. Graham Brown settled on Noel Odell and Peter Lloyd as first choices, the former's experience combining with the latter's youth to meet Emmons's criteria. Odell, aged forty-six, had spent almost a fortnight above 7,000 metres on Everest in 1924 and had been the last person to see Mallory and Irvine alive. Lloyd, aged twenty-nine, had no experience of high altitude but was out of the Cambridge University Mountaineering Club stable and had acquired a reputation as a 'very good mountaineer'.

'Would the possibility of joining a Himalayan expedition this summer attract you?' Graham Brown asked, adding conspiratorially:

The thing (a 'big one') is not my proposal, and so I must not speak freely, but it is roughly this: an ultra-first-class peak to be tried in July (project quite feasible); private show with no publicity (or a minimum); composition of party – Anglo-American; the names I know are the best of good fellows; no leader; money already raised, but subscription of 300 dollars would be asked; I don't know anything

else about finances, but assume that travelling expenses there and
back would be private; no women to be taken.[33]

Odell replied that he would love to go but did not know how he would raise
the funds and, a month later, still had to 'square it' with his wife whom he
hoped would be 'sensible'. Lloyd, who was also married, seemed able to
accept without demur. When Houston learned of Odell's selection he asked
Graham Brown, 'Isn't he a little old for 28,000 feet? Or has he taken his
age as you have? I believe you could make the top alright, but you're phe-
nomenal.'[34] Graham Brown, now aged fifty-four, considered that he was
climbing better and with less fatigue than he had done before passing fifty;
a twenty-hour day did not bother him at all, although his recovery was not
as rapid as previously. For an objective assessment, he submitted himself
to the same physiological tests administered to candidates for Everest, passing 'with flying colours', and noted with obvious satisfaction that 'a neutral
puts my condition as exceptional even for a man of 35'.[35]

From the outset, Odell queried the young Americans' competence to
tackle Kangchenjunga and his doubts were reinforced by a letter from Terris
Moore, the expedition's éminence grise in America, who commended their
enthusiasm and sense of responsibility, but considered Kangchenjunga too
great a challenge. Furthermore, they had left applying for permission to
approach the mountain through Sikkim very late and it was likely to be
refused. An alternative objective was required. Nanda Devi (7,816 metres),
situated in the Garwhal Himalaya in British India, did not require special
permission and, two years earlier, Shipton and Tilman had solved the problem of the approach to its base. It was a more realistic proposition.

Loomis, who had travelled to England to advance preparations, and
Graham Brown met Tilman for dinner at Simpson's in the Strand. Nominally, Kangchenjunga remained the objective but the possibility of Nanda
Devi was discussed as an alternative. They invited Tilman to join the expedition and deputed him to speak to Shipton to ensure that he had no objection to the expedition switching to Nanda Devi if permission for Kangchenjunga was refused. The expedition was a private venture and its members
were responsible for the cost, estimated at £1,600 in total. Each was asked to
contribute what they could afford but this gentlemanly arrangement would
lead to some financial wrangling after the expedition. Graham Brown acted
as treasurer, a role for which he was not best suited; by his own admission,

accounts and money matters bored him to tears. Loomis was quarter-master and Tilman organised the transport and supplies in India. There was no titular leader of the expedition. The young Americans were comfortable with an egalitarian approach and the old hands had either been involved in the controversies that had surrounded the leadership of the Everest expeditions or had been victims of leadership decisions and were happy to do without. 'The general idea is to have a small party of good people without any tomfoolery about a leader,'[36] wrote Graham Brown. The group was also averse to the perceived publicity excesses which had surrounded the large national expeditions to the Himalaya but there was still a need to balance the books and Graham Brown negotiated with *The Times* on behalf of the expedition. The £350 offered was less than that paid to Smythe's expedition to Kamet causing him to complain, 'it is a little disappointing that you rate our attempt on Nanda Devi, even if successful, on so much a lower scale. Our mountain is higher, and also much more difficult than Kamet.'[37]

In March 1936, with Kangchenjunga still the expedition's goal, Tilman departed for India to make preliminary arrangements, hiring Sherpas and porters. But on arriving in Calcutta, he learned that permission for Kang-chenjunga had been refused. 'Like most oracular pronouncements no reasons were given,' Tilman recalled, and:

> there was nothing to be done except write a 'forlorn hope' of a letter asking for reconsideration and the reply to that was merely an official 'raspberry'.[38]

Nanda Devi became their objective. Shortly before his own departure for India at the end of May, Houston wrote to Graham Brown, 'In just about two or three weeks I will be seeing you and we shall have some awful scraps; do you suppose we can avoid being BM this summer?'[39] To which Graham Brown replied,' I shall look out for you very eagerly at Marseille. I am very fit and strong – quite able to put you in your proper place when necessary, so mind your manners and be a good boy.'[40]

Chapter 15

Nanda Devi

Graham Brown sailed from Tilbury on 12 June 1936 accompanied by Lloyd. By the time they reached Gibraltar, Graham Brown had regaled him with the shenanigans concerning the Everest Committee, narrated the story of Waller and Smythe on the Grépon in 1928 and described the frailties of Knubel and Aufdenblatten on the *Pear Buttress*; by Suez, both he and Odell, who had joined ship at Marseilles, had been told the Smythe saga 'in detail'. Charlie and his family also came aboard at Marseilles. Oscar's intention was that his wife and daughters should holiday on the lakes in Kashmir while he accompanied the climbing expedition to the base of Nanda Devi. Charlie doubted that his father could cope with the rigours of the approach march and secretly hoped that he would fail a medical assessment, but to improve his fitness, Oscar had stopped smoking, given up alcohol and ran daily. Charlie, indebted to his father, had been unable to refuse him, but Odell and Graham Brown opposed the plan. Graham Brown noted in his diary that Oscar, aged fifty-two and two years younger, was 'bitterly jealous' of him, 'thinks where I can go he can go' and did not allow that he was 'a recognised mountaineer'.[1] Oscar was extremely disappointed to be rejected and threatened to return home from Aden. Odell mollified him. On the eve of their arrival in Bombay, Graham Brown joined the Houston family for champagne cocktails and, a few days later, shared with them the 'wonderful' sight of the Taj Mahal by moonlight. But Oscar's resentment persisted and six months after the conclusion of the expedition, he did not contact Graham Brown when he travelled to England on business. On learning that Oscar had been in England, Graham Brown wrote to his informant:

I had not heard that Mr Houston Snr. had been in Town … He is very unlike his son, who takes after his mother, but the father is a very interesting and well-informed man. He is not a mountaineer, but he came out to India last summer with the intention of forcing himself on our party. He gave me quite a lot of difficulty and it was not a pleasant business ... I had to hold the baby, of course, as I usually have to do ... but I expect it has blown over by this time.[2]

The climbing party, except for Carter who was in Shanghai – which as Tilman wryly observed 'seemed a bit far from Nanda Devi' – gathered on 6 July in Ranikhet, a hill station and cantonment town in the Almora district of India. The first leg of the expedition was a ten-day march to Joshimath during which it rained incessantly, the tents leaked and leeches plagued them. Houston, who had been responsible for obtaining the tents, which had performed well in Alaska, became the butt of some merciless teasing: 'Were they equally good in snow? Was the rain in Alaska very dry?'[3]

On 21 July seven sahibs (Carter was still catching up), six Sherpas and forty-seven porters set out for the Rishi Gorge, the key to the approach to the mountain, which had been penetrated for the first time by Shipton and Tilman in 1934. Steep-sided and in places 3,000 metres deep, the gorge carves through the barrier of mountains that encircles Nanda Devi. For the first few days the party followed traces of a herdsmen's track; thereafter they had to forge their own way through increasingly difficult terrain. They groped their way through thickets of rhododendron and struggled up 'vertical' grass. Graham Brown tersely described the ascent of the 'grass cliff' in his diary: 'like Lliwedd but much grass. The ascent was very exposed and sensational. In places dangerous.'[4] He noted that 'one coolie funked the grass cliff and had to be got up without a load'. (Tilman generously excused the porter who was burdened with an unruly load of telescopic tent poles, 'which at the slightest provocation telescoped out again'.)[5] Their route continued above drops of several thousand feet into the gorge below. They balanced along narrow ledges and across steep slabs, covered with semi-liquid mud that gave them 'heart failure at every step'. As well as being nerve-wracking the march was physically punishing. Following the dismissal of thirty-one porters who refused to cross the Rhamani torrent, which was in spate and blocked the route, the climbers shouldered loads of 60lb and the party resorted to relaying. Even the famously tough Tilman suffered: 'at the end of a long day one's back felt as though it had been flagellated'.[6] Graham Brown observed that on several occasions Lloyd 'packed light', remarking in extenuation that he had developed piles. It took five days to gain the five miles through the upper gorge and the mental and physical strain took its toll on Graham Brown who felt 'morose and irritable'.[7]

On 1 August they emerged from the confines of the gorge and entered the sanctuary – eight miles of rolling meadow, studded with blue poppies and edelweiss, on which mountain goats and sheep grazed unafraid of man – dominated by the great mass of Nanda Devi rising 3,900 metres from its base to summit. The vista had changed dramatically but the hard labour of carrying heavy loads continued. Base camp was finally established at about 5,100 metres on 7 August. The remaining porters were paid off and sent down, leaving seven climbers (Carter had at last caught up with the team; Emmons stayed at base camp to undertake survey work) and six Sherpas to attempt the climb.

Their route of ascent lay up the narrow, serrated south ridge, on which Camps I (5,850 metres) and II (6,220 metres) were placed, leading to a snow arête where they sited Camp III (6,460 metres). The arête broadened into a snow saddle, the site of Camp IV (6,645 metres). Above this, 1,000 metres of steep, mixed ground led to the summit. The climbing was difficult. Odell judged the difficulties to be comparable to one of the 'stiffer' ridges of the Dent Blanche and Graham Brown thought they were similar to those encountered on the Aiguille Blanche de Peuterey. Rotten rock on the ridge made the climbing precarious and dangerous. Tilman noted laconically, 'Noel came off with a loose rock but I had a good axe anchorage' and 'I ... nearly killed Noel with a rock.'[8] Subsequent expeditions fixed ropes for security over long stretches of the ridge. Sickness amongst the Sherpas resulted in them providing minimal support to the climbers who had to ferry their tents, food and equipment up the mountain. One pair prospected the route whilst the others established and stocked the camps. Tilman made five journeys between Camps I and II; Houston and Graham Brown did six trips between II and III. During his first climb from Camp II to Camp III, Graham Brown painstakingly recorded the time taken for each stretch of 100 steps and the halts in between. The 850 steps from the foot of the snow ridge to the site of Camp III took seventy-two minutes, at an average rate of twelve steps per minute, and forty-two minutes were taken in rests, a rate of progress that suggests he was not yet acclimatised and Houston observed that he was slow, 'grouchy' and 'very cyanotic'.

Both men's diaries include a disproportionate number of comments about each other compared with the rest of the team. Houston found numerous reasons to be irritated by Graham Brown: he was slow and lazy; his heavy breathing disturbed him; even his sunburnt face – 'a horrible mess' – was an annoyance and eventually they had a 'huge row'. But such irritations are commonplace when living at close quarters at altitude. 'All manner of things, great and small, are liable to promote discord,' wrote Shipton, a veteran of many Himalayan expeditions,

> Garrulity is notoriously hard to bear; silence can be no less trying. Even an unconscious display of virtue can be as intolerable as any vice, gentlemanly poise as hasty temper, efficiency as clumsiness, knowledge as ignorance, energy as sloth. In conditions of boredom or nervous strain one is quick to resent the way a man drinks his soup or wears his hat, or the silly manner in which his beard has grown, or a thousand other trifles that in normal circumstances would pass unnoticed. When one is short of rations it generally seems that one's companion has secured the larger part of a meal; and he invariably occupies more than his share of the tent.[9]

Graham Brown made frequent reference to Charlie's bad temper, of which he was generally forgiving, but he was disconcerted by Houston's volte-face in wishing to appoint a leader and aggrieved that he should propose Tilman for the role.

The issue of leadership came to a head on 21 August. The summit was within striking distance of one additional camp and a decision about who should make the bid for the top was needed. The night before, Loomis and Houston had discussed privately the performances of their companions and possible pairings for the attempt on the summit. They agreed that Graham Brown was not going well: 'Both of us feel that Tim is at about his top … he can't seem to do other than go up and go to bed.'[10] The team gathered in the large tent at Camp III and had 'a very congenial and profitable conference'[11] – Houston later described it as 'an hilarious debate'[12] – but Graham Brown was 'very quiet and obviously displeased'.[13] After Odell had declined the role, Tilman 'was given the invidious job of leader, that is to say decide who goes first'.[14] He chose Odell and Houston for the 'first shot'.

More than fifty years later, Houston made clear in reported interviews and letters that Graham Brown had insisted that he was the strongest and most experienced in the group and should be in the party to make the first bid for the summit. In one of the interviews Houston even suggested that a ballot was instigated in response to Graham Brown's 'delusions'.[15] When the expedition was over much was made of the unity and teamwork of the party. Houston wrote that 'despite the intense desire of each man ... there was no grumbling or expressed regret (with one mild exception) when the team was chosen. We all felt so closely identified with the mountain that the question of what individuals should actually reach the top was purely academic.'[16] In the official account of the expedition, Tilman quoted Kipling: 'the game is more than the players of the game and the ship is more than the crew'.[17] But Graham Brown wrote in his diary that he was 'nearly heartbroken'.

On 25 August Houston and Odell, supported by Loomis, Lloyd and Tilman, set out on their summit attempt. Five hours of laborious step-kicking led to the foot of a rock tower which was climbed by a chimney that required Lloyd's rock-climbing expertise to overcome. Above this was a more broken ridge on which Houston and Odell pitched their tent at about 7,150 metres. The others descended to Camp IV where Graham Brown had arrived. The next day Houston and Odell reconnoitred the ridge above. That night Houston became acutely unwell with vomiting and diarrhoea and the following morning had to descend. Tilman took his place and on 29 August he and Odell reached the summit where Tilman recalled, with now legendary understatement, 'I believe we so far forgot ourselves as to shake hands on it.'[18]

The descent proved trying for everyone and almost disastrous. They were all very tired and the weather and snow conditions were poor. Houston went down with Graham Brown who resented having to accompany him and abandon his own chance to go for the summit. 'Tim and I down over bloody ridge to Camp 2. Tim shaky, nearly killed us both,'[19] Houston noted in his diary. A step had given way and Graham Brown fell, pulling Houston off. Graham Brown's version, inked into his diary and therefore added sometime later with a hint of self-justification, ran, 'I went along in old steps. They broke, but I stopped myself before reaching rocks. On looking up saw C[harlie] falling and his ice axe left behind. Held him but shocked at his insecurity.'[20] The unannotated entry reads, 'Slip on descent. C. bad.'

They reached base camp mentally and physically exhausted, but the next day they set off on separate journeys back to Ranikhet, Graham Brown returning down the gorge and Houston over Longstaff's col. Their parting was tense. 'C[harlie] would not look at me in the face when saying goodbye, obviously ashamed, poor fellow,'[21] noted Graham Brown, in a pencilled addendum to his diary. Houston, recalling their final conversation, wrote,

'I am not quite sure what your attitude toward me is … I don't suppose it is too good. For which I am sure I can't blame you very much.'[22] Graham Brown's journey back through the gorge proved slow and painful; suffering with blistered feet and a sore leg, he limped into Ranikhet on 21 September.

News of the successful ascent appeared in *The Times* of 9 September. The names of the summit pair had not been given and Tom Longstaff, doyen of Himalayan exploration and patron saint of the small expedition, applauded the simple announcement as 'a grand gesture' against the pernicious effect of publicity. Shipton called it 'the finest achievement that has ever been done in the Himalaya' and wished he had been with them instead of wasting time 'on that ridiculous Everest business'.[23] Congratulatory telegrams, addressed to Graham Brown, were received from the Viceroy of India and the Alpine and Himalayan clubs. The long-suffering Welsh National School of Medicine also sent its congratulations to their absentee professor of physiology.

Graham Brown arrived back in England on 10 October. Before returning to Cardiff he met Strutt at the Alpine Club and agreed to read a paper to the club in the near future. When Odell discovered this arrangement he reminded Graham Brown, in unambiguous terms, that the team had agreed previously that Tilman should give the paper, in recognition of his contribution to the success of the expedition. The task of writing the expedition's book also fell to Tilman who sent proofs to Graham Brown and regretted doing so: 'Like a B[loody] F[ool] I sent Timmy the proofs and today comes a letter pointing out many places in which he thinks his doings have not received sufficient notice … I have told him it doesn't accord with his views on being <u>impersonal</u>. They only apply to others apparently.'[24] Graham Brown's comments ranged from the pedantic to self-serving. In particular he was critical of Tilman's view on age and high-altitude mountaineering. Tilman had written, 'Another interesting point is that the age limit for high climbing, previously put at 35, seems to have expanded, for our party was of all ages from twenty-two to over fifty, but I do not want to imply that either of these extremes is recommended.' Graham Brown struck back:

> This will be read as meaning that a man over 50 is not to be recommended on a high expedition, and I don't like it. I hope that you will cut it out. I went six times from Camp II to Camp III and carried loads five times which was the same as the number carried by Charlie and yourself, and no others carried more than three loads.

He added the barb, 'This as you know was my first experience of high-altitude work, and I would rate my physical performance as better than your own at your first visit.'[25] An irritated Tilman replied:

> Your rather unimportant corrections have given me a lot of work. I threw no bouquets to anyone and tried to be as impersonal as possible which I believe is your strong suit when it comes to writing accounts.

He continued, 'I agree as you know that your performance was remarkable and gladly admit that it was better than my own on whatever occasion you refer to.'[26] Graham Brown's self-esteem would not allow him to let his achievements pass unnoticed, his desire for recognition conflicting with his declared antipathy to publicity. In a moment of vanity, he sat for a portrait, executed in crayon by the fashionable artist Kathleen Shackleton[a], adding to her 'collection of famous persons'.

After some pestering by the assistant editor, Graham Brown produced a series of articles for *The Times*, which appeared over five consecutive days at the end of November. The final article was largely devoted to his views on the merits and success of their small expedition compared to the excesses and failures of the large national expeditions, particularly to Everest, of which he wrote, 'These extravagant and formal affairs, with their publicity, their cohorts of trained porters, their armies of coolies, their squadrons of yaks, and their small achievement have caused most of us to wonder what mountaineering is coming to and whether failure may not be inherent in the method.'[27] His remarks were opportune. Following the failure of the expedition to Everest earlier in the year, the constituency and direction of the Everest Committee were under renewed attack. Commenting on the expedition in an interview for the *Morning Post*, George Finch, who had reached 8,300 metres on Everest in 1922, had said, 'Our present position is that we are beginning to look ridiculous.' Meade, who had resigned from the Alpine Club's committee in protest over relations with the Everest Committee, thought Graham Brown's article was 'magnificent', adding, 'You have discredited the *ancien regime* but its flunkeys may yet sabotage its successors.'[28]

---

a   Kathleen Shackleton (1882–1961), sister of the polar explorer Sir Ernest Shackleton. Other sitters included Arthur Conan Doyle and W.B. Yeats.

Odell also expressed approval: 'Congratulations on the articles: v. good. Yesterday's should give the MEC etc. much good food for thought.'[29] The success of the Nanda Devi expedition provided a persuasive example of the merits of a small expedition and influenced the reformed Everest Committee, on which the climbers now held greater sway. The 1938 expedition was cheaper and leaner, to the point of frugality some considered.[b] The party, under Tilman's leadership, included Lloyd and Odell. Graham Brown's omission is noteworthy because he was the only other eligible climbing member of the Nanda Devi expedition – the Americans being disqualified because climbing Everest was still regarded as a strictly British affair. But his performance on Nanda Devi had not overcome the objection of his age and there may have been doubts about his temperament and willingness to work in a team, especially one that included Smythe.

Meanwhile settlement of the expedition's finances dragged on and Graham Brown's dilatoriness was seen to be the problem. 'Do let us have this business resolved and finalised on a satisfactory basis to all, so that there is no unpleasant flavour left after what was a delightful show,'[30] urged Odell, and Tilman considered 'the whole arrangement is very un-businesslike'.[31] The final disbursements to the British members were made in January 1938, more than a year after the expedition's return, and three months later, Houston was still chasing Graham Brown on behalf of the Americans.

The expedition to Nanda Devi proved to be the watershed of the friendship between Houston and Graham Brown. Houston broke silence at the beginning of November. He had hesitated to write because he suspected that their parting at base camp had signified rupture of their friendship: 'I was much afraid we had split up for good, something I should hate to see happen.' As usual he blamed himself: 'Somehow I guess we will always quarrel when together – it's largely my fault and I suppose I won't change much.'[32] Graham Brown brushed off Charlie's concerns and turned to making plans for climbing together again but Houston wrote, 'your attitude was so uncordial that I made no plans for your company this summer'.[33] Graham Brown proffered reassurance: 'If you think my feelings of friendship for you have changed even a little, you are quite wrong because they are as strong as ever.'[34] Houston replied:

---

b   Odell complained that the rations had been meagre. Tilman retorted that Odell 'has not yet finished criticising the food we ate on Nanda Devi in 1936 and ... in spite of his semi-starved condition, succeeded in getting to the top'. (Tilman H., *Mount Everest 1938*, p. 124)

You and I have had some funny times together, Tim; I sometimes feel that we are too much alike ever to get along in each other's company for very long at a time without a scrap, but that does not alter the fact that I feel closer to you than to almost anyone else I know. Without getting drippy about it you really are my closest friend, and I value your opinion and friendship more than anyone's, my father included … I hope it will be the last [letter] that I write to apologise for all the wrongs and misunderstandings I have caused and that we are back on the old Foraker footing again.[35]

But he excused himself from joining Graham Brown in the summer, saying that his medical studies were increasingly time consuming. Graham Brown pressed him to agree plans for climbing together in 1938. Houston had been invited to join a party sponsored by the American Alpine Club to attempt K2 and asked tentatively whether Graham Brown would be interested in going, while making it clear that he was not in a position to make a firm offer. Graham Brown replied that he would be 'delighted'. Later, Houston was obliged to withdraw the offer, explaining that another candidate who was forty-seven years old was to be rejected on the grounds of his age and therefore Graham Brown's inclusion could not be justified. Furthermore, he had doubts about Graham Brown's ability to acclimatise: 'I don't feel you would be able to make the top … and I don't believe you yourself think you could get extremely high.'[36] Graham Brown's reaction is not documented but it is inconceivable that he received the decision equably and his prompt resolve to join an expedition to Masherbrum in the Karakoram suggests that he wished to prove a point. Houston certainly felt that from that moment a frostiness developed on the part of Graham Brown, whose correspondence with Houston, always erratic, dwindled and ceased. Three years later Houston wrote wearily:

This is the last time I shall bother you with a letter, because after shooting so many in the air futilely I begin to think you do not want to hear from me anymore … I am used to your casualness about letters, and for a long time I excused it on the grounds of the war etc. etc.; but I have not heard from you for over a year now, though I have written several times both before and after my marriage.[37]

Chapter 16
Masherbrum

Let down by Houston, Graham Brown arrived alone in Grindelwald at the end of July 1937. He asked the proprietor of his hotel to recommend 'a young, good, ambitious guide' and was introduced to Albert Schlunegger, 'a nice fellow of about 32 years old' whom he engaged for 'fourteen days at 30SF (he wanted 35)'.[1] Schlunegger was wary of his new client's proposal to attempt the classic testpieces of the *Nollen Route* on the Mönch and the *Guggi Route* on the Jungfrau as a party of two, prompting Graham Brown to remark in his diary that his guide seemed 'rather frightened'.

In the summer of 1937 the North Face of the Eiger was still unclimbed. The discovery at the beginning of July of Andreas Hinterstoisser's corpse, lying on a patch of snow at the foot of the wall, recalled the previous year's tragic disaster which had claimed his life and that of his three companions – Toni Kurz freezing to death while dangling on a rope just feet away from rescue. On 11 August Matthias Rebitsch and Ludwig Vörg set out to attempt the face and Graham Brown joined the crowds of onlookers at the telescopes to follow their progress. The Austrian-German pair climbed almost two thirds of the way up the face, passing the site of 'Death Bivouac' where Max Sedlmayer and Karl Mehringer, the first to dare to attempt the face, had perished in 1935, before turning back in torrential hail and sleet and descending safely. A few days later Graham Brown went up to Alpiglen to study the face from close at hand. He summed up his month at Grindelwald in a letter to Houston:

> I didn't try the climbs I really wanted to do, because the weather made them hopeless and eventually after a final week of rain, I came home in disgust. The North Face of the Eiger was not one of the climbs on my list, or rather I took it off. I spent two days under it in a very careful examination, and so many stones fell on the second day that I decided the climb was a sheer gamble and not legitimate.

In the same letter he asked about climbing together the following year:

> Well Charlie I don't want to be left at a loose end again … Can we fix
> something up? I want to climb with you if we can fix it. I am just as
> keen on unexplored country as you are, and Alaska would be fine if
> that could be managed.[2]

But Houston's plans for 1938 did not include him, so when Graham Brown
learned of an opportunity to join an expedition to Masherbrum (7,821
metres) in the Karakoram Himalaya, he applied.

The expedition was conceived and organised by James Waller, a gunner
subaltern stationed in India. Prior to his arrival in India in 1932, aged twenty,
Waller's mountaineering experience had been limited to three weeks in the
Alps climbing with a guide, but over the next few years he had undertaken
several audacious, exploratory trips in the mountains of Kashmir and the
Karakoram. In 1934, together with another young officer, J.B. 'Jock' Harrison, he had attempted to climb Nun (7,135 metres) supported only by some
local porters. Neither of the self-confessed tyro mountaineers had camped
above the snow line before. Waller recalled that their outlook 'was that mere
altitude could not have as much effect as is normally attributed to it, and
that if a lady, Mrs Bullock Workman, had achieved 22,800 feet in 1909, Jock
and I should be able to reach 23,400 feet in 1934.' He continued, flippantly:

> Mrs Bullock Workman had climbed in a long tweed skirt and a large
> hat with a veil; we could not believe that anyone so clad could have
> done anything of great difficulty, and we were fairly sure that the
> fuss made about high altitude climbing must be some sort of racket
> designed to keep other people from trying it and so spoiling the
> market for those who had already been high. We were young and
> very inexperienced.[3]

By 1938 they had 'both learned a lot'. Harrison had been on an expedition to
the Kangchenjunga massif; Waller and John Hunt[a] had reached 7,300 metres
on Saltoro Kangri before turning back in deteriorating conditions, their
prudence drawing praise from Strutt, who, in his presidential valedictory

---

a   John Hunt (1910–1998), leader of the successful Everest expedition in 1953.

address to the Alpine Club, complimented them on their 'splendid attempt' and 'extraordinary insight'. But, apart from Harrison, none of Waller's previous companions were available for an attempt on Masherbrum so he recruited Lieutenant J.O.M. Roberts, aged twenty-one, a close friend of Harrison's and who had recently been elected to the Alpine Club on the strength of climbs achieved as a minor, and wrote to the Alpine Club requesting help with finding two more climbers to join the team.

Robin Hodgkin, who 'had been polite to Strutt in Edinburgh and friendly with Dr Longstaff at the Alpine Club'[4] was nominated. Aged twenty-two, he was in limbo between university and a career in teaching. Whilst at Oxford he had made the first ascent of the Radcliffe Camera[b], several new and difficult rock climbs on Clogwyn Du'r Arddu and the first British ascent of the South Peak of Ushba (4,696 metres) in the Caucasus, by a bold and technical new route. In his letter of invitation to Hodgkin, Waller wrote, 'Harrison, Roberts and I are all as keen as mustard, but I would hesitate to call us an experienced trio, and your joining would add great strength to the party.'[5]

Strutt passed Waller's invitation on to Graham Brown who wrote to Waller asking to be considered, saying, 'I think that I can fit in fairly well with a young party.'[6] The disparity between Graham Brown's age and experience and that of the rest of the party caused Waller to prevaricate but, having sounded out Harrison and Roberts, he extended a firm invitation to Graham Brown, writing deferentially:

> The party will be very pleased if you will consent to join us … I sincerely hope, sir, that you will decide to give us a trial … I am afraid I cannot guarantee any startling performances, and the general climbing standard will be below what you are used to … We are very young but I hope you will forgive that.[7]

He outlined his views on leadership and his intention that the expedition should be run 'as a soviet':

> The party chooses its own leader … The party is all very young and should instinctively turn to the right man to lead … My opinion is that the leader should be the man who will get the party to the top by

---

b   Hodgkin and his companion were in two minds about whether to hoist a Red Flag or a Union Jack. Patriotism prevailed and the *Daily Mail* decided that perhaps Oxford wasn't decadent after all.

sheer character and example. He will probably be the strongest climber, least affected by altitude.[8]

His letter to Hodgkin was more dogmatic: 'The technical leader should be the best climber and the fellow with most guts; the latter being the most important!'[9] In a typed circular to all the team, he extolled the need for teamwork and warned of the effects of altitude:

> Every expedition must have as its primary object the getting of a pair of climbers to the top. If more reach it so much the better. But every man must work to get a pair there … We will have our chance of discussion before major decisions are arrived at; once the discussion has finished we must obey the majority decision.
>
> The most difficult thing at high altitude is to remain normal mentally. We must make up our minds beforehand that we will not allow ourselves to show irritability with the peculiarities of another member. It is criminal not to be good tempered and cheerful whatever the provocation … [and] high altitudes dull the brain and deaden the sense of fear. They make for dangerous climbing.[10]

He added a hand-written postscript to Graham Brown's copy, saying, 'I hope that you agree with me, sir?' Given Graham Brown's behaviour later on the expedition the remark proved to be unintentionally ironic.

With less than a week to go before sailing for India, Graham Brown wrote to the principal of the university to seek official leave of absence and suggested that he had a secret commission:

> two objects call for my presence in India, can I be spared, … both of which must (for different reasons) be kept as confidential as possible. One of these, as you know, concerns high altitude. The second has to do with anti-aircraft defence, with which I am intimately concerned as chairman of a committee which has had that as its chief function for the past 10 years or more.[11]

Graham Brown was being economical with the truth. It was true that secrecy was being observed regarding Masherbrum being the expedition's objective because Waller had neglected to obtain permission from the

Indian authorities and they were proceeding under the pretext of a hunting trip. It was also true that Graham Brown was the chairman of the Medical Research Council's committee on the physiology of hearing and that the committee had oversight of some experiments on sound localisation in connection with the development of 'sound mirrors'[c] to detect approaching aircraft. But he did not have a brief to investigate anti-aircraft defences. To lend some veracity to his story, on the day that his ship sailed he wrote to a contact at the Air Defence Experimental Establishment, Biggin Hill, asking whether he could 'be of any use in connexion with anti-aircraft defence' during his visit to India, and confessed that he had already 'informed one person in Cardiff, privately and confidentially, that there are anti-aircraft problems of great importance in India, and that during my visit I shall not be wholly engaged with that other problem as to how high it is possible to get without the aid of aeroplanes!'[12]

The response was curt: 'The R[oyal] E[ngineer] Board did not see any application to war purposes for your possible activities'[13] and the query was passed to the director of scientific research at the Air Ministry, D.R. Pye, a former climbing companion of George Mallory and a member of the Alpine Club, who was puzzled by Graham Brown's offer: 'I am not clear from your letter what are the types of information which might be useful in connection with anti-aircraft defence that you thought you might be able to get while in India' adding, 'how one envies you the opportunity of getting away on such a jaunt'.[14]

Hodgkin and Graham Brown travelled out together, sailing to Bombay, via Suez, on the P&O liner *Strathnaver*. Recalling the voyage, Hodgkin wrote:

Graham Brown was good company. He talked a bit about that villain F.S. Smythe but more about Nanda Devi in 1936; how he should have been on the assault party, and I can't quite recall the reason why he wasn't. And advice about girls: 'Watch out for that lass at the swimming pool, Robin, not too much "spooning".' That was a new word to me and I don't think that G.B. quite realised how inexperienced this

---

[c]   They worked by focusing sound waves on the central point of a large concrete dish and were manned by trained operators listening through a stethoscope, who could detect aircraft 15–20 miles away. Between the wars, a number of 'mirrors' were built on the south coast.

young mountaineer was. 'Yes, and watch out for that friendly Indian girl. Mixed marriages with natives can be pretty disastrous.'[15]

They arrived in Srinigar on Sunday 17 April 1938 and spent ten leisurely days in this enchanting place, residing on a houseboat on the nearby lake. They bathed frequently, 'great dives in very deep water', and were paddled to the city in shikaras, local gondolas, to shop for personal supplies – tobacco for Graham Brown – and to take tea in the ornamental gardens.

On 28 April Graham Brown, Hodgkin, Harrison and Waller set off for Masherbrum (Roberts left four days later and caught up with the main party en route), marching in short stages to get fit without tiring themselves, a policy approved by Graham Brown who liked Waller's 'ideas in general about fitness' and confessed that 'I never under any circumstances do any training myself.'[16] They shared a riding pony and were pampered by their personal Sherpas who 'tend to our every need and tuck us up in bed'.[17] On 2 May they reached the Zoji La, a high pass (3,530 metres) linking Kashmir to Ladakh; Waller described the crossing, which was made at night because of the risk of avalanche:

> The ascent of the Zoji La gorge next morning was as unpleasant as it usually is at this time of year. It seemed very cold at one in the morning when we ate our breakfast and dressed by the light of a single candle. By two-thirty the whole party was on the move. The sky was cloudless and the stars very bright; the Milky Way lighted the snow vaguely. We stumbled up over the avalanche rubble in the bottom of the gorge, the walls of which closed blackly about us. A cold breeze was blowing. Occasionally a torch flashed, but for the most part we ascended in the dark. The coolies went up in a series of fifty-yard rushes, after which they would sit down and rest. Graham Brown and I followed slowly after them; ... By the time we reached the top of the pass the sun was colouring with gold the snow peaks above us. As soon as we began to descend the climbers put on their skis; all except Graham Brown whose bindings had been lost, and who had to wait until we could unearth some string. Hodgkin was our expert skier; the only time he fell was when I was taking a carefully staged shot on my cinema film! Harrison was the next best, getting along at a great rate, but looking and being more insecure.

Graham Brown had only worn skis on one occasion previously, and he found that two Sherpas were required to keep him on his feet; his progress was somewhat stately.[18]

They descended into the valley of the river Shingo where the weather was springlike – 'we pitched camp under apricot trees which were shedding their blossom, so that the beach was like snow'[19] – and followed it into the valley of the Indus where the climate turned to summer and it was warm enough to swim – 'we immediately threw off our clothes and had a marvellous bathe, swimming and diving off the rocks'.[20] The path along the Indus climbed up and down, clinging precariously to the steep cliffs of the gorge, which in places was so narrow that Harrison claimed that he could spit a stone across it, and dropped down on to flats and plains, passing through orchards of apricot which provided welcome shade from the oppressive heat. They crossed the Indus on a punt. As they poled and drifted to the opposite bank, the crew sang; Graham Brown tried unsuccessfully to memorise the tune, which reminded him of the refrain 'two lovely black eyes'. The party turned east, crossing the river Shyok on rafts made of branches of poplar and inflated goatskins, which had a distressing tendency to deflate in the middle of the stream and required repeated re-inflation by the ferryman who crawled from skin to skin. During the trek the party's mood was lighthearted. 'Robin, Tim and I behaved like children,' observed Harrison, as they trundled boulders that 'bounced magnificently and disappeared with a most satisfying splash'.[21] At the end of the day's march, they relaxed together completing crosswords 'by committee' and reading 'a thriller' aloud. Harrison thought it 'a grand life'.

Graham Brown's assessments of his young companions reveal him as censorious and a snob. Waller 'had a rather chubby face – 'babyish', and rather prominent blue eyes. He looked neither interesting, athletic nor intellectual':

> His great interest was in organisation. He had great files of correspondence about our present expedition, and he told me later on that, at high altitudes, his mind became so absorbed with such fancies as the organisation of an hotel that he could not sleep but had to take drugs. He spoke much about the present expedition and about his own past exploits (<u>very</u> much!), but would not speak much about

mountaineering as such. I found later on that he had two interests: one was to write, but some of his writing that I and RH accidentally came across in one of his Masherbrum files was quite childish. His second interest was horses, especially in connexion with polo and steeple-chasing. He knew his subject and his great ambition was to ride in the Grand National! J.W. was 26 years of age. His father had died when he was young, and his mother (I judged) was not one who would give the tone of good breeding to her son. But J.W. had acquired very strongly the 'army' tone, and had excellent manners, restraint, and code of behaviour – all superficial rather than ingrained. He has his mother's habit of resentment, but 'sublimes' it by putting down his feelings in his diary, so he told me, there giving them free rein.

Harrison 'was a very tall man with a charming manner and intonation' and 'his manner gave the impression of very strong character and pushfulness – a "leader"'.

He was 30 years of age and good-looking. From the moment of our first meeting I felt that I would like him, but that he himself had some sort of reserve towards me. Were this true, it might be due to the age difference; or were it not so, my feeling about it might be due to J.H.'s overpowering height. His father had risen from the ranks to a commission (Ordinance, I think) and had educated J.H. to a commission – a fine story.

'Hodgkin was a pleasant "stable companion", and his personality interested me,' Graham Brown recorded.

He had good manners and could be charming if he liked. He was a communist, but gave me the impression that his personal advantage was of more importance to him than his convictions. His memory was very retentive, and he had an amazingly accurate memory for topographical detail. His interests were many and widespread, but did not go deep. He was good at doing anything with his hands, and liked intricate manual work. He was very self-contained and selfish, for instance, he took the best of everything whilst we lived together on the houseboat at Srinigar. I doubt if I have met a more selfish man.

He was easily affected by criticism or a hint, and rather charmingly apologetic.[22]

Of Jimmy Roberts, Graham Brown observed simply that he had climbed the Dent Blanche the day after he had done so in 1935.

Hodgkin's impressions of his companions were more generous:

Jock Harrison and Jimmy Roberts are both hellish good blokes ... Graham Brown continues to be pleasant and tolerable. He may irk before the show is finished but it should never get bothersome. James (Waller) ... is a very worthy bloke. Being small he is sometimes a bit aggressive but this is his only noticeable drawback. We have had no quarrels and I don't think they will be likely occurrences.[23]

On 15 May they glimpsed Masherbrum for the first time and the next day established their base camp between the village of Hushe and the snout of the Masherbrum Glacier, at an altitude of 3,250 metres, camping on grass, which they had hardly seen since crossing the Zoji La, amongst 'a delightful jungle' of juniper trees. They spent the next ten days in reconnaissance for there had been no previous attempt on Masherbrum and their only information was an old photograph, taken twenty years earlier. The only feasible route appeared to be via a branch of the Masherbrum Glacier which led up to a snow basin, from where a steep snow slope led to a hog's-back of snow, dubbed the Dome, above which towered the south-east face and summit of Masherbrum, but the ground between the Dome and south-east face was hidden from view.

They worried whether a safe way could be found through the crevasses and séracs of the branch glacier that descended from the snow basin for about 900 metres in a series of icefalls. But, on 26 May, Harrison and Hodgkin returned to base camp with the news that they had managed to reach the rim of the snow basin. Graham Brown noted in his diary:

They had reached the plateau of the 'Brenva' glacier [Graham Brown idiosyncratically used the nomenclature of the Mont Blanc region] by what must have been a fine piece of work, bivouacking on the way. The difficulty lay in the first 20 minutes, and the route led (as I thought it would, and so advised) up the true L[eft] edge of the glacier.

It appears that there may be some sérac danger. JH came to my tent and we had a long talk about the routes.[24]

The difficult section was a steep, icy gully exposed to the risk of falling stones and rock, which they named 'Scaly Alley', and was the key to the route up the glacier. Their discovery engendered an air of anticipation amongst the team. Harrison noted that they were all 'in good spirits' except for Graham Brown, who did not 'seem to be himself', observing that Graham Brown, who had come in from his reconnaissance a few days earlier, appeared 'pretty done but won't admit it'.[25]

After spending the night at an intermediate camp, the entire party, climbers, Sherpas, porters and cook reached the site of Advance Base Camp (4,220 metres), at 9.30 a.m. on 29 May. The camp was situated about an hour's walk over snow from the foot of the Sérac Glacier and the climbers pressed on to secure the route to Camp I for the porters, cutting steps and fixing ropes in Scaly Alley. As the day advanced, Graham Brown became concerned about the increasing risk from falling stones and ice. Hodgkin paused to supervise the Sherpas while Graham Brown and Roberts climbed on for twenty-five minutes before turning back. It was after midday and Graham Brown considered that 'nobody who had been up that trough should have suggested an ascent in the <u>afternoon</u>, tho' it looked to be safe enough in the morning.'[26] Graham Brown had a point. On returning to camp he 'spoke forcibly (perhaps too forcibly) about the plan to force this place at any time save in the morning' and was severely critical of Harrison and Hodgkin:

> I had not until then realised how completely ignorant of mountaineering both of them were … I now lost confidence in both of them and began to fear the inexperience of the party.[27]

Henceforth their judgement would be scrutinised by Graham Brown who found fault with all their decisions.

The weather was poor throughout the climb. Snow fell almost every day and progress was usually through knee-deep and sometimes thigh- or waist-deep snow – punishing and dispiriting toil:

> We could realise in every limb the pain of lifting a leg till the knee almost touches the chin, then the agony of tightening the various

muscles till one's weight is fairly raised upon it, followed by the heart-breaking squash as the snow gives way, and a hole eighteen inches deep remains almost the only result of the effort.[28]

It was risky, too: snow slides were frequent and mindful of the recent disaster on Nanga Parbat,[d] the party worried continually about avalanches. Graham Brown and Roberts were slower to acclimatise than the others and, writing in his diary, Harrison expressed concern about Graham Brown: 'I think he believes himself capable of getting to the top and I am sure he is not. I only hope he has the sense to admit it if he feels it too much but he won't admit anything which might be interpreted as weakness, which is stupid.'[29]

After ten days on the mountain, they had established Camp III at the top of the Dome (6,300 metres) from where, through breaks in the cloud, it was now possible to see the terrain that had been invisible from below. A snowfield rose gently towards the foot of the south-east ridge. Above the snowfield steeper slopes led up to a plateau beneath the south-east face. On 10 June Graham Brown and Roberts set out, in doubtful weather and poor visibility, to prospect a route to Camp IV. Harrison insisted on accompanying them, prompting Graham Brown to remark peevishly that Harrison 'regarded himself as a "driving force", and was coming out to see that something was done',[30] but heavy snowfall and worsening visibility limited progress.

The next day they were joined by Waller, Hodgkin and their porters and they all set out to establish Camp IV. There was a dispute about the route. To reach the upper basin, Harrison proposed climbing a gully which was threatened by unstable ice cliffs lurching over it and which Graham Brown considered unacceptably dangerous. Graham Brown was overruled, leaving him to ponder on 'the advantages and disadvantages of any system of counting heads'. His concern proved well founded. Three days later a massive fall of ice swept the route, obliterating their tracks, the debris reaching just fifty yards from Camp III, 'the air was filled with gleaming ice crystals … the wind struck the tent like a blizzard'.[31] On 13 June the entire climbing party was storm-bound at Camp IV (6,490 metres). The wind was 'terrific';

---

d   The previous year seven Germans and nine Sherpas had been killed when an avalanche overwhelmed Camp IV. Diaries had been written up on the evening of 14 June. Their watches had stopped just after midnight.

the tents flapped wildly threatening to rip the fabric and break the tent poles. It was bitterly cold. Graham Brown had the misfortune to develop diarrhoea and suffered all the miseries associated with defecating at altitude in a storm: 'Poor old man, he nearly got a frostbitten bottom and even then I don't think he got out in time,'[32] Harrison noted sympathetically.

The way forward was uncertain. Poor visibility had restricted the views of the upper reaches of the mountain and they were still relying on impressions formed from studying the mountain from the Hushe valley, fifteen miles away. From that distance the south-east ridge had seemed the most practicable route of ascent, but steep walls of granite and a huge gendarme barred access to it from their current camp. During their discussions, Hodgkin mooted the south-east face as an alternative line, drawing scornful comment from Graham Brown:

> That RH should discuss the possibilities of this face before having seen it would have had little significance had it not been for the fact that, on other occasions, RH had expressed strong admiration for 'face' climbs in general ... The attitude was that of the novice ...

And he was concerned about Harrison:

> I had begun to think that JH (who seemed sane and sober enough) was unduly influenced by his friendship for RH ... that night, I took the opportunity of warning JH. He is 10 years the senior of RH, has much Himalayan experience and is apparently sane, or so I thought.[33]

Graham Brown's opinion prevailed and the plan agreed was to find a way on to the south-east ridge from the upper basin:

> JH and RH were to take a light camp to the basin and try to find a way on to the south arête. They were to take 4 days' food for themselves and two Sherpas, and were to attempt to establish a camp VI on the arête itself. Once this was established and sufficiently consolidated the first actual attempt upon the summit would be made by pushing a bivouac tent further up the arête, whence the summit would be reached if we were to be lucky; but we agreed that if JH and RH found a site on the arête for camp VI and saw that the summit could

be reached directly from it without undue difficulty they were at liberty to make the attempt.[34]

Privately, Waller intimated to Hodgkin and Harrison that he thought the expedition was losing its impetus and urged them to press the attack home.

On 14 June Harrison, Hodgkin and two Sherpas, Dawa Tsering and Passang Phutar, set out, accompanied by Waller who broke trail in knee- and thigh-deep snow gaining 250 metres of height before turning back and leaving them to make Camp V at 6,850 metres. Over the next two days of better weather Camp VI was established and Harrison and Hodgkin pressed on up the lower part of the south-east face to place Camp VII at 7,500 metres, from where they examined the possible ways ahead. The route to reach the favoured south-east ridge would have necessitated a lengthy and possibly dangerous traverse and they estimated that climbing the ridge itself would require at least one more camp whereas the rocky east ridge led directly to the summit, was much closer and offered a much shorter route to the summit, 300 metres above. The morning of 17 June dawned fair and with Waller's encouragement in mind, Harrison and Hodgkin determined to make a bid for the summit via the east ridge. They ploughed through waist-deep snow and tried to climb the rocks which proved much more difficult than they appeared. At about 7,600 metres, exhausted – 'will power was weak' – and with incipient frostbite, they turned back to their high camp where they spent the remaining day massaging their frozen hands and feet.

As Waller observed philosophically, 'weather and luck on a high mountain are so much alike as almost to be the same thing'.[35] That night a tempest enveloped the mountain with disastrous consequences. The storm was the fiercest that they had experienced on the mountain and it pinned down the climbers in their respective camps: Harrison and Hodgkin at VII, Waller and three porters at VI, and Graham Brown and Roberts, who spent the next day 'hanging on to the tent poles' at Camp V.

During the course of the next day Harrison and Hodgkin, whose tent had been buried by a snowslide, excavated themselves and tried to descend to Camp VI but became completely lost in a white-out and, in desperation, sought shelter in a crevasse. Late in the afternoon Waller heard shouts and he set out to look for them but conditions were appalling: waist-deep snow, a wind that obliterated their tracks almost immediately and no visibility.

It was hopeless. Prolonging the search simply risked being overtaken by disaster and Waller turned back. The next morning, during a slight clearing in the weather, Harrison and Hodgkin emerged from the crevasse and struggled down to Camp V, accompanied by Waller and his porters, arriving, according to Graham Brown, in a 'state of demoralisation and hysteria' similar to 'cases of <u>mild</u> shell shock such as I saw often in the war.'[36] Graham Brown treated the situation 'in as matter of fact and unemotional manner as possible', leading Waller to conclude that he was simply callous, and wrote accusingly in his journal that 'by their decision to go for the east ridge', Harrison and Hodgkin had 'sacrificed the party and our agreed plan for their personal attempt.'[37] Years later, Hodgkin recalled with restraint, that on reaching the camp, they had 'enjoyed a drink and G.B. was cross and said it would have been all right if we had taken his advice.'[38] Harrison and Hodgkin were exhausted and badly frostbitten: their hands were going black and their toes were 'like ivory'. It was clear that they needed to descend as soon as possible and would need assistance, so the party agreed to quit the mountain, but not before Graham Brown had proposed that he and Roberts remain to make another attempt since, in his opinion, he was still in fine condition:

> I was feeling extraordinarily fit ... my appetite was good – almost ravenous ... I slept very soundly and I greatly enjoyed my pipe ... I moved slowly at that height, but above all, my mental state was one of real eagerness ... [39]

But Harrison observed that Graham Brown 'was behaving queerly', 'was in a foul temper' and 'very disgruntled that his chance of climbing Masherbrum was lost'.[40] Graham Brown had exhibited similar behaviour on Nanda Devi when his deluded assessment of his physical condition and anger on being passed over for the leadership and for the summit party had led Houston to describe him as 'paranoid'.[41] Its recurrence, high on Masherbrum, suggests that his behaviour was a manifestation of altitude-related illness. Some days later and at lower altitude, Graham Brown reflected on his proposal:

> I think the idea of so small a party staying alone on the mountain at that altitude and thus making an attempt on the summit unsupported

was almost as rash as anything I have criticised in the adventures of JH and RH, but at any rate it was not selfish. I blame myself for the project however and believe that the altitude effect had increased the influence of my ambition upon my judgement. It is a queer thing.[42]

But his resentment persisted, even at sea level.

The next morning, 20 June, the party retreated. The wind had moderated but it snowed heavily and it was intensely cold. They floundered down through deep snow, Harrison and Hodgkin suffering considerable pain in their feet and taking all day to reach Camp IV. Passang Phutar's hands and Graham Brown's big toes were frostbitten. 21 June was 'mercifully fine' and they all descended to Camp I. Roberts and Passang, who had broken trail almost all the way down, pressed on to base camp to send a request for assistance to Waller's mother and stepfather, both of whom were practising doctors and were trekking in the vicinity. That night, Hodgkin, whose hands were useless, shared a tent with Graham Brown, who noted, unsympathetically, that he was 'an exacting partner … always asking me to do this or that for him'.[43] The party broached a bottle of rum. Acting as the expedition's doctor, Graham Brown rationed the amount given to Harrison and Hodgkin but gave himself 'a stiff dose' which 'went through me grandly' with the result that 'even my feet became warm and cozy. So, very comfortable for the first time in many days I dropped off to sleep.'[44]

The next day they all reached base camp where Graham Brown resurrected his basic skills in first aid to re-dress Harrison's fingers, which appeared septic. Before leaving Camp IV, Graham Brown had gathered up some medical supplies, for which he was nominally responsible, but left behind the bottle of iodine, which had leaked, and their only antiseptic was some tablets of boracic acid, which he ground into a powder and sprinkled on Harrison's fingers. Out of his depth, he was 'thankful indeed' to hand over Harrison's care to the 'capable hands' of Dr Teasdale, Waller's stepfather. Teasdale amputated all Harrison's toes and the tips of his fingers, except from his left thumb, without anaesthetic or pain relief, their supply of morphine having been lost on the mountain, and lacking cotton wool and dressings he improvised; clothing was torn up to make bandages and sterilised inner tubes of bicycle tyres and rubber tobacco pouches were utilised as dressings.

Roberts, whose leave was over, made haste to rejoin his regiment; the rest of the party took two and a half weeks to cover the 250 miles back to Srinigar.

Harrison was carried the whole way on a stretcher. Hodgkin rode a pony and, unable to use his hands or feet, needed support from two Sherpas. Graham Brown whose frostbitten toes were painful also rode. Each member of the party proceeded at their own pace. Graham Brown deliberately distanced himself from the others because 'the journey and getting over each spell of riding was almost more than I could manage ... and also because I felt that my temper might get too short under the strain'.[45] His diary entries became increasingly querulous, resentful and self-pitying. He grumbled that he did not get his fair share of the 'chocolate and other dainties' which were being 'reserved' for Hodgkin and Harrison, and that Hodgkin 'got his Sherpa ... to spread the jam on very thick and quite regardless of the quantity in the jar'.[46] He brooded on the injustice of having been denied the opportunity of a bid for the summit of Masherbrum or the consolation of an attempt on a neighbouring mountain or passage of a new pass to the Baltoro Glacier. And he suffered alone: 'I sometimes lay with my face buried in a shirt and allowed myself to groan'.[47]

The fortitude and cheerfulness displayed by Harrison and Hodgkin elicited expressions of admiration from Roberts and Waller, but Graham Brown considered Hodgkin made 'as much as possible of his condition' and 'has no pain and is in no discomfort save that his fingers are too bandaged up to be used and he cannot walk for fear of damaging his injured toes'.[48] Hodgkin would later require partial foot amputations and lose most of his fingers. The suggestion that Hodgkin had no pain was cruelly unsympathetic.

On 16 July the party was met by two cars to transport it the last few miles to Srinigar. Graham Brown described the arrangements, which illuminate the state of relations at the end of the journey: Harrison and Hodgkin 'were put in a big car on couches in part made of their personal luggage, Dr T going in front with Major Landor, who drove. The second car was a smaller four-seater, carrying much of the T's luggage. Mrs T rode in front with a native driver, JW sat behind, and the fourth seat was occupied by – "Jock" (dog)!'[49] Graham Brown was left behind to ride six miles and then take a lorry to the town the next day.

Graham Brown's attitude and behaviour had alienated his companions. Waller suspected him of disloyalty. He was concerned that Graham Brown had criticised the mountaineering judgement of Harrison and Hodgkin in a letter to H.E.G. Tyndale, editor of the *Alpine Journal*, and worried that any criticism would jeopardise their careers. In an icily correct letter, in which he politely enquired about the state of Graham Brown's toes, Waller wrote, 'there are signs that an adverse and, as you will doubtless agree, inaccurate story about the climb has got about in England' and, believing that Graham Brown was the source, added, 'I think it would be to the advantage of all members of the party if you were to try to put the matter straight.'[50] Graham Brown pleaded innocence and Tyndale, naturally emollient, wrote reassuringly to Waller, but that the suspicion had arisen at all was a measure of Waller's distrust. And Harrison had no time for him. For obvious reasons, his diary entries stopped on the day before the summit attempt, but writing almost three years later, he recalled the bitterness he had felt towards Graham Brown:

> I ... told him that from the beginning he had not done a stroke towards helping the expedition along since he joined it and that he was a selfish old man who had no thought beyond his own personal comfort and success ... So much for Tim.[51]

On 20 February 1939 Graham Brown read a paper on the expedition at the Royal Geographical Society. Hodgkin, the only other member of the expedition in the audience, was invited to say a few words. He described the events above Camp IV matter of factly and concluded with his opinion on the best route of ascent for future attempts, maintaining the view he had expressed on the mountain and which had caused Graham Brown to accuse him of irresponsibility:

> Captain Harrison and I both agree in thinking that the east face would probably be the quickest route to the top. Though the south ridge would be less laborious and possibly safer, it would be a roundabout approach and would involve traversing the south lower summit before the true summit could be gained. Our attempt by the east ridge seems to suggest that its angle and general difficulty would discount any advantage it might gain from its directness.[52]

A line up the south-east face was followed on the first and second ascents of Masherbrum in 1960 and 1983, vindicating Hodgkin's opinion; the south ridge, advocated by Graham Brown, remains unclimbed.

Shipton highlighted the significance of the expedition, remarking that it 'was very different from most mountaineering expeditions that we hear of in this hall':

> The tackling of a mountain on the scale of Masherbrum or of any of the other great Himalayan giants without previous reconnaissance was a courageous effort[53]

for which Waller, Harrison and Hodgkin must surely deserve the credit.

Chapter 17

Interlude

After the expedition had broken up, Graham Brown remained in Srinigar, nursing his frostbitten toes aboard a houseboat for six weeks. He was attended by Dr Rowland and Dr Flower. Rowland, Graham Brown's contemporary at medical school in Edinburgh, but 'not so thorough or neat as Flower',[1] gave his prognosis: the tip of the right great toe, the bone of which was exposed and septic, would be lost but the left would be preserved. After a fortnight, Graham Brown was still confined to the houseboat, 'scarcely able to walk'.[2] He tried to work but the pain from his feet impaired his concentration and made him querulous. Commenting on Waller's draft of an article reporting the expedition for the *Alpine Journal*, he wrote, 'I think you might give Jimmy and me the credit for the exploration of the north-east glacier, it was the most interesting piece of route finding we came across.'[3]

On 10 September he set sail for England. It was a miserable journey. His diary contains daily records of the condition of his feet and his pain: 'dreadful night with continuous pain, sometimes almost unbearable'.[4] Three months later he was still unable to get his right foot into a slipper and hobbled about with a bag around it. Despite their more extensive injuries, Hodgkin and Harrison were making swifter progress. Hodgkin provided an update:

> I hope your feet behaved themselves and are now quite healed. Mine are pretty good but the final stages are rather long. I am getting about quite a bit now though I can't walk much more than a mile. Jock also is getting on pretty well and mercifully but with difficulty succeeded in brow-beating his medical board into not kicking him out of the army.[5]

And in April 1939 he wrote that he had managed to do some climbing and had been 'braced to find how little harder it seemed than usual', but added, 'I don't intend to do anything more like that for some time. It was just bravado.'[6] By the summer of 1939 Graham Brown was able to wear a shoe and could walk short distances; by June 1941 his toe had finally healed.

The state of his feet precluded an Alpine holiday in 1939. Instead he visited Palestine, staying with his sister, Janey, and brother-in-law and second cousin, George Graham Brown, the Anglican Bishop in Jerusalem. He sailed for Egypt on 21 July and immediately sought advice on the management of his feet from the ship's surgeon, who prescribed salt baths and sunbathing. On 23 July Graham Brown noted in his diary, 'first salt bath yesterday – my first total immersion since mid April 1938, fifteen months ago.'[7] From Port Said he travelled by train to Katara from where he crossed the Suez Canal by ferry, continuing his journey by train to Jerusalem, arriving on 3 August.

Palestine was in a turbulent state. In response to increasing numbers of Jewish immigrants and the threat of partition, the Palestinian Arabs had revolted. Ambushes, explosions and assassinations had become everyday events during the preceding three years. The British had retaliated with harsh reprisals and Graham Brown's brother-in-law complained of their severity to the general commanding the Eighth Division, Bernard Montgomery, who was uncompromising, replying, 'I shall shoot them.'[8] By the beginning of 1939, Arab violence had diminished but the British Government's publication of a White Paper in May, reversing the policy of partition and imposing strict limits on Jewish immigration, provoked attacks on the British by the Jews. Graham Brown's sightseeing was conducted against a background of sporadic gunfire and with the protection of armed escorts. Meanwhile the prospect of war between Britain and Germany drew closer, and on 29 August Graham Brown wrote in his diary, 'It was now pretty clear that my time in Palestine might be cut short.'[9] He booked a passage on a P&O ship sailing from Suez on 4 September but the declaration of war the day before meant no P&O boats or other British ships were sailing, and he had to wait several days at Port Said until he obtained passage to Marseilles on a small Danish cargo boat. The rail journey to Paris was 'wearisome' and on reaching the capital, he learned that he would have to wait four days to obtain an exit visa, but somehow he wangled a flight in an RAF aeroplane, managing 'to avoid all formalities'. The flight was 'extremely interesting and amusing, and even luxurious'.[10]

Back in Cardiff he prepared for war. While barrage balloons were being deployed above the docks and city centre, his lecturer and deputy, John Pryde, ordered 5,000 sandbags for the department's protection and Graham Brown, 'alarmed that pipe tobacco might become scarce, mustered the technicians and set off to buy out Cardiff's tobacconist shops. Many tins were acquired and carried back to the department where he opened the safe, swept all the papers on to the floor, put the tobacco inside, locked the door and put the key in his waistcoat pocket and walked off.'[11] Regarding war work, he wrote with a trace of self-importance:

> I am taking over the medical students from University College London. In addition, I am an Assoc. Member of the Royal Engineers and Signals Board, and will have advisory work to do. Also my laboratory is ear-marked as a unit (under my direction) for tackling any problems which may arise in connection probably with anti-aircraft defence. I fancy, therefore, that we may be fairly busy here.[12]

But the evacuation of the London medical students to Cardiff proved temporary and the work on sound mirrors with which he had been connected was superseded by the development of radar. George Finch, now professor of applied physical chemistry at Imperial College and a scientific adviser to the Ministry of Home Affairs, proposed Graham Brown as a potential member of a subcommittee on incendiary projectiles. Graham Brown was grateful for the nomination but unprepared: 'I cannot tell you how much I appreciate your kindness in putting me on to this ... could you drop me a hint as to whether the object is offence or defence?'[13] Nothing came of it.

An early British casualty of the war was Graham Brown's twenty-one-year-old nephew, Lachlan Graham Brown, who had followed his father into the Royal Navy and was a sub-lieutenant on HMS *Royal Oak*, the battleship in which Thor had served at Jutland. On 14 October 1939 *Royal Oak* was anchored at Scapa Flow, the base for the British Home Fleet, when she was torpedoed by U-47. Lachlan Graham Brown and 832 of his shipmates died when the ship was wracked by internal explosions and rapidly sank.

Following the fall of France in May 1940, Cardiff came within range of German bombers based in Brittany and air raids on the city commenced. In September 1940, Graham Brown wrote to a mountaineering friend:

Life is considerably disturbed here these days with petty annoyances, of which we had five daylight ones yesterday, and several at night. Nothing serious has happened to anyone I know thank goodness, but conditions generally make me feel rather as if upon a slope exposed to falling stones.[14]

The intensity of the raids increased in 1941 and attacks continued through 1942. The final air raid over Cardiff occurred in March 1943, lasted eighty-three minutes and involved no more than fifty bombers but caused widespread destruction: over 4,000 houses were destroyed and forty-five people were killed. Most of the windows of Graham Brown's laboratory were broken and the Royal Hotel, where he lived, was hit by a bomb that failed to detonate. Throughout the war, Graham Brown remained sanguine. In response to a gloomy letter from Peter Lloyd, written soon after the fall of Tobruk, he wrote, 'I cannot feel that the war is going at all badly for us ... our setbacks have been excessively annoying, but not, I think of any real importance in the long run – save only that they have made the end of the war a little further off.'[15] He distracted himself by writing a book.

In writing *Brenva*, Graham Brown sublimated his case concerning the issues of priority and leadership that had fuelled his feud with Smythe. He had been preparing his position for ten years. In April 1932 he had promised himself that he would 'someday make my own claim clearly', confident that 'based on the facts' his claim 'would convince all', but with latent malice had been content with 'the mere power of being <u>able</u> at any time to do so'.[16] During a week in March 1933, he composed a series of three letters to Strutt, whom he now regarded as 'one of my very best friends in the club', giving his version of his climbs with Smythe and demonstrating how Smythe had manipulated the facts to present himself in a more favourable light. The analysis is painstaking, repetitive and lengthy, amounting to seventy-three pages of foolscap. In the first letter he complained that Strutt's editorial note, stating that Blakeney had been the first to point out the line of *Route Major* to Smythe, had been 'unfair' – Strutt had joked previously that the error could always be corrected in Graham Brown's obituary – and presented a detailed case for his being acknowledged as the originator of the lines of *Sentinelle Rouge* and *Route Major*. In the second letter he scrutinised Smythe's accounts for any inaccuracy, inconsistency or hint of exaggeration and in the third instalment offered an explanation for what he considered to be

Smythe's tendency to self-delusion:

> I think myself that Smythe must invent romantic stories to himself,
> and with himself as the hero ... At first he will know the difference
> between the truth and the romance; but later on, the frontier
> between the two will fade with repetition of the 'play' to himself.
> He will then come really to believe that the romance is true, and at
> that stage he will have destroyed the truth, and all the pain which it
> must give him.[17]

He observed that he had spent longer writing the three letters than it had
taken to climb the two routes on the Brenva Face but did not think it was
time wasted, and concluded:

> I do not know, my dear Strutt, if I shall really send these letters to you,
> nor (should I send them) when I shall do so. But if they come to you,
> and if you can spare the time to read them, I trust that they will be
> of sufficient interest to compensate you for your trouble.[18]

The letters were probably never sent but their content was the *raison d'être*
of *Brenva*.

That Smythe's character would be subjected to critical examination is
apparent from his preliminary notes. The headings include Smythe's ambition, bravado, egotism, evasions, incidents, inventiveness, selfishness and
vanity. Graham Brown commenced the first draft on Christmas Day 1933
and by the next day had written eighteen pages, which were promptly discarded and burnt. By May 1936 he had completed a draft of 166,595 words,
amounting to 440 pages of typescript, which he showed to his colleague,
Pryde, who foresaw trouble and his comments caused Graham Brown
to reflect:

> Whatever the merits may be people will say 'this is terribly unkind,
> why is this man so detailed and smashing in his attack?' The careful-
> ness of case and analysis of detail would of itself help to convey this
> impression, one of bitterness, a terribly smashing legal attack. This
> might react unfavourably on me. This would be the more likely if

Smythe made an apparent or actual success on Everest and became a national hero.[19]

The manuscript lay untouched until 1939.

The structure of *Brenva* is underpinned by his vision of a triptych, formed by his three routes on the face: the *Sentinelle Rouge* rising to the summit of Mont Blanc and the *Via della Pera* which goes to the summit of Mont Blanc de Courmayeur, forming the right- and left-hand panels respectively, and *Route Major* leading to Col Major between the two summits, the magnificent centrepiece. This was a contrivance for if Smythe had agreed to climb *Route Major* in 1927, as Graham Brown had urged, there would not have been a right-hand panel. Furthermore, their success on the *Sentinelle Rouge* had been due to Smythe's leadership and Graham Brown was never going to give his partner's role prominence in his imaginary picture. He all but painted out the right-hand panel, writing of the *Sentinelle Rouge* that although 'it had been a glorious thing to have won the Brenva Face by whatever route',

> My dream had, above all, created imaginary intricacy, difficulty and uncertainty – places which would call for thought, trial, and action ... That fancy was a cherished part of the dream, and it had been destroyed by the straightforward nature, not of the route (which in itself might be called complicated), but of the climbing – the certainty of outcome, and the absence of unavoidable difficulty,

insinuating that Smythe's lead had been a cakewalk, and concluded: 'the fine route had given us a great expedition indeed, but the climbing itself had not been quite worthy of the route'.[20]

Each chapter of *Brenva* is introduced with a poem of his own composition. Graham Brown's first extant poem was written in 1898 when he was still at school. Whilst at university he wrote a few verses concerning the sea and hills, and a humorous poem describing life as a resident in the Royal Infirmary. Encouraged by Sherrington, who was a published poet, he began writing poetry regularly. During 1914 he wrote nineteen poems and thereafter produced about six per year over a period of fifteen years. Drafts were made on the backs of envelopes, invitations, bills and receipts and the agenda for Academic Board. In 1931 he had selected forty-eight poems from almost 100 and submitted them for publication, only to receive a standard rejection slip. Some of the poems in *Brenva* had been written twenty years earlier, others were written specially for the book. In the preface, Graham Brown acknowledged the 'kindly and valuable advice' of Canon Adam Fox, professor of poetry at Oxford.

His narrative is ponderously factual and understated. Although his account of the events at the final buttress on the first ascent of *Route Major* made his publisher 'sweat at the palms' every time he read it, there are few other occasions when the reader's pulse quickens. And there was no place for 'uplift', the suspect quality, embracing 'moral, poetical, sentimental and even spiritual levitation'[21] – that was Smythe's preserve. Graham Brown makes his view plain in the preface:

> The way in which the climber is absorbed in the climbing on all routes worthy of the name deserves notice, because that absorption is an important aspect of mountaineering, but has been overshadowed by the emphasis now conventionally given to what are displayed as higher and more spiritual interests. It must therefore be stressed that climbing for its own sake (with everything thereby implied) is, and always has been, the chief motive in pure mountaineering. We are all moved by Alpine scenery; but the pleasures of scenery and contemplation remain the predominant memories of the day only on those occasions where the action has required small effort from the climber – that is, where the going has been straightforward and easy. Days of this sort often give memorable pleasure, but also feelings of incomplete achievement; and it is then that romantic or poetic fantasies are likely to suggest themselves as substitutes for the good climbing which the day has lacked.[22]

For him, 'the intrinsic pleasures of climbing ... consist in the physical pleasure of action and the intellectual pleasure of outwitting dangers'.[23]

In May 1940 he sent a copy of the manuscript to Tyndale, who had succeeded Strutt as editor of the *Alpine Journal*, asking for his comments, saying:

> It has been very difficult for me to write of Smythe's part in my climbs, and if you knew the story you would agree that he has been treated

with restraint and generosity. But I do not want you to read the book with my knowledge on these points because what I know to be restrained may yet appear to an ordinary reader to be unrestrained, and it is just on this that I would dearly like to have a friendly opinion.[24]

Tyndale, who had a reputation for being a gentle critic, responded bluntly:

> I cannot feel that you are right in submitting Smythe's narratives to such detailed criticism ... The ordinary man will certainly get the impression that all was not well between you and Smythe, and the conclusion he will draw is that either one or both of you wish to establish priority for himself ... I do beg you to look very closely into this matter. By all means refer to any major discrepancy between your narrative and Smythe's, but do so as rarely as possible and in the briefest manner ... I do regard this analysis as a serious weakness in the book and I think it ought to come out.[25]

Graham Brown accepted that his analysis had been 'very pedantic' and agreed to address his 'treatment of Smythe's narratives'.[26] On Tyndale's advice he approached E.F. Bozman, a partner in the publishing firm, J.M. Dent & Sons, and a fellow member of the Alpine Club, regarding possible publication. When still only halfway through the manuscript, Bozman also felt obliged to question Graham Brown's anti-Smythe stance, commenting, 'bottom of page unpleasant reading', 'these pages make Smythe look foolish' and 'is this a private dispute or a matter for the general public?' As for Graham Brown's assessment of Smythe's account of the ascent of *Route Major*, he considered it 'very scathing' adding, 'I do not imagine that F.S. could take it.'[27] Bozman's anxiety is understandable for Graham Brown had written:

> Smythe's lively Irish pen vivified those by no means hazardous or arduous passages with difficulties and dangers, such as falling ice and stones during our walk across the great couloir, where my own more prosaic memory recalled none. His recital of dramatic exploits in such a setting gave an enthralling and exciting picture of a long, dangerous and difficult expedition ... But, to be frank, I could not quite recognise in it my own memories either of the climbing or the climb.[28]

Bozman, who knew Smythe personally and had published one of his books, did not want 'to be involved in a public controversy' or 'injure him in any way'[29] and asked whether Graham Brown would be willing to allow Smythe to see the proofs. Graham Brown replied that he would appreciate Bozman's 'advice concerning passages that might be altered' but 'under no circumstances'[30] would he permit Smythe to see any proofs.

As the war continued, shortage of labour and supplies of paper made printing problematic and Bozman warned that publication was in doubt. Nevertheless, in August 1942, Graham Brown submitted a revised manuscript which Bozman considered 'a fine piece of work', but he was still bothered by the anti-Smythe sentiment, 'in spite of our efforts to lay this ghost'.[31] He sought another opinion from R.L.G. Irving, retired schoolmaster, mountaineer and author, who wrote:

> I have read G-B's book with much interest. After the first half which I read in conjunction with Smythe's account … I said 'One or both of these two must be a bit of a liar' and on the photographic evidence G-B was a good deal more accurate in his statements … Smythe has 'written up' his, G-B has written down his a good deal I daresay, to get his own back on Smythe. But the evidence of subsequent events and of the photos shows that G-B is substantially accurate where he can be checked.

He continued:

> Perhaps one can sympathise just a bit with G-B in Smythe having got far the largest share of fame out of these climbs when actually his own contribution to the success was the larger. To have expurgated all the possible suggestions of anti-Smythe would have taken much of the psychological interest out of the book …

And in an aside, observed acutely:

> His meticulousness over times and measurements is almost exasperating and induces the idea that his climbing is the serious business of life, not its refreshment.[32]

Bozman reiterated his wish to give Smythe the opportunity of seeing the manuscript or proofs and Graham Brown's refusal aroused his suspicions. He wrote, 'May I ask what exactly it is you are after in this book?'[33] Graham Brown replied, 'I want to tell as true a story as possible; I think that some people will read it (if published) alongside of Smythe's story, and I want the truth to prevail … What you have read is overgenerous to Smythe.'[34] But he undertook a further revision and six months later a relieved Bozman wrote, 'my first impression of the latest version is that you have surmounted the Smythe difficulties'.[35] And Graham Brown finally agreed to Smythe seeing this revised version, which Smythe's wife forwarded to him in Canada, where in September 1943 he had been posted as chief instructor in high-mountain warfare. In her letter to Bozman informing him that she had despatched the manuscript, she added sarcastically, 'knowing Graham Brown so well it will no doubt amuse him very much.'[36]

Smythe was anything but amused. Bozman reported that Smythe 'seems to be rather distressed'[37] and had asked him to contact his solicitor, E.S. Herbert, Graham Brown's erstwhile climbing companion. In his memoir of Graham Brown, Herbert recalled that Smythe had threatened legal proceedings but had eventually agreed to accept publication 'in any form I approved'. Herbert claimed to have rewritten 'considerable elements'[38] of the early chapters but in his account of his 'most pleasant chat'[39] with Herbert, Graham Brown stated that the suggested alterations had been few and 'trivial' and he had accepted them all. One of the changes to which Graham Brown finally agreed was excision of a lengthy footnote in which he had disparaged Smythe's climbing achievements. Previously he had resisted Bozman's request to omit it, saying:

> I put this footnote in as a sort of self-defence. Smythe is <u>now</u> so well known to the public that the ordinary reader will not realise that he was little more than a novice in 1927 and that his record (on a count of peaks) was not quite equal to my own.[40]

This change resulted in an inconvenient gap that would have required fresh typesetting, so Graham Brown filled it with some banal text and quipped to Bozman, 'By the way, have you thought of asking Smythe to foot the bill for alterations?'[41]

At the end of September 1944, Bozman showed a prepublication copy to Graham Brown pointing out that the tops of the pages had been gilded, which he supposed was 'an extravagance in war time' but declared that 'in this case I could not resist it'.[42] *Brenva* was published the following month. Graham Brown sent copies to a number of his friends including Leslie Letts and Charles Houston, both of whom interpreted the gesture as indicating a rapprochement. Letts wrote:

> I appreciate the book for more than just a gift. When we parted some twenty years ago it seemed to me that you took my 'desertion' amiss and I hope that any soreness has long since healed, as indeed your gift would seem to show.[43]

And Houston:

> Your book is the first word I have had from or of you since 1939 … Even for so poor a correspondent as you would consider five years a long time, so I have been forced to conclude that you wished to cut me off completely. Your very kind thought leads me to believe that perhaps this is not the case.[44]

A.E.W. Mason, whom Graham Brown had credited with igniting his passion, was admiring:

> You must have had many tense and unforgettable moments especially on the final buttress of *Route Major* when you were cutting through the verglas down to the tongue of rocks and were afterwards doubtful – or Smythe was doubtful, for I don't think you ever were – whether the chimneys above would go. There was … a long stretch over 3,000 feet of vacancy which must have called upon you for all you had got to give.[45]

Graham Brown must have purred.

Longstaff liked his verse: 'I do envy you of the power of writing "narrative" poetry so poetically'.[46] Strutt was glad that he had 'let Smythe down very gently and given the "Teutonics" what for' but added a pedantic postscript, 'is it not Jétoula with the acute accent?'[47] All the reviewers agreed that the book was distinguished by attention to topographical and historical detail, testimony to Graham Brown's 'scientific' approach to climbing. Lord Chorley, writing in the *Manchester Guardian*, did not consider it suitable for the general reader – Smythe's constituency – but within three months of publication a reprint was in preparation, and by May 1945 more than 2,000 copies had been sold, earning Graham Brown £428-5-0 in royalties.

As for the feud, the moderating influence of Tyndale and Bozman had resulted in a dilution of Graham Brown's bile. But Lloyd, whose friendship went back to the expedition to Nanda Devi, wrote fairly:

> The story that Brenva conceals, though it peeps through in places, is that of Tim G-B's long feud with Smythe. This is something one cannot ignore for it was far more than just a clash of temperaments or of climbing styles. It arose from something fundamental in Tim's character, from the scientist's inability to compromise on matters of fact and his rejection of romantic interpretations of events seen through the haze of memory.[48]

At last, Graham Brown's version of the discovery and ascent of the climbs on the Brenva Face had received wide recognition and would go unchallenged. In 1949 Smythe died prematurely. Graham Brown's reputation was secure.

Chapter 18
Return to the Mountains

A ten-year absence had not diminished his enthusiasm or ambition and, with his frostbitten feet healed, Graham Brown returned to the Alps in 1948, aged sixty-six. He had volunteered to participate in the inaugural, post-war Alpine Club meet to introduce a new generation of climbers to the Alps. During a fortnight's poor weather in Kleine Scheidegg, he and his 'recruits' ascended the Mönch and Finsteraarhorn by the normal routes, as well as several lesser peaks. At the conclusion of the meet he joined Peter Lloyd, with whom he had been to Nanda Devi, and Neil Hanson, a promising Alpine novice, and travelled to Courmayeur with ambitions to climb one of his routes on the Brenva Face. Walking along Val Veni, stripped to the waist in the heat, Graham Brown appeared 'immensely enthusiastic',[1] revelling in his knowledge of the region and his rediscovery of it. Uncertain weather deterred them from attempting Mont Blanc and instead they set out to climb the Aiguille Blanche de Peuterey, only a slightly less serious proposition. At the bivouac hut at the Brèche des Dames Anglaises it snowed heavily overnight. The next morning they decided to retreat. It began to snow again and powder-snow avalanches swept the couloir they were descending. Progress was insecure and painfully slow. It took eight hours to descend the 300 metres to the Frêney Glacier, which they groped their way across in fading light. They bivouacked, huddled around a candle, which soon sputtered out, and shivered their way through the night. The following day, they struggled to find a way up to the Col de l'Innominata. Thick snow obscured the route and made climbing the rotten rocks even more precarious. They reached the col in the late afternoon and fought their way through a blizzard and waist-deep snow to the Gamba Hut. Their retreat had taken thirty-six hours. Years later Lloyd paid tribute to Graham Brown's indefatigability on this expedition, saying that he was 'a great companion and game to the end'.[2]

At Whitsun 1949 Graham Brown found himself the sole representative of the Alpine Club at a joint meet with the Scottish Mountaineering Club based at the Kings House Hotel, Glencoe. He walked over to the SMC hut at Lagangarbh in search of climbing companions and met Gordon Parish, currently serving as a medical officer in the RAF, having recently qualified from Edinburgh University where he had been a founder member of the university mountaineering club. Their chance meeting led to friendship and Graham Brown's introduction to the RAF Mountaineering Association and the Edinburgh University Mountaineering Club, in whose affairs he took an active part for the rest of his life.

They climbed together on Buachaille Etive Mòr. Both men were out of training and Graham Brown vented his frustration with his lack of form in 'luxuriant expletives'.[3] Later that summer they explored Beinn Trilleachan. On his retirement two years earlier, Graham Brown had acquired a converted lifeboat, *Marion of Lorne*, which was moored at Taynuilt on the shore of Loch Etive and served as their base and means of crossing the loch to the mountain. They noted the extensive granite slabs that now provide rock climbs of the highest standard and recognised their potential and difficulty, but were drawn first to investigate the numerous gullies seaming the east flank of the mountain. They prospected a huge, branching gully, which they named Golden Eagle Chasm, and made a route up it.

The following summer they returned with two of Parish's friends, Johnnie Lees[a] from the RAF and Dan Stewart, a member of the EUMC. Carrying their equipment down to the lochside at Taynuilt, 'Graham had a huge kit bag across his shoulders but pressed on quite cheerfully – remarkable for a chap of sixty-eight,' noted Lees, admiringly, and the next day when it proved necessary to tow the boat out with the dinghy, 'Graham took the oars and pulled like a hero!'[4] On the mountain they repeated the route Graham Brown and Parish had climbed the year before but took a direct line up the short steep wall that they had avoided previously. Lees described the crux:

> Dan, in vibrams, managed it nicely, and I soon followed, having to scratch one hold so that I could see it when I was five feet above it with my eyes, and get the edge of a tryke[b] on it. Gordon didn't have much

---

a   J.R. Lees (1927-2002). He led the mountain rescue team based at RAF Valley, Anglesey, for a number of years and received the George Medal for his part in a rescue on Amphitheatre Buttress in 1958.

b   'Tryke' or Tricouni and clinker are different styles of nails used on climbing boots.

trouble either – it's Severe – but Graham needed a rather tight rope, and then came off it! He uses clinkers and couldn't get the right foot on at all, apart from having a reach roughly a foot shorter than us![5]

Their return across the loch turned into a struggle with the temperamental *Marion*. A mile from the anchorage, the engine cut out and the wind and tide proceeded to take them in the wrong direction. Lees tried unsuccessfully to restart the engine, observing, ruefully, 'surprisingly enough Graham knows nothing whatsoever about engines'.[6] Stewart, Parish and Lees, who had trains to catch and a three-mile walk to the station, rowed ashore, abandoning Graham Brown to be rescued by a local farmer with a motor-launch.

Graham Brown continued to visit the Alps, participating in subsequent training meets organised by the Alpine Club and RAFMA. One beginner, whom Graham Brown mentored, recalls fondly 'the amount of time he spent in tutoring an alpine novice with kindness, wit and great good humour'.[7] Graham Brown seems to have enjoyed the role of instructor in the mountains. For several years he spent a fortnight at the recently established centre for outdoor activities at Glenmore Lodge, in the Cairngorms, where his 'salty tang of wisdom and experience' was appreciated. The lodge's director hoped 'we managed to dispel some of your doubts about the wisdom of the Glenmore experience and the opening up of mountaineering to the masses'.[8]

In the summer of 1952 Graham Brown joined an EUMC meet in the Alps. In stark contrast to his pre-war routine of dinner and billiards at the Athenaeum before boarding the boat-train, he spent the night on a bench in St James's Park and had an early breakfast at a Lyon's corner-house. He fared little better in Switzerland as the plans for accommodation were based on the youthful premise 'that sleeping out will not prove too uncomfortable. If it rains we can all crowd into Arthur's tent'.[9] Graham Brown climbed the Pigne d'Arolla and the Dent Blanche. Both routes resulted in long days. Going slowly and, at the end of the day, alone, he was forced to sleep out in fields in just his clothes, complaining that he 'scarcely slept for cowbells'.[10]

On 25 July he made his first and only ascent of the Matterhorn, teaming up with a member of the Rucksack Club whom he considered had got the 'wind up' for wanting the services of a guide. Their respectable time of ten hours from hut to hut included delays due to congestion on the route and an hour spent on the summit. This proved to be the last climb of the season, his extraordinarily ambitious plan to climb Mont Blanc via the frontier ridge of Mont Maudit and descend the *Route Major* being thwarted by bad weather.

Graham Brown had been elected honorary vice-president of RAFMA at the beginning of 1951 and six months later dined with Air Chief Marshal, the Honourable Sir Ralph Cochrane[c] at the Athenaeum. They had met to discuss the future of the RAF Mountain Rescue Service. In March 1951 an RAF Lancaster bomber had crashed on Beinn Eighe in Torridon. The site was remote and difficult to access, especially under the prevailing wintry conditions, and the local RAF team from Kinloss had been shown up as lacking in the necessary mountaineering expertise to effect a timely search and rescue. The RAF had resisted posting keen mountaineers to bases with mountain rescue, fearful that they would take advantage, but the accident on Beinn Eighe brought about a softening of this view. Graham Brown advocated encouraging young doctors to join the RAF, identifying those with mountaineering experience and posting them accordingly. Cochrane welcomed him acting as a 'recruiting sergeant' and Graham Brown used this influence to the benefit of his young friends called up for National Service, who soon learned that a word with 'Graham' could result in a more congenial posting.

Graham Brown also still enjoyed some influence within the Alpine Club and he proposed some of his new companions for consideration as members of the 1953 expedition to Everest. 'Will you please tell me the names of the young climbers in Scotland that you would like to be given a chance,' asked Lieutenant Colonel H.W. Tobin, ex-Indian Army and member of the Joint Himalayan Committee, 'Craig Dhu was one if I remember right.'[11] Tobin, ignorant of the contemporary climbing scene, had not recognised that Craig Dhu [sic] was the name of a mountaineering club that was the antithesis of the Alpine Club: founded in 1930s Glasgow, the Creagh Dhu had a reputation for hard climbing, hard drinking and brawling. None of its members were selected but Charles Evans, an Oxford-educated trainee surgeon whom Graham Brown had befriended after a fatal accident to Evans' partner on the Brouillard Ridge in 1949, reached the south summit of Everest and on the journey back from the mountain, wrote from Darjeeling

c   Sir Ralph Cochrane (1895–1977). Vice-chief of the Air Staff. During the war he had commanded No.5 Group, Bomber Command, which included 617 Squadron, responsible for the Dambusters' raid.

to thank Graham Brown 'for starting the process that put me on this last expedition.'[12]

The year 1953 ended badly for Graham Brown with his only serious accident in the mountains. Returning in poor light to a cave bivouac in the Lost Valley, Glencoe, he slipped on the edge of a collapsed path, slid on steep grass to the top of a rocky gully and fell outwards about five metres over a vertical cliff on to scree, down which he rolled and bounced before being stopped by a large boulder. He hobbled very slowly back to the cave and after a bad night – 'could not move for pain and severe headache'[13] – descended to the road but missed the bus and was given a lift to Belford Hospital in Fort William. He had suffered multiple cuts, mainly to his scalp, bruising and a sprained ankle. He remained in hospital for ten days and it was during this period, when his whereabouts was unknown, that he was sacked as editor of the *Alpine Journal*.

Graham Brown received numerous requests from climbing clubs to lecture on his past exploits, which he never refused, although sometimes his acceptance was conditional on being taken for a day's climbing. His last climbing expedition abroad resulted from one such invitation and in 1954 he joined members of Sheffield University Mountaineering Club on a trip to the Lyngen Alps in Norway. It was not a success; dismal weather – mists and rain – prevailed and little climbing was done. But he would continue to climb in Britain for several more years.

Chapter 19
Editor of the Alpine Journal

Meanwhile, as Graham Brown made his return to the mountains, the death of Tyndale in 1948 caused the editorship of the *Alpine Journal* to fall vacant and, on the face of it, Graham Brown was well suited to fill the role. Recently retired, he had wide mountaineering experience, an extensive network of contacts, including foreign mountaineers, and a serious interest in Alpine history. But he was not keen. In response to a sounding letter from Blakeney, now the salaried assistant secretary of the club, he wrote, 'Long-staff [President, 1947–1950] asked me a year ago if I would be willing to edit the journal, and quite a lot of other people have asked me the same thing since Tyndale's death. In every case I have said "No" emphatically'[1] and explained, 'I do not feel well fitted for the work, which I also dislike.'[2] Furthermore, he was nursing a grievance. In October 1947 he had received a telegram from the honorary secretary, asking, 'If nominated would you accept vice-presidentship Alpine Club'[3] to which Graham Brown had replied immediately, 'with great pleasure'. But he was not nominated and learned subsequently that 'there had been a difference of opinion amongst the office bearers',[4] with the result that Raymond Greene had been elected instead.

Longstaff continued to press Graham Brown, offering the support of an assistant and reminding him that the honorary editor was routinely co-opted on to the club's committee, where he would enjoy some influence. Having received a formal request from the committee expressing its unanimity in asking him to accept the post, Graham Brown relented, saying, 'I feel that I can no longer allow my private feelings to sway me, and it is therefore with feelings of inadequacy that I accept.'[5] Longstaff advised, 'Use anybody and everybody you like: delegate but remain the autocrat'[6] and added the warning, 'you are pathologically sensitive to the exact truth. Speaking – or writing – the exact truth just breeds SWARMS of enemies.'[7] Despite the warning, Graham Brown was not about to change the habit of a lifetime.

His first number led with an article entitled 'Alpine Uplift', written by Geoffrey Howard[a], but could just as well have been by Graham Brown, who shared his views. Its theme was that contemporary mountaineering literature was tending to become too concerned with 'mystical emotions and elevated thoughts'[8] rather than climbing action. No names were mentioned but the purveyors of 'uplift' recognised themselves. Arnold Lunn, who 'had an almost mystical apprehension of eternal beauty as he contemplated his beloved mountains',[9] thought the article was 'a good-humoured but definite attack on the Schuster – Young – Lunn school of alpine writers, to say nothing of Smythe', and wrote, 'our bunch cannot let our case go by default'.[10] Graham Brown published Lunn's rejoinder but gave Howard the last word: 'I believe that our members would generally deplore any tendency to allow metaphysics to be accepted as a satisfactory substitute for hard physical achievement. After all, this is the Alpine Club, not the Authors' Club.'[11]

Given his own obsession with accuracy, Graham Brown should have been prepared for criticism for any failures on that score, but the degree of pedantry may have surprised him. P.J. Unna, known for his 'trenchant criticisms, so often right and so often pointing out defects that others had not observed'[12], wrote that a misplaced accent or umlaut could change the identity of a peak or a pass and concluded, 'I therefore venture to suggest that you adopt a system of checking.'[13] And Blakeney devoted a paragraph of a letter to the correct spelling of 'defecation'. His contributors required careful handling, too. The immediate past president of the club, L.S. Amery, ex-secretary of state for India, condescendingly conceded a grammatical point: 'I am quite willing to accept your correction, though I consider the genitive, i.e. treating "referring" like a substantive, equally legitimate.'[14] Amery had taken a double first in 'Greats' at Oxford so probably knew his genitive from substantive. Douglas Busk submitted an article in which he had employed the Christian names of his companions. Graham Brown indicated that he did not favour their use but allowed them to appear in the proofs, which were approved by Busk, and then deleted them. Busk was livid and wanted to escalate the matter to the committee. Tom Brocklebank[b] expressed annoyance at changes made to a review he had written: 'alterations have been made in it – quite arbitrary ones, I consider'.[15] This perceived editorial

---

a   G.E. Howard (1877–1956), vice-president of the Alpine Club, 1952–1953.

b   T.A. Brocklebank (1908–1984). A celebrated oarsman, Eton schoolmaster and another good chap who, despite limited mountaineering experience, had been selected for the 1933 expedition to Everest.

high-handedness would be used against him in the future.

If his first number had ruffled a few feathers, the second raised a furore. Graham Brown included an article which he had written on the history of climbing on the Innominata Face of Mont Blanc. Geoffrey Winthrop Young wrote to Claude Elliott[c], the current president of the Alpine Club, saying that the article, 'from the nature of its assertions and innuendo, was clearly intended to belittle my mountaineering reputation', and constituted 'a breach with our club tradition and a grave discourtesy to a member of the club'.[16] Elliott, a friend of Young who had been his best man, remonstrated with Graham Brown, saying, the article 'has caused more feeling than I realised [and] the present situation, tho' it has not reached the dimensions of a general row, might well do so'.[17] And in a letter to Young, wrote, 'The sooner he [TGB] ceases to be editor the better'.[18] Later, Elliott would recall that his presidency was blighted by having to deal with Graham Brown, whom he found 'abominable' and endeavoured to avoid, employing coded messages to determine whether Graham Brown was attending the Alpine Dining Club for the dinner that preceded a meeting of the Alpine Club. Twenty-four hours beforehand, the secretary of the Alpine Dining Club would telegraph either 'N.B.G.', which meant 'no bloody good' and Elliott dined elsewhere, or 'N.G.B.', which meant 'no Graham Brown', and he could attend.

To a dispassionate reader, the article provides a detailed and rather tedious account of the exploration of the Innominata Face. Even reading between the lines it is difficult to see what caused such offence and Graham Brown claimed not to understand what the fuss was about. He wrote to Elliott, saying, 'I have already asked you for the specific points to which GWY objects, because my only aim is accuracy in all matters of history and I shall of course correct any mistakes which I have made inadvertently,'[19] adding, 'it is quite unfair to challenge my accuracy or my disinterestedness as an Alpine historian in general terms, and to refuse to state the specific points to which objection is taken.' He concluded, somewhat disingenuously, 'You write … as if there was some sort of feud between us.'[20]

But there was more to Young's outrage than a concern for historical niceties. A rumour was circulating within the club that Young had removed a page from Sir Edward Davidson's diary because the entry depreciated his

---

c   C.A. Elliott (1888–1973). Headmaster and provost of Eton.

performance on the South Face of the Täschhorn in 1906. This climb had become a legend of Alpine achievement, not least due to Young's account in his book, *On High Hills*. Pasted into the back of Davidson's diary is a letter from Young to Elliott, written at the beginning of 1950, in which he denied having tampered with the notebook and attacked Graham Brown, whom he suspected, probably correctly, of initiating the rumour, calling him 'base-minded' and a 'liar'.[21] From the chronology of the letters to Elliott, it seems that it was the discovery of this rumour that enraged Young and subsequently he saw malice in anything Graham Brown wrote concerning him. But, however much he impugned Graham Brown, there remained the inconvenient fact that the page that had previously been present was now missing, and that in the interval the notebooks had been in Young's possession for safekeeping during the war.

Smythe's death in 1949 necessitated an obituary notice in the journal, another potentially incendiary subject. Blakeney, who was assisting Graham Brown with production of the journal, moved rapidly to neutralise him, writing, 'I think you will agree that as death cancels all scores, you would not wish your old differences with Smythe to interfere in any way with him getting a full notice in the AJ'[22] and composed the notice himself, as he explained in a letter to Smythe's widow:

> ... since I had promised I wd. try and keep Graham Brown out of it, the obvious thing was to present him with a complete notice, which I did, by getting everything into slip-proof before he even saw it. Then, he wd. have to accept it ... I got Dr Longstaff to have a word with Graham Brown to ensure that he kept himself in the background.[23]

In the meantime Graham Brown was faced with the challenges of delivering the journal within budget and on time, difficulties familiar to his predecessors: in 1920 Farrar had been forced to recommend almost doubling the price from 3s 6d to 6s 6d and, in 1934, Strutt had complained, 'some of our members are simply b[lood]y and they grumble like hell if A.J. is late'.[24] In the aftermath of the Second World War the club's financial situation was precarious. Recruitment of members had fallen off and the income from subscriptions had not kept pace with increasing costs.

The famously parsimonious honorary treasurer, R.W. Lloyd,[d] reprimanded Graham Brown: 'in spite of the united efforts of Mr Blakeney and myself, the rising costs of running the club have made it difficult to balance. One of these charges is an extra £100 on the AJ ... I fear we cannot afford it.'[25] He went on, 'I'm getting very anxious at the delay of the journal ... You have plenty of enemies, don't give them big handles to get at you.'[26]

A subcommittee was formed to identify the factors contributing to the delay in production of the journal. It recognised that the schedule required to produce two issues each year, in May and November, was difficult to adhere to and aired the possibility of introducing some leeway over the dates of publication, simply producing a summer and winter edition, or even reducing the frequency to a single issue, but concluded illogically by recommending a more stringent timetable. Graham Brown protested that it was unreasonable to expect an amateur editor to work during August when any self-respecting member of the Alpine Club should be in the Alps.

Blakeney soon grew weary of Graham Brown's dilatoriness and the difficulties in communicating with him. Although still living in Cardiff, Graham Brown often disappeared to Scotland on climbing and sailing trips and was incommunicado for long periods, his correspondence accumulating at the Marine Hotel in Mallaig. Blakeney felt imposed upon and later claimed that the fact that the journals appeared at all 'owed little to the Editor's efforts and much to those who assisted him.'[27] Although he expressed the wish 'to preserve a reasonable atmosphere of good-will towards him, because I have to do so for all the members of the Club, and because I have to work with him'[28], Blakeney did not scruple to disparage him in his correspondence. He wrote, at length and in detail to Lunn, denigrating Graham Brown's climbing ability and his contribution to the Brenva Face routes, saying that 'he was incapable of taking any share in the work.'[29] When he learned that Smythe's widow was preparing a biography of her husband, he advised, 'You will have to slaughter him' but warned he 'is unreasonable and has a malicious mind' and 'remember, that if you knocked G-B and there was the slightest loophole for him to make a legal case of it, you should reckon on him taking the opportunity. He is no fool, however much a rogue.'[30] He wrote to Goodfellow, now honorary secretary of the club, setting out

---

d   R.W. Lloyd (1868–1958). A personally wealthy man, his administration of the finances of the club and Himalayan Committee admitted no laxity. When Ed Hillary submitted his expenses incurred on the 1951 Everest reconnaissance expedition, which included numerous receipts from Nepali and Indian tea-houses, Lloyd admonished him: 'Gentlemen pay for their own cups of tea.' (Confrey M., *Everest 1953*; p. 94)

Graham Brown's 'defects' and suggested 'that it may be necessary to get rid of G-B as editor.'[31]

Young's second volume of autobiography, *Mountains with a Difference*, was published in 1951. The possibility that Graham Brown would review it for the journal caused panic in the club. Elliott begged him not to do so and denied his request was special pleading for a friend, but rather an attempt to fend off another row. Even Graham Brown's friends were alarmed. Lloyd wrote:

> I cannot tell you how worried I am over the matter … I have inti-
> mated very plainly that if an attack is made upon you unfairly, there
> will be a split in the club. Now this is most undesirable and for a
> miserable little thing like a review of a book by Young.[32]

In the end, C.F. Meade wrote a generous review.

At the beginning of 1952, Graham Brown recorded that the meeting of the Alpine Club Committee in February 'went well' and the 'atmosphere was much improved', such that afterwards he could enjoy a 'very pleasant'[33] dinner with Elliott and vice-president, Leslie Shadbolt. But on 23 September 1952, the editorship of the journal was once again an item on the committee's agenda. Lloyd reported the meeting to Graham Brown:

> … a perfect storm blew up over the journal, your enemies had a first
> class innings. I was the only one out of eleven members of committee
> present who stood up for you and even I could not defend the last
> journal … They want your resignation.[34]

For the time being, Graham Brown continued as editor but the senior officers of the club heaped more pressure on him.

Wanting to capitalise on the first ascent of Everest in May 1953, Sir Edwin Herbert, who had succeeded Elliott as president, wrote urging Graham Brown to ensure that the journal containing articles reporting the climb appeared at the end of October or at the latest, the beginning of November, and crucially, before the *Geographical Journal* in order to scoop the rival Royal Geographical Society. As ever, Lloyd was interested in improving the club's finances. Anticipating a large demand for the journal and anxious to get the extra money, he pressed Graham Brown to meet the deadline.

But the schedule was impractical; from the outset, there was delay in obtaining vital copy. 'As regards the M.S. for the A.J., I am desperately hard-pressed and really in a fix,'[35] wrote Hunt, and Ed Hillary asked, 'I wonder if you are still needing my article for the *Alpine Journal*? If you can possibly manage without it for the time being, I should be most grateful as I really have no time at all.'[36] Eventually, at the beginning of September, Hunt submitted an article, 'a terribly rushed job', saying,

> I am sending a copy of this to 'Alpinisme' and also 'Die Alpen'. In doing so I am fulfilling urgent requests by the Presidents of the GHM and the SAC, and presuming on the kindness of the Alpine Club and on the spirit of comradeship which exists between all mountaineers, to allow this to be translated and published.[37]

The club could hardly refuse. Graham Brown now found himself in an unwanted race with foreign journals to publish first.

The October deadline was missed and there were more delays, some of which were outside Graham Brown's control, but there had also been a lack of editorial focus. The journal eventually appeared on 15 December, after its continental competitors but still just in advance of the *Geographical Journal*. Smarting from the loss of priority and prestige, and reacting to a number of complaints from members of the club, Herbert wrote to Graham Brown, saying, 'I have come to the conclusion that the time has arrived to make a change in the editorship of the journal.'[38]

The dossier of 'serious complaints' that Herbert had received comprised just ten letters, all written in December 1953. Young and his friends, Brockle-bank, Busk and Lunn, were responsible for eight. Blakeney, exasperated and disaffected, orchestrated the protest and connived with Busk. The late appearance of the journal was a common theme of the complainants. Young had found additional reason to take offence. He criticised Graham Brown for publishing a brief article, written by Blakeney, in which it was correctly pointed out that Young had erroneously claimed the first descent of the Schaligrat in his books. Young angrily demanded to know from Herbert whether Graham Brown was to continue as editor because if he were, he threatened to take further action.

One letter, written by W.H. Murray, who was not allied to Young, was completely different in tone and content and raised an important concern: the club and the journal were preoccupied with the past. 'I am at last compelled to write you despite a very natural reluctance – for I count Graham Brown as a friend whom I deeply respect,' he wrote:

> The Editorship of the Journal has been too long uncreative and has formed for itself a rut that grows annually deeper. I and several other members of the Club who joined the recently formed Alpine Climbing Group were impelled to do so because it had become no longer possible within the AC to keep ourselves adequately informed about Alpine climbing developments ... The AJ has become the last place one looks to get news of routes and reconnaissances.[39]

The committee meeting at which Graham Brown's position as editor would be decided was scheduled for 12 January 1954. Graham Brown was invited to attend but failed to turn up as he was still recovering from the fall that had put him in hospital in Fort William. In anticipation of the meeting and the result, Busk, who was serving as HM Ambassador to Ethiopia, wrote to Herbert from Addis Ababa, saying, 'I have arranged for prayers to be said in all Coptic churches.'[40] The committee, with one dissenting voice [Lloyd's], agreed to dismiss Graham Brown and appointed F.H. Keenlyside in his place.

Graham Brown suspected intrigue: 'There is (to me) obviously a good deal behind all this, and I must say that I suspect the grey eminence [Young] and his friends, and what I cannot quite understand is how Herbert has come to lend himself to it.'[41] True to form, he made a forensic examination of the evidence against him and prepared a defence. Having seen the letters of 'serious complaint', he maintained that his published statements concerning Young's climbs were historically accurate and he thought it 'absurd' that he should have to apologise for them. Thinking that the late delivery of *Alpine Notes* prepared by John Emlyn Jones, the assistant editor, had been critical in delaying production of the November issue and wishing to shift some of the blame, Graham Brown wrote to the printers for a detailed timetable of production. Warily, they first sought Herbert's permission before replying that the late receipt had added only a week to the already delayed publication date. But Graham Brown still considered Emlyn Jones to have been at fault and mounted a spiteful campaign to prevent his election to the exclusive Alpine Dining Club. Even Graham Brown's friends thought he was being unreasonable: J.C. Eaton, secretary of the Alpine Dining Club, 'beseeched' him not to use his veto and Lloyd asked to be excused from his promise to black-ball Emlyn Jones.

At the beginning of March 1954 Graham Brown made a statement to a general meeting of the club. Herbert thought 'the general feeling after your statement the other night was that it was a pity in your own interests that it should have been made',[42] whereas Lloyd's impression was that Graham Brown 'had the sympathy of the room'.[43] Graham Brown's support lay mainly with those members who considered that during his presidency Young had sacrificed the prestige of the Alpine Club to realise his vision of forming an alternative national body to represent all mountaineers, which became the British Mountaineering Council. Those who had aligned themselves with Young saw this group, whose attitudes were seen to be reflected in the journal, as reactionary. Although Herbert and the committee maintained the fiction that the reason for Graham Brown's sacking was the 'impracticability of carrying on the journal with the editor so far away from London',[44] in fact it was the result of an old-fashioned Alpine Club row in which a member's *amour propre* was the issue. However, in dismissing Graham Brown the committee had taken a necessary step towards modernisation, for which the recent formation of the Alpine Climbing Group[e] and Murray's letter had been a wake-up call. Graham Brown was not a reforming editor: his lineage was that of W.A.B. Coolidge and Strutt – 'the awkward squad'[45].

Herbert recalled that Graham Brown took his dismissal 'very badly', refusing to speak to him or even acknowledge his presence. But, five years later, Graham Brown sought a reconciliation: 'I wonder if it would be possible to dine together at the Athenaeum and dissolve any clouds which may have come between us in a bottle of wine?'[46] And they lunched together 'as though nothing had happened and our friendship was thus resumed.'[47]

---

e   Membership required evidence of climbing at a high standard and lapsed automatically on reaching the age of forty.

Chapter 20
Alpine Historian

When his physiological research waned during the 1930s, Graham Brown turned to Alpine history, becoming a serious student for the rest of his life. His chief interest was in Mont Blanc, particularly the history of climbing on its Italian side. He ferreted through back numbers of the *Alpine Journal* and the journals of the French, Swiss and Italian Alpine clubs, examined the club's collection of *führerbuchs*, making copious notes, and started to collect the books that would form his valuable library.

He also undertook an extensive correspondence. In 1932, during his two-week stay at the Gamba Hut on the south side of Mont Blanc, Graham Brown had made a record of the hut's visitors and their explorations during the preceding twenty years. Later he wrote to them, explaining and excusing himself: 'I am very greedy for information' and 'I do trust you will humour my fad' because 'I find trying to discover the answer to such problems is far more interesting than any crossword puzzle or detective novel.'[1,2,3] The motive behind this exhaustive research was not entirely disinterested scholarship. He wanted to establish the originality of his routes on the Brenva Face and there is a note of undoubted satisfaction in his conclusion that 'the Brenva Face was generally thought to be so impracticable that its possibilities were neither recognised nor discussed save by the very few'.[4]

Sometimes his inquiries were pursued simply out of spite. In Smythe's case he could at least claim to have been traduced, but his forensic examination of Young's climbing career seems to have been driven by pathological dislike. Graham Brown trawled through Young's writings and identified fifty examples of 'exaggerations, false claims, mis-statements etc.' in his climbing autobiography, *On High Hills*, and his second volume, *Mountains with a Difference*, describing his climbs with an artificial leg, received similar treatment; the margins of Graham Brown's copy are littered with exclamation marks. He suspected that Young had exaggerated the difficulties encountered on the South Face of the Täschhorn to excuse his inept per-formance and that the disappearance of the note concerning the climb from Davidson's diary indicated that there was more to the story than simply Ryan's uncomplimentary remark about Young's climbing ability. The bait was irresistible and he set out to discover more. Ryan had died in 1947 and the few records of his climbs that he had kept had been passed to Young who had been reluctant to hand them over, adding to the suspicion that he was engaged in a cover-up. After several false leads, Graham Brown traced Ryan's widow to a hotel in South Kensington but she was unable to provide any information and merely expressed a dislike of Young, apparently shared by her late husband. When Graham Brown eventually extracted Ryan's notes from Young's clutches he was disappointed to find no account of the ascent of the Täschhorn. It is possible to sympathise a little with Young who had concluded that Graham Brown was a 'vicious lunatic'.[5]

In July 1953 Graham Brown and Gavin de Beer wrote to the president of the Alpine Club pointing out the coincidence of the club's centenary year in 1957 with the bicentennial anniversary of the birth of Michel-Gabriel Paccard, who with Jacques Balmat made the first ascent of Mont Blanc in 1786. To mark the occasion, they suggested publication of 'some of the manuscript treasures belonging to the club, such as Dr Paccard's journal and other basic documents relating to the early history of the ascent of Mont Blanc',[6] adding, importantly, that no financial burden would fall on the club – a welcome inducement given the parlous state of the club's finances. Nevertheless, it would take more than eighteen months and de Beer's threat to withdraw from the project before the club's committee gave its official approval and, having done so, managed to give de Beer the impression that the club had also endorsed a rival publication from Arnold Lunn, necessitat-ing an emollient letter of explanation from the president.

De Beer, trained in zoology, became professor of embryology at Univer-sity College London, and subsequently director of the Natural History Museum. He was fluent in three foreign languages and noted for his prodi-gious memory; his interests were many and various, literary and historical: famously, he re-opened the debate about the route of Hannibal's crossing of the Alps, making the case for the Col de la Traversette. But 'his didactic tenacity' and 'brushings aside' of the opinions of others were remarked on, even in the soft focus of an obituary.[7] He was not a mountaineer but rather an inveterate walker and gave 'wandering about' as his recreation for

Who's Who. He had been elected to the Alpine Club on a literary qualification and had published a number of articles on the history of Mont Blanc in the *Alpine Journal*, under Graham Brown's editorship.

For more than a century after the first ascent of Mont Blanc on 8 August 1786 by Paccard, Chamonix's doctor, and Balmat, a local crystal hunter, the credit for discovering the route, reaching the summit first and leading his exhausted companion to the top was Balmat's; when a commemorative statue was erected in Chamonix in 1887, Balmat not Paccard was the subject. But in the last decades of the nineteenth century, with mountaineering an established pastime, an interest in its history had developed and the events leading to the first ascent of the highest mountain in Europe naturally attracted the attention of scholar-mountaineers. Contemporary documents were unearthed and evidence emerged that it was Paccard who, as a result of patient observation of the mountain over several years, had discovered the route of ascent that led to success and, far from being a passenger on the climb, had played an equal role in the expedition and had been the first to arrive at the summit.

Graham Brown and de Beer set out to sift and weigh all the evidence and deliver the last word on the subject. Their approach was a paradigm of thoroughness. Close examination of the original text of Balmat's witnessed affidavit revealed that a crucial word – *presque* – had been omitted in published reproductions and hence its significance missed, for Balmat had actually admitted that he *'nearly'* reached the summit at the same time as Paccard. Meticulous analysis of recorded times and progress of the ascent combined with Graham Brown's knowledge of the terrain enabled them to show conclusively that it would have been impossible for Balmat to have reached the summit and then descend to drag the flagging doctor to the top, as was later claimed, in the period before both men were observed by telescope together on the summit. As for Balmat's claim to have explored the higher reaches of the mountain and shown Paccard the way, scrutiny of a near contemporaneous account by Professor de Saussure,[a] who almost certainly had been in possession of the facts, disclosed that Paccard and Balmat went there together and for the first time.

The tone of their collaboration is exemplified in a letter from Graham Brown to de Beer on the subject of the height of Mont Blanc, an issue that

---

a   Horace-Bénédict de Saussure (1740–1799), professor of philosophy and natural science at the Academy of Geneva. In 1760 he offered a prize, said to have been one or two guineas, for the discovery of a practicable way to the summit of Mont Blanc, subsequently claimed by Balmat, and made the third ascent of the mountain in 1787.

perhaps should have been agreed upon earlier than three months before publication of their book. 'Many thanks for your list of corrections, all of which are excellent. I have only challenged your proposed arrangement of brackets on page 60,' he wrote graciously but continued:

> With regard to the height of Mont Blanc (in feet) ... The only place where I give the height of Mont Blanc (so far) is on page 6 '(4,807m = 15,772ft)'. This is correct if the equation which I always use, 1m = 3.281ft, is correct (4,807m = 15,771.767ft). I of course have no objection whatsoever to using '15,771', and have used this for the correction on page 24.
>
> But these figures in general raise another question. They depend on the now accepted height of Mont Blanc as 4,807m in place of the former, and now abandoned, 4,810m. The reduction by 3m is not peculiar to Mont Blanc, but is common to all former Alpine altitudes.
>
> Thus the elevation of Chamonix must now be taken to be 1,037m ... In your discussion ... you assume the obsolete figure for Chamonix ... I assume that the difference of only 4m in the altitude of Chamonix ... does not materially alter the calculations for Paccard's various elevations ... [8]

Touché. But the collaboration between these two opinionated and pedantic scholars proceeded without major disagreement. Unsurprisingly, de Beer had to chivvy Graham Brown to meet deadlines: 'we must stick to this time-table so as to avoid the galling calamity of A[rnold] L[unn]'s book stealing our thunder',[9] and curb his prolixity – 'your 400 pages of manuscript include over 132,000 words and this is without counting the footnotes'[10] – but he was enthusiastic about their work: 'the book continues to read like a detective story in which the reader awaits the next instalment impatiently'.[11]

The villain of the piece was Marc-Théodore Bourrit[b], 'the dark, frustrated figure spitting venom'.[12] Bourrit had made several attempts to climb Mont Blanc. Envious of Paccard's success and fearful that his proposed book would expose the accounts of his own attempts as exaggerated or false, Bourrit had set out to denigrate Paccard's role in the first ascent, and his distorted account that gave all the credit to Balmat, published six weeks

---

b   M.T. Bourrit (1739–1819), precentor of Geneva Cathedral. He travelled widely in the Alps and did much to popularise the mountains through his writings, paintings and genius for self-promotion.

after the event and widely circulated, became the authorised version for 100 years. Graham Brown considered Bourrit was 'one of those men who, while having a true interest in mountains, cannot write of them without exaggeration and bombast, and must use them, perhaps unconsciously, as a means for personal parade'.[13] And Smythe had been the same. Graham Brown's efforts to vindicate Paccard echo his own crusade to establish priority in respect of the routes on the Brenva Face. Commenting on the discovery of the successful line of the first ascent, Graham Brown and de Beer wrote, 'What was hidden from everyone but Dr Paccard was a quality and not a material form, the quality of practicability and accessibility – the fact (or probability) that the *Passage* could be climbed, and climbed safely in certain conditions of the snow'.[14] Substitute Graham Brown for Paccard and *Route Major* for the *Passage* and the similarity is striking.

Deadlines were met and *The First Ascent of Mont Blanc* was published in time for the club's centenary celebrations, which reached a climax with a reception at the Great Hall of Lincoln's Inn, at which the Queen and Prince Philip were present. An enraptured member of the club described the Queen's appearance in a style more suited to readers of *Vogue* than the *Alpine Journal*: 'wearing a lovely, full-skirted dress of cream and gold brocade, diamond tiara, necklace and ear-rings of diamonds, and the star and blue sash of the Order of the Garter, Her Majesty, vivid, smiling and relaxed, clasping a charming bouquet of edelweiss, deep-blue trumpet gentians and other alpine flowers made a radiant picture'.[15] Graham Brown, in white tie, presented a copy of the book, specially bound in Morocco, to Prince Philip, who had accepted honorary membership of the club the year before.

But this moment in the limelight can hardly have recompensed for the snubs he had received from the club. The offer of the vice-presidency made and withdrawn in 1947 was repeated in 1956 but not fulfilled, and the committee's decision to appoint Zürcher as one of the three extra vice-presidents[c] for the centenary year must have rankled. The following year Graham Brown began negotiations with the National Library of Scotland regarding the destination of his library on his death, rescinding his intention to leave it to the Alpine Club, as expressed to Sydney Spencer on his departure for Alaska, more than twenty years earlier.

---

c   C.S. Houston was another. He dined with Graham Brown and enjoyed 'a delightful evening ... good food, wonderful wine and edifying talk'. (11/11/57; NLS Acc 4338/14)

Chapter 21
Vagabond Professor

After a lifetime of controversy, Graham Brown's last years were surprisingly tranquil. Following his retirement in 1947, Graham Brown moved from the Royal Hotel, Cardiff, where he had lived for thirty years, into a large, single room above his laboratory in the tower of the Institute of Physiology. The room overlooked the Bristol Channel and was filled with 'stacks of books, periodicals and papers, some of them physiological, most of them Alpine. Behind the stacks his camp bed and his belongings were invisible, and he himself (for he was of short stature) hardly to be seen until a visitor was close upon him.'[1] It is here that he must be imagined, seated in a large armchair, surrounded by the detritus of an inveterate smoker – used matches, dottle and empty tins of tobacco – cataloguing, collating and cross referencing the records of his climbs, photographs, reprints and newspaper cuttings. According to his chief laboratory technician, the only time Graham Brown was seen in public was about nine o'clock each morning when, dressed in an old but expensive three-piece suit and wearing a homburg hat, he would walk to a coffee stall under the old railway bridge 100 yards away and breakfast with the labourers.

In the same year Graham Brown had acquired the converted lifeboat *Marion of Lorne* in a joint venture with his old friend, Roy Stewart, with whom he had served in the RAMC during the First World War. Thirty years previously, they had shared the ownership of an unreliable motorbike, which had proved a source of trouble and expense; *Marion* was no different. On her trial run she required pumping-out for half an hour and a further hour was needed to start the engine. Rotten timbers were soon discovered and it took over eighteen months to render her seaworthy, only for her to be damaged irreparably at her mooring in October 1950. Undeterred, Graham Brown bought a replacement which proved no less a liability. Originally the lifeboat, *Cyril & Lilian Bishop*, and one of the small boats used during the evacuation from Dunkirk, Graham Brown had her converted and renamed *Thekla* (his father had owned a yacht of the same name).

In July 1951, instead of instructing in the Alps as in the previous three summers, he set out with a crew of three to sail *Thekla* from Wallasea, in Essex, where she had been commissioned, up the east coast to Edinburgh. On the second day they ran into rough seas and took on water; the pump seized and they baled with buckets, eventually reaching safety in Yarmouth. Graham Brown took her in for repairs. The vendors of the boat, who had also carried out the modifications, pursued Graham Brown in court for unpaid bills, but he countered that the conversion had been shoddy, and the judgement went in his favour.

Thekla was subsequently moored at Mallaig and Graham Brown started to spend the summer months aboard, undertaking a series of lengthy cruises around the west and north coast of Scotland. In 1959 he crossed the North Sea to Norway in a three-month round-trip to Tromsø, beyond the Arctic Circle. His crews comprised mainly Edinburgh University students who found him an amenable and generous skipper. Several accompanied him on more than one trip; 'It would be wonderful to be back on *Thekla* again, I must say last year was one of my best holidays,'[2] wrote one of them. Graham Brown's frequent absences at sea led him to declare that he had 'No Fixed Abode', to the disbelief of HM inspector of taxes with whom he was often in dispute. The number of uncompleted tax returns, tax demands and letters regarding late payment amongst his papers suggest he was un-cooperative rather than simply inefficient. In 1939 he had had the temerity to ask for a tax rebate in respect of his six-month absence abroad on the expedition to Masherbrum. The request was summarily dismissed.

Graham Brown had been elected honorary president of the EUMC in 1951. He was not simply a figurehead: in 1957, the club's secretary, Robin Smith[a], wrote 'there can't be many honorary presidents running around today with half the kick or half the history you have.'[3] He attended the club's meets regularly, often cadging a lift from one of the students – he never learned to drive – travelling as a passenger in a side-car or riding pillion on a motorbike. Here he is arriving in North Wales from Edinburgh:

---

a   Robin Smith (1938–1962). An extraordinarily talented climber whose exploits are legendary, he was killed, aged twenty-three, in a fall from Pik Garmo in the Pamirs. He was a favourite of Graham Brown who was greatly upset by Smith's death.

Just as we were leaving, an old Indian combination rolled up and a pinched wee man crawled out of the sidecar ... When he crawled out of his balaclava as well I recognised one of the grandfathers of mountaineering – the finest of the lot – Professor T. Graham Brown – still rushing about mountaineering at 72! ... such a grand old chap – still with that scruffy little stub of a nose-warming pipe.[4]

He continued to climb at a moderate standard, usually as second on the rope. In wet conditions he favoured wearing baggy shorts; a woolly bala-clava was his trademark headgear and he was inseparable from his pipe. He enjoyed the unruly atmosphere, campfires, singing and playing poker, although he was less comfortable when women were in the party, the increasingly relaxed relations between the sexes contrasting with his own Victorian upbringing. Successive generations of students actively sought his company; many wrote telling him of their plans, their climbs and the progress of their careers. They admired his enthusiasm and held him in warm affection.

In 1961 Graham Brown moved to Edinburgh, where he had purchased a Georgian flat, 20 Manor Place, in the 'posh' West End of the city, a quarter of a mile from his childhood home. He occupied the ground floor in eccen-tric squalor and let the basement free-of-charge to members of the EUMC, several of whom have provided a vivid and similar picture of his quarters:

The whole flat was covered in a very thick layer of dust – particularly the carpets. Cobwebs were everywhere ... [Graham Brown] had installed himself in a vast room overlooking the weed-infested garden at the back and there was a 'footpath' from this room to the front door. Another track led through the dust to the toilet and from there to his bedroom, where he slept in a sleeping bag.[5]

Graham Brown had, by now, given up climbing but he joined members of the club at their weekly meetings.

He loved the rendezvous in pubs or at his place, where discussions could extend through the night on big Alpine lines, old and new, of which he had such an extensive knowledge. He in turn took great pride in the young blood's endeavours, delighting in their successes or their sometimes more interesting failures. There was total empathy on both sides of the relationship.[6]

And when the talk turned to the past, 'Graham was always ready to remove his pipe to tell improbable stories to the discredit of his contemporaries ... Frank Smythe bore more than his fair share of these calumnious attacks.'[7]

In 1962 he had a brief resurgence of interest in physiology. Anders Lundberg, professor of physiology at Göteborg University, had travelled to Edinburgh, hoping to meet Graham Brown and discuss his film of a decerebrate cat walking on a treadmill, demonstrated at a meeting of the Physiological Society twenty years earlier. But Graham Brown was absent aboard *Thekla*. When he heard of Lundberg's visit he set about trying to recall his observations, but, now aged eighty, found that his 'memory was not good enough' and instead offered to sail to Sweden in his boat and explain the film in person, but he was unable to assemble a crew and they never met. Nevertheless, Lundberg played a leading role in re-evaluating Graham Brown's research and drawing attention to its importance.

Graham Brown's cruising days were over. His health declined. The students moved out of Manor Place and a nurse moved in. Robin Campbell, the last of the EUMC residents, took Graham Brown to Fort William to view his boat, moored on Loch Lochy, for the last time and poignantly recalls, 'He stared at it from the shore for a minute or so and turned away, unable to get aboard.'[8] Graham Brown died in the small hours of 28 October 1965. His ashes are buried in the family plot situated in a corner of the Dean cemetery, a burial ground made fashionable by the professional classes of Victorian Edinburgh.

It was never likely that it would end there. His whole life had been one of endless contradictions, of warm friendships and bitter enmities, of great generosity and petty jealousies, and these were all reflected in his will. He had not forgotten the slights and the library that had been intended for the Alpine Club was left instead to the National Library of Scotland (along with a bequest of £60,000) and his Edinburgh flat to the University of Edinburgh for use as a student residence, preferably members of the mountaineering club.[b] It was his last gesture to a mountaineering world that could still not quite make up its mind about him.

---

b   Manor Place was eventually sold and the 'spiritual home' of the EUMC moved to a flat in Nicholson Street that still provides accommodation for six students.

The Times published an obituary notice, written by Blakeney who stoked the embers of the feud with Smythe, using calculated nuance to give the credit for the climbs on the Brenva Face to Smythe. Referring to *Route Major*, he wrote, 'again with Smythe's leadership, he made the first ascent by a more direct route' and continued, 'the partnership then broke up, for Graham Brown was not well suited to guideless climbing'. As for Graham Brown's editorship of the *Alpine Journal* that had caused Blakeney trouble, it had been 'somewhat turbulent', and although 'whatever he wrote himself was distinguished by its scholarship ... his judgement was less sound, particularly of individuals, and he was capable of violent likes and (more frequently) dislikes'.[9] Meanwhile the then editor of the *Alpine Journal*, David Cox, fretted, 'I have given a good deal of further thought to the tiresome Graham Brown problem ... the crucial question ... has all along been what weight should be attached to GB's wishes?'[10] Graham Brown had stipulated that his obituary notice in the *Alpine Journal* should comprise simply a complete list of his climbs in that remarkable year, 1933, and only the unusual climbs in other years, to be compiled by his friend Charles Evans.[c]

Evans took his responsibility for overseeing Graham Brown's wish and posthumous reputation seriously. He had already submitted a supplementary notice to *The Times* as a corrective to Blakeney's view on the Brenva Face routes:

> Pioneering climbs of this nature have it in common with the earlier great Alpine first ascents that distinctions between 'guided' and 'guideless' and between leader and led have little meaning. Inspiration, meticulous planning and timing, and technical expertise were all essential to the successful outcome of the series of explorations which Graham Brown and his associates carried out on the Brenva face.[11]

When he learned of Cox's intention to publish an 'appreciation' of Graham Brown by Lord Tangley, he objected, but Cox held his ground: 'it seems to me far better that the story should be put on record accurately and sympathetically than that it should be left for some future alpine historian to give a distorted version of it'.[12] And Blakeney, now assistant editor of the journal, quipped, 'dear old GB is being as great a nuisance dead as he was alive'.[13]

---

c   Sir R. Charles Evans (1918–1995), president of the Alpine Club 1967–1970.

References

Abbreviations

AC   Alpine Club
AJ   *Alpine Journal*
BL   British Library
IWM   Imperial War Museum
MHT   Mountain Heritage Trust
NLS   National Library of Scotland
TGB   T. Graham Brown

Introduction

1. AJ 71: 51
2. Band G., *Summit: 150 Years of the Alpine Club*; p. 98

Chapter 1: Early Influences

1. TGB to Dr Klebs 6/10/31; NLS Acc. 4338/2
2. Father to TGB 5/9/98; NLS Acc. 4338/1
3. Father to TGB undated; NLS Acc. 4338/16
4. Magnusson M., *The Clacken and the Slate: the Story of The Edinburgh Academy 1824–1974*; p. 231
5. Ibid. p. 26
6. Ibid. p. 229
7. Ibid. pp. 227, 228
8. Ibid. p. 245
9. Ibid. p. 248
10. TGB to Thorburn 11/98; NLS Acc. 4338/1
11. TGB's *Brenva* manuscript; NLS Acc. 4338/166
12. Ibid.
13. Ibid.
14. Ibid.
15. TGB's diary 1898; NLS Acc. 4338/17
16. Father to TGB undated; NLS Acc. 4338/16
17. TGB's diary 1899; NLS Acc. 4338/19
18. Father to TGB 9/4/99; NLS Acc. 4338/1
19. Father to TGB 13/5/99; NLS Acc. 4338/1
20. Father to TGB 13/8/00; NLS Acc. 4338/1
21. Father to TGB undated; NLS Acc. 4338/16

Chapter 2: First Steps in Physiology

1. Bonner T., *Becoming a Physician*; p. 275
2. *Obituary Notices of Fellows of the Royal Society* 1935; 1:400

3. Drennan 10/5/03; Lothian Health Services Archive GD9/44

4. Drennan 10/8/03; Lothian Health Services Archive GD9/44

5. TGB's diary 1906; NLS Acc. 4338/20

6. Ibid.

7. Ibid.

8. Ibid.

9. Ibid.

10. Bonner T., op. cit. p. 254

11. Sherrington to TGB 27/5/07; NLS Acc. 4338/1

12. *Biographical Memoirs of Fellows of the Royal Society* 1966 12: 22

Chapter 3: Sherrington and Liverpool

1. Cathcart to TGB 5/12/19; NLS Acc. 4338/1

2. *Obituary Notices of Fellows of the Royal Society* 1952 8: 241

3. Eccles J. & Gibson W., *Sherrington: His Life and Thought*; p. 185

4. *British Medical Journal* 1947; ii: 810

5. *Proceedings of the Royal Society (B)* 1911 84: 308

6. Mclean Watson to TGB 16/1/12; NLS Acc. 4338/1

7. Cathcart to TGB 5/12/19; NLS Acc. 4338/1

8. TGB's diary June 1916 – May 1917; NLS Acc. 4338/23

9. NLS Acc. 4338/1

10. King, C.M. & H., *The Two Nations: The Life and Work of Liverpool University Settlement and Its Associated Institutions 1906–1937*; p. 12

11. Woolton Earl., *The Memoirs of the Rt. Hon. The Earl of Woolton*; p. 26

12. Ibid.

13. TGB's *Brenva* manuscript; NLS Acc. 4338/166

14. Father to TGB 2/2/13; NLS Acc. 4338/1

Chapter 4: Physiologist at War

NOTE: All the unreferenced quotations in this chapter are from TGB's diary (June 1916 – May 1917); NLS Acc. 4338/23

1. Cathcart to TGB 4/2/15; NLS Acc. 4338/1

2. Father to TGB 14/2/15; NLS Acc. 4338/1

3. Sherrington to TGB 18/3/15; NLS Acc. 4338/1

4. Myers to TGB 9/5/15; NLS Acc. 4338/1

5. Elliott to TGB 22/4/15; NLS Acc. 4338/1

6. Jones E., *Journal of the History of Medicine and Allied Sciences*; 65: 368

7. Pear T., *Journal of the Royal Anthropological Institute*; 90: 227

8. Shephard B., *A War of Nerves*; p. 81

9. Munk's Roll; 5: 397

10. *British Medical Journal* 1964 i 1573

11. Graham Brown T. & Stewart R., *Brain* 39: 348

12. D.T. Graham Brown to his wife 1/6/16; IWM docs 15427

13. Paton to TGB 27/5/19; NLS Acc. 4338/1

14. Father to TGB 22/6/15; NLS Acc. 4338/1

15. Southborough Lord, *Report of the War Office Committee of Enquiry Into 'Shell-Shock'*; p. 3

16. Shephard B., op. cit. p. 2

17. Graham Brown T., *Journal of Neurology & Psychopathology*; 8: 146
18. NLS Acc. 4338/16
19. Bradley to TGB 25/4/34; NLS Acc. 4338/4

Chapter 5: Professor
1. Cathcart to TGB 18/5/20; NLS Acc. 4338/1
2. Roberts A., *The Welsh National School of Medicine 1893–1931: the Cardiff Years*; p. 83
3. *Biographical Memoirs of Fellows of the Royal Society 1966*; 12: 22
4. TGB to the Secretary, University of Wales 28/5/47; Cardiff University Institutional Archives UCC/per/emp/14
5. Memorandum 3/11/50; Cardiff University Institutional Archives UCC/per/emp/14
6. Calvert H., *Smythe's Mountains*; p. 82
7. Roberts A., op. cit. p. 226
8. Cathcart to TGB 5/12/19; NLS Acc. 4338/1
9. Brocklehurst to Blakeney 7/11/65; BL Add 63123
10. Roberts A., op. cit. p. 255
11. Ibid. p. 229
12. Sherrington to TGB 27/4/19; NLS Acc. 4338/1
13. Dale to TGB 5/8/30; NLS Acc. 4338/2

Chapter 6: A New Direction
1. TGB's *Brenva* manuscript; NLS Acc. 4338/166
2. Ibid.
3. TGB's diary 1906; NLS Acc. 4338/20
4. Chorley Lord, *Fell & Rock Climbing Club Journal*; 20: 263
5. Petty W., *Gritstone Club Journal* 1923; No. 1 Vol. 2
6. Basterfield G., *Gritstone Club Journal*, 1925–6; 2/3: 5
7. Letts to TGB 17/10/24; NLS Acc. 4338/2
8. TGB to Letts 24/4/25; NLS Acc. 4338/2
9. Basterfield to TGB 8/5/25; NLS Acc. 4338/2
10. Warren C., AJ 88: 252

Chapter 7: To the Alps
1. Smith J.A., *Mountain Holidays*; p. 129
2. Letts to TGB 20/5/24; NLS Acc. 4338/2
3. Letts to TGB 22/5/24; NLS Acc. 4338/2
4. Quoted in Ring J., *How the English Made the Alps*; p. 190
5. Letts to TGB 22/5/24; NLS Acc. 4338/2
6. Ibid.
7. Ibid.
8. NLS Acc. 4338/205
9. Letts L., *Gritstone Club Journal* 1924; 2 (2): 12
10. Letts to TGB 7/8/25; NLS Acc. 4338/2
11. Letts to TGB 15/6/26; NLS Acc. 4338/2
12. Graham Brown T., *Brenva*; pp. 3–4
13. Ibid. p. 2
14. Blakeney to Lunn 11/8/49; Sir Arnold Lunn papers, box1/folder57 Georgetown University, Washington

15. Tangley Lord, AJ 71: 52
16. Letts to TGB 3/2/27; NLS Acc. 4338/164
17. TGB's climbing diary: Col du Géant 1927; NLS Acc. 4338/41
18. Ibid.

Chapter 8: Climbs with F.S. Smythe

1. *The Times* [London] 26/7/49
2. Greene R., AJ 57: 234
3. TGB's climbing diary: Col du Géant 1927; NLS Acc. 4338/41
4. TGB's *Brenva* manuscript; NLS Acc. 4338/166
5. Smythe F., AJ 40: 75
6. TGB to Gask 4/9/27; AC archives: Tracts T442
7. Ibid.
8. Smythe to TGB 22/9/27; NLS Acc. 4338/164
9. Smythe to TGB 15/10/27; NLS Acc. 4338/164
10. Smythe to TGB 30/10/27; NLS Acc. 4338/164
11. Gask to TGB 23/12/27; NLS Acc. 4338/164
12. Smythe to TGB 13/2/28; NLS Acc. 4338/164
13. Smythe to TGB 29/2/28; NLS Acc. 4338/164
14. Smythe F., *Blackwood's Magazine* 224: 19
15. Quoted in Hankinson A., *Geoffrey Winthrop Young: Poet, Mountaineer, Educator*; p. 243
16. Young G.W., Sutton G., Noyce W., *Snowdon Biography*; p. 40
17. TGB's climbing diary: Alps 1933; NLS Acc. 4338/50
18. Waller to TGB 23/12/32; NLS Acc. 4338/164
19. TGB's *Brenva* manuscript; NLS Acc. 4338/166
20. Smythe F., *Blackwood's Magazine* 224: 726–727
21. TGB to Gask 9/8/28; AC archives: Tracts T442
22. Graham Brown T., AJ 40: 373
23. Smythe T., *My Father, Frank*; p. 106
24. Smythe to TGB 12/9/28; NLS Acc. 4338/164

Chapter 9: Fallout

1. Smythe to Strutt 11/9/28; NLS
2. Gask to TGB 8/10/28; NLS Acc. 4338/164
3. Strutt to TGB 8/10/28; NLS Acc. 4338/164
4. Strutt to TGB 22/10/28; NLS Acc. 4338/164
5. Strutt to TGB 8/10/28; NLS Acc. 4338/164
6. Strutt E., AJ 40: 375
7. Notes of a conversation with Herbert 12/5/32; NLS Acc. 4338/164
8. Blakeney to TGB 4/2/32; NLS Acc. 4338/164
9. Smythe to TGB 19/10/29; NLS Acc. 4338/164
10. Spencer to TGB 3/10/32; NLS Acc. 4338/164
11. Strutt to TGB 25/9/32; NLS Acc. 4338/164
12. Smythe to Young 1928; AC Archives 1922/B63
13. TGB to Smythe 24/12/32; NLS Acc. 4338/164
14. Smythe to TGB 28/12/32; NLS Acc. 4338/164
15. TGB to Smythe 3/2/33; NLS Acc. 4338/164

Chapter 10: Alpine Heyday

1. Graham Brown T., AJ 43: 14
2. Young G.W., *On High Hills*; p. 113
3. TGB's diary of Brenva climbs: 1929–1931; NLS Acc. 4338/191
4. Waller to TGB 23/12/32; NLS Acc. 4338/164
5. TGB to Ogier Ward 23/4/32; NLS Acc. 4338/164
6. Ward to TGB 29/4/32; NLS Acc. 4338/164
7. Goodfellow to TGB 24/1/33; NLS Acc. 4338/3
8. Unsworth W., *Savage Snows*; p. 136
9. Graham Brown T., AJ 45: 231
10. TGB to Goodfellow 8/10/31; NLS Acc. 4338/2
11. Graham Brown T., AJ 45: 243
12. TGB to Strutt 2/8/32; NLS Acc. 4338/3
13. TGB to Knubel 22/12/32; NLS Acc. 4338/3
14. TGB's climbing diary: Alps 1933; NLS Acc. 4338/49
15. Blakeney to Lunn 11/8/49; Sir Arnold Lunn papers; Georgetown University Library, Box1/folder57

Chapter 11: The Alpine Club

1. Collie N., AJ 35: 1
2. Wilson C., AJ 44: 11
3. Russell S., In: G.I. Finch, *The Making of a Mountaineer*; p. 10
4. TGB to Strutt 11/3/33; NLS Acc. 4338/187
5. Graham Brown T., Early Mountaineering; In: Spencer S. (ed.) *Mountaineering*; p. 33
6. Graham Brown T., AJ 45: 121
7. TGB to Strutt 12/1/33; NLS Acc. 4338/3
8. TGB's diary of Brenva climbs: 1929-31; NLS Acc. 4338/191
9. Ibid.
10. TGB to Spencer 30/9/32; NLS Acc. 4338/3
11. TGB's diary of Brenva climbs: 1929-31; NLS Acc. 4338/191
12. Graham Brown T., AJ 45: 128
13. Spencer to TGB 13/1/34; NLS Acc. 4338/164
14. TGB to Goodfellow 20/12/32; NLS Acc. 4338/164
15. Notes of Conversations at the Athenaeum and Alpine Club; NLS Acc. 4338/191
16. Ibid.
17. TGB to Meade 2/11/35; NLS Acc. 4338/5
18. TGB to Meade 10/1/36; NLS Acc. 4338/6
19. Meade to Herbert 3/2/36; NLS Acc. 4338/6
20. Quoted in Unsworth W., *Everest: the Mountaineering History*; p. 570

Chapter 12: Annus Mirabilis

1. Strutt to TGB 24/9/33; NLS Acc. 4338/4
2. TGB to Zürcher 11/3/33; NLS Acc. 4338/3
3. NLS Acc. 4338/125
4. TGB to Kay 3/3/32; NLS Acc. 4338/3
5. TGB to Foot 4/3/33; NLS Acc. 4338/3
6. Foot to TGB 26/2/33; NLS Acc. 4338/3
7. TGB to Foot 11/3/33; NLS Acc. 4338/3
8. Foot to TGB 26/2/33; NLS Acc. 4338/3

9. Graham Brown T., *Rucksack Club Journal*; 7 (2) 1932, 182
10. Graham Brown T., AJ 53: 285
11. TGB to Miss Whymper 19/5/33; NLS Acc. 4338/3
12. Graham Brown T., *Brenva*; p. 128
13. TGB's climbing diary: Alps 1933; NLS Acc. 4338/51
14. Ibid.
15. Graham Brown T., *Brenva*; p. 148
16. TGB's climbing diary: Alps 1933; NLS Acc. 4338/52
17. Ibid.
18. TGB's climbing diary: Alps 1933; NLS Acc. 4338/46
19. TGB's climbing diary: Alps 1933; NLS Acc. 4338/47
20. TGB's climbing diary: Alps 1933; NLS Acc. 4338/52
21. Graham Brown T., *Brenva*; p. 162
22. Ibid. p. 166
23. Ibid. p. 169
24. Ibid. p. 170
25. Ibid. p. 172
26. Miss Whymper to TGB 22/4/34; NLS Acc. 4338/5
27. TGB's climbing diary: Alps 1933; NLS Acc. 4338/47
28. TGB to Gask 6/8/33; NLS Acc. 4338/4
29. Lunn A., *New English Review* 11: 514
30. TGB's climbing diary: Alps 1933; NLS Acc. 4338/55
31. TGB's climbing diary: Alps 1933; NLS Acc. 4338/54
32. TGB's climbing diary: Alps 1933; NLS Acc. 4338/55
33. Ibid.
34. TGB's climbing diary: Alps 1933; NLS Acc. 4338/44
35. TGB's climbing diary: Alps 1933; NLS Acc. 4338/56
36. TGB's climbing diary: Alps 1933; NLS Acc. 4338/57
37. Ibid.
38. Ibid.
39. Goodfellow B., AJ 46: 49
40. Climbing diary: Alps 1933; NLS Acc. 4338/58
41. TGB to Strutt 12/8/33; NLS Acc. 4338/4
42. Aufdenblatten to TGB 4/10/33; NLS Acc. 4338/4
43. NLS Acc. 4338/125
44. Perrin J., *The Climbing Essays*; p. 117
45. TGB's *Brenva* manuscript; NLS Acc. 4338/166
46. Hallward B., *Oxford & Cambridge Mountaineering*, 1921; p. 46
47. Longland J., AJ 62: 97

Chapter 13: C.S. Houston and Mount Foraker

1. Quoted in Isserman M. & Weaver S., *Fallen Giants*; p. 314
2. Houston to TGB 8/12/37; NLS Acc. 4338/7
3. Houston C., diary: Europe 1932
4. TGB's climbing diary: Alps 1932; NLS Acc. 4338/44
5. Houston C., diary: Europe 1932
6. TGB to Strutt 19/6/34; NLS Acc. 4338/4
7. Houston to TGB 10/1/33; NLS Acc. 4338/3

8. A.J. Dimond to the Principal, UCSW 18/4/34; NLS 4338/4
9. Houston to TGB 11/2/34; NLS 43338/4
10. Tilman H., *Nepal Himalaya*; p. 213
11. TGB to Wilson 9/3/34; NLS Acc. 4338/4
12. TGB's climbing diary: Alaska 1934; NLS Acc. 4338/61
13. TGB to Strutt 19/6/34; NLS Acc. 4338/4
14. Ibid.
15. Graham Brown T., AJ 47: 24
16. *Idem*
17. Houston C., *American Alpine Journal* 2: 286
18. Houston C., diary: Foraker 1934
19. Graham Brown T., AJ 47: 25
20. Ibid. pp. 29, 30
21. Ibid. p. 27
22. Ibid. p. 37
23. TGB to Strutt 29/8/34 – 11/9/34; NLS Acc. 4338/4
24. Graham Brown T., AJ 47: 47
25. Ibid.
26. Houston C., diary: Foraker 1934
27. TGB's climbing diary: Alaska 1934; NLS Acc. 4338/62
28. Graham Brown T., AJ 47: 47
29. TGB's climbing diary: Alaska 1934; NLS Acc. 4338/62
30. Waterston to TGB (post-marked 27 Sept.); Acc. 4338/16
31. TGB to Houston 23/10/34; NLS Acc. 4338/4
32. Houston C., diary: Foraker 1934
33. Houston to TGB 10/1/35; NLS Acc. 4338/5
34. TGB to Houston 23/10/34; NLS Acc. 4338/4
35. Mrs Houston to TGB 11/12/34; NLS Acc. 4338/4

Chapter 14: Himalayan Prospects
1. TGB to Houston 23/10/34; NLS Acc. 4338/4
2. TGB to Houston 12/11/34; NLS Acc. 4338/4
3. Houston to TGB 10/1/35; NLS Acc. 4338/5
4. Houston to TGB 11/12/34; NLS Acc. 4338/4
5. TGB to Houston 14/11/34; NLS Acc. 4338/4
6. TGB to Houston 12/1/35; NLS Acc. 4338/5
7. Houston to TGB 15/1/35; NLS Acc. 4338/5
8. Strutt to TGB 23/1/35; NLS Acc. 4338/5
9. Houston to TGB 25/2/35; NLS Acc. 4338/5
10. Houston to TGB 18/4/35; NLS Acc. 4338/5
11. TGB to Houston 8/3/35; NLS Acc. 4338/5
12. Mrs Houston to TGB 29/6/35; NLS Acc. 4338/5
13. TGB to Houston 13/6/35; NLS Acc. 4338/5
14. TGB's climbing diary: Alps 1935; Acc. 4338/67
15. Houston C., *American Alpine Journal* 2: 485
16. Graham Brown T., AJ 53: 293
17. TGB's climbing diary: Alps 1935; NLS Acc. 4338/67
18. Roberts D., *Moments of Doubt & Other Mountaineering Writings*; p. 90

19. TGB's climbing diary: Alps 1935; NLS Acc. 4338/68
20. Ibid.
21. Houston to TGB 16/8/35; NLS Acc. 4338/5
22. TGB to Houston 15/11/35; NLS Acc. 4338/5
23. Houston to TGB 7/1/36; NLS Acc. 4338/6
24. TGB to Houston 15/1/36; NLS Acc. 4338/6
25. Houston to TGB 17/1/36; NLS Acc. 4338/6
26. TGB to Houston 23/1/36; NLS Acc. 4338/6
27. Houston to TGB 6/5/33; NLS Acc. 4338/3
28. Houston to TGB 26/5/36; NLS Acc. 4338/6
29. Houston to TGB 2/12/35; NLS 4338/5
30. Houston C., Heyday Climbs; In: Bonington C. (ed.) *Great Climbs*; p. 154
31. Houston to TGB 2/12/35; NLS 4338/5
32. Emmons to TGB 6/12/35; NLS Acc. 4338/5
33. TGB to N. Odell 10/1/36; Odell papers, AC Archives B74
34. Houston to TGB 17/1/36; NLS Acc. 4338/6
35. TGB to Odell 13/2/36; Odell papers, AC Archives B74
36. TGB to Lloyd 14/1/36; NLS Acc. 4338/6
37. TGB to Asst. Editor of *The Times*, 9/6/36; NLS Acc. 4338/6
38. Tilman H., *The Ascent of Nanda Devi*; p. 25
39. Houston to TGB 26/5/36; NLS Acc. 4338/6
40. TGB to Houston 31/5/36; NLS Acc. 4338/6

Chapter 15: Nanda Devi
1. TGB's climbing diary: Nanda Devi 1936; NLS Acc. 4338/69
2. TGB to Oughton 10/2/37; NLS Acc. 4338/73
3. Tilman H., *The Ascent of Nanda Devi*; p. 73
4. TGB's climbing diary: Nanda Devi 1936; NLS Acc. 4338/70
5. Tilman H., op. cit. p. 99
6. Ibid.
7. TGB's climbing diary: Nanda Devi 1936; NLS Acc. 4338/70
8. Tilman H., diary; AC Archives D106/2
9. Shipton E., *Upon that Mountain*; p. 207
10. Houston's diary: Nanda Devi 1936
11. Ibid.
12. Houston C., *American Alpine Journal*, 3: 13
13. Houston C., diary: Nanda Devi 1936
14. Tilman H., diary; AC Archives D106/2
15. Roberts D., *Moments of Doubt & Other Mountaineering Writings*; p. 91
16. Houston C., *Appalachia* 4 (new series): 301
17. Tilman H., op. cit. p. 232
18. Ibid. p. 196
19. Houston C., diary: Nanda Devi 1936
20. TGB's climbing diary: Nanda Devi 1936; NLS Acc. 4338/70
21. Ibid.
22. Houston to TGB 8/11/36; NLS Acc. 4338/6
23. Quoted in: Steele P., *Eric Shipton: Everest and Beyond*; p. 73
24. Tilman to Odell 6/3/37; Odell papers, AC Archives B74

25. TGB to Tilman 2/3/37; NLS Acc. 4338/7

26. Tilman to TGB 6/3/37; NLS Acc. 4338/7

27. *The Times* 27/11/3628.

28. Meade to TGB 3/12/36; NLS Acc. 4338/629.

29. Odell to TGB 28/11/36; NLS Acc. 4338/6

30. Odell to TGB 26/11/37; NLS Acc. 4338/7

31. Tilman to TGB 25/11/37; NLS Acc 4338/7

32. Houston to TGB 8/11/36; NLS Acc. 4338/6

33. Houston to TGB 1/4/37; NLS Acc. 4338/7

34. TGB to Houston 14/6/37; NLS Acc. 4338/7

35. Houston to TGB 25/6/37; NLS Acc. 4338/7

36. Houston to TGB 8/12/37; NLS Acc. 4338/7

37. Houston to TGB 24/12/41; NLS Acc. 4338/8

Chapter 16: Masherbrum

1. TGB's climbing diary: Alps 1937; NLS Acc. 4338/73

2. TGB to Houston 14/10/37; NLS Acc. 4338/7

3. Waller J., *Everlasting Hills*; p. 27

4. Hodgkin R., AJ 103: 218

5. Ibid., p. 220

6. TGB to Waller 9/1/38; NLS Acc. 4338/7

7. Waller to TGB 27/1/38; NLS Acc. 4338/7

8. Waller to TGB 22/1/38; NLS Acc. 4338/7

9. Hodgkin R., AJ 103: 219

10. Waller to TGB 14/3/38; NLS Acc. 4338/7

11. TGB to Principal, University College Cardiff 24/3/38; NLS Acc. 4338/7

12. TGB to Tucker 26/3/38; NLS Acc. 4338/7

13. Tucker to TGB 7/4/38; NLS Acc. 4338/7

14. Pye to TGB 6/4/38; NLS Acc. 4338/7

15. Hodgkin R., AJ 103: 220

16. TGB to Waller 23/3/38; NLS Acc. 4338/7

17. Hodgkin R., *Playing. Robin Hodgkin's Mountaineering Letters* 1937-47; p. 36

18. Waller J., op. cit. pp. 128–129

19. TGB's climbing diary: Karakoram 1938; NLS Acc. 4338/79

20. Harrison J., Masherbrum diary; AC archives

21. Ibid.

22. TGB's climbing diary: Karakoram 1938; NLS Acc. 4338/79

23. Hodgkin R., op. cit., p. 47

24. TGB's climbing diary: Karakoram 1938; NLS Acc. 4338/80

25. Harrison J., op. cit.

26. TGB's climbing diary: Karakoram 1938; NLS Acc. 4338/80

27. Ibid.

28. Mummery, A.F., *My Climbs in the Alps and Caucasus*; p. 162

29. Harrison J., op. cit.

30. TGB's climbing diary: Karakoram 1938; NLS Acc. 4338/80

31. Ibid.

32. Harrison J., op. cit.

33. TGB's climbing diary: Karakoram 1938; NLS Acc. 4338/80

34. Ibid.

35. Waller J., op. cit. p. 164

36. TGB's climbing diary: Karakoram 1938; NLS Acc. 4338/80

37. Ibid.

38. Hodgkin R., AJ 103: 223

39. TGB's climbing diary: Karakoram 1938; NLS Acc. 4338/81

40. Harrison J., op. cit.

41. Houston C., In *Nanda Devi: Exploration and Ascent*, Shipton, E. & Tilman, H.; p. 13

42. TGB's climbing diary: Karakoram 1938; NLS Acc. 4338/81

43. Ibid.

44. Ibid.

45. TGB to Waller 9/8/38; NLS Acc. 4338/7

46. TGB's climbing diary: Karakoram 1938; NLS Acc. 4338/81

47. Ibid.

48. Ibid.

49. Ibid.

50. Waller to TGB 31/7/38; NLS Acc. 4338/7

51. Harrison J., op. cit.

52. Graham Brown T., *Geographical Journal* 95: 93

53. Ibid., p. 94

Chapter 17: Interlude

1. TGB's climbing diary: Karakoram 1938; NLS Acc. 4338/82

2. TGB to Waller 9/8/38; NLS Acc. 4338/7

3. TGB to Waller 24/8/38; NLS Acc. 4338/7

4. TGB's climbing diary: Masherbrum 1938; NLS Acc. 4338/76

5. Hodgkin to TGB 14/9/38; NLS Acc. 4338/7

6. Hodgkin to TGB 27/4/39; NLS Acc. 4338/8

7. TGB's climbing diary: Palestine 1939; NLS Acc. 4338/84

8. Brandon P., *The Decline and Fall of the British Empire 1781–1997*; p. 469

9. TGB's climbing diary: Palestine 1939; NLS Acc. 4338/85

10. TGB to Henderson 30/9/39; NLS Acc. 4338/8

11. Jones J., Tansey E., Stuart D., *Journal of the History of Neuroscience*; 20: 188

12. TGB to Henderson 30/9/39; NLS Acc. 4338/8

13. TGB to Finch 16/10/43; NLS Acc. 4338/8

14. TGB to Stevens 28/9/40; NLS Acc. 4338/8

15. TGB to P. Lloyd 8/8/42; NLS Acc. 4338/8

16. TGB's *Brenva* manuscript; NLS Acc. 4338/190

17. TGB to Strutt 11/3/33; NLS Acc. 4338/187

18. Ibid.

19. TGB's *Brenva* manuscript; NLS Acc. 4338/167

20. Graham Brown T., *Brenva*; p. 14

21. Howard G., AJ 57: 1

22. Graham Brown T., *Brenva*; p. xii

23. Graham Brown T., NLS Acc. 4338/204

24. TGB to Tyndale 27/5/40; NLS Acc. 4338/165

25. Tyndale to TGB 10/8/40; NLS Acc. 4338/165

26. TGB to Tyndale 9/11/40; NLS Acc. 4338/165

27. Bozman to TGB 3/12/40; NLS Acc. 4338/165
28. TGB's *Brenva* manuscript; NLS Acc. 4338/190
29. Bozman to TGB 3/12/40; NLS Acc. 4338/165
30. TGB to Bozman 25/11/40; NLS Acc. 4338/165
31. Bozman to TGB 6/10/42; NLS Acc. 4338/165
32. Irving R; NLS Acc. 4338/165
33. Bozman to TGB 29/10/42; NLS Acc. 4338/165
34. TGB to Bozman 21/11/42; NLS Acc. 4338/165
35. Bozman to TGB 14/4/43; NLS Acc. 4338/165
36. Bozman to TGB 3/12/43; NLS Acc. 4338/165
37. Bozman to TGB 10/3/44; NLS Acc. 4338/165
38. Langley Lord, AJ 71: 57
39. TGB to Bozman 3/5/44; NLS Acc. 4338/165
40. TGB's *Brenva* manuscript; NLS Acc. 4338/190
41. TGB to Bozman 8/5/44; NLS Acc. 4338/165
42. Bozman to TGB 29/9/44; NLS Acc. 4338/165
43. Letts to TGB 27/12/44; NLS Acc. 4338/165
44. Houston to TGB 31/1/45; NLS Acc. 4338/8
45. Mason to TGB 21/11/44; NLS Acc. 4338/165
46. Longstaff to TGB 10/12/44; NLS Acc. 4338/165
47. Strutt to TGB 15/12/44; NLS Acc. 4338/165
48. Lloyd P., In *Thomas Graham Brown 1882–1965*; p. 5

Chapter 18: Return to the Mountains
1. Hanson N., AJ 57: 26
2. Lloyd P., op. cit. p. 3
3. Parish G., Conversation with author 2/4/14
4. Lees J., Papers of Johnnie Lees; MHT: GB 3075 JRL
5. Ibid.
6. Ibid.
7. Pettigrew R., Letter to author 12/2/15
8. Glenmore Lodge to TGB 24/5/51; NLS Acc. 4338/10
9. Mill to TGB 2/7/52; NLS Acc. 4338/11
10. TGB's diary 1952; NLS Acc. 4338/30
11. Tobin to TGB 25/9/52 NLS Acc. 4338/11
12. Evans to TGB 19/8/53; NLS Acc. 4338/12
13. TGB's diary 1953; NLS Acc. 4338/32

Chapter 19: Editor of the Alpine Journal
1. TGB to Blakeney 30/9/48; NLS Acc. 4338/12
2. TGB to Oughton 7/10/48; NLS Acc. 4338/12
3. Donkin to TGB October 1947; NLS Acc. 4338/8
4. TGB to Longstaff 7/10/48; NLS Acc. 4338/8
5. TGB to Malcolm 11/10/48; NLS Acc. 4338/8
6. Longstaff to TGB 31/12/48; NLS Acc. 4338/8
7. Longstaff to TGB 11/2/50; NLS Acc. 4338/9
8. Howard G., AJ 57: 1
9. *Dictionary of National Biography 1971–1980*; p. 523

10. Lunn to TGB 15/8/49; NLS Acc. 4338/9
11. Howard G., AJ 57: 565
12. Ling W., AJ 58: 117
13. Unna to TGB 21/9/50; NLS Acc. 4338/10
14. Amery to TGB 16/10/50; NLS Acc. 4338/10
15. Brocklebank to TGB 4/2/50; NLS Acc. 4338/9
16. Young to Elliott 17/2/50; NLS Acc. 4338/9
17. Elliott to TGB 12/2/50; NLS Acc. 4338/9
18. Quoted in Hankinson A., *Geoffrey Winthrop Young: Poet, Mountaineer, Educator*; p. 326
19. TGB to Elliott 1/3/50; NLS Acc. 4338/9
20. TGB to Elliott 31/3/50; NLS Acc. 4338/9
21. Young to Elliott 5/2/50; in Davidson Sir E., Notebook Vol. 8; AC archives C35
22. Blakeney to TGB 18/8/49; NLS Acc. 4338/9
23. Blakeney to Nona Smythe 10/1/50; Blakeney papers: BL Add MS 63125
24. Strutt to TGB 14/3/34; NLS Acc. 4338/4
25. Lloyd to TGB 10/1/51; NLS Acc. 4338/10
26. Lloyd to TGB 18/6/52; NLS Acc. 4338/11
27. Blakeney T., AJ 81:160
28. Blakeney to Nona Smythe 24/10/50; AC archives 1922/B63
29. Blakeney to Lunn 11/8/49; Sir Arnold Lunn papers; Georgetown University Library, Washington, Box1/folder 57
30. Blakeney to Nona Smythe 27/10/51 and 6/12/51; Blakeney papers: BL Add MS 63125
31. Blakeney to Nona Smythe 24/10/50; AC archives 1922/B63
32. Lloyd to TGB 31/1/52; NLS Acc. 4338/11
33. TGB's diary 1952; NLS Acc. 4338/31
34. Lloyd to TGB 24/9/52; NLS Acc. 4338/11
35. Hunt to TGB 5/8/53; NLS Acc. 4338/12
36. Hillary to TGB 1/10/53; NLS Acc. 4338/12
37. Hunt to TGB 1/9/53; NLS Acc. 4338/12
38. Herbert to TGB 16/12/53; NLS Acc. 4338/12
39. Murray to Herbert 1/12/53; AC Archives B59 (1)
40. Busk to Herbert 2/1/54; AC Archives B59 (1)
41. TGB to Wordie 29/1/54; NLS Acc. 4338/13
42. Herbert to TGB 8/3/54; NLS Acc. 4338/13
43. Lloyd to Herbert 10/3/54; AC Archives B59 (1)
44. Herbert to TGB 14/1/54 and Goodfellow to TGB 15/2/54; NLS Acc. 4338/13
45. Goodwin S., *Himalayan Journal*, 60: 5
46. TGB to Herbert 14/11/59; NLS Acc. 4338/15
47. Tangley Lord, AJ 71: 57

Chapter 20: Alpine Historian

1. TGB to Mazzuchi 6/10/32; NLS Acc. 4338/3
2. TGB to Porter 6/11/33; NLS Acc. 4338/4
3. TGB to Elliott 18/11/33; NLS Acc. 4338/4
4. Graham Brown T., *Brenva*; p. 109
5. Quoted in Hankinson A., *Geoffrey Winthrop Young: Poet, Mountaineer, Educator*; p. 326
6. TGB & de Beer to President of AC 17/7/53; NLS Acc. 4338/12
7. Anon., AJ 78: 282

8. TGB to de Beer 14/2/57; NLS Acc. 4338/163

9. de Beer to TGB 14/2/57; NLS Acc. 4338/14

10. de Beer to TGB 8/9/56; NLS Acc. 4338/14

11. de Beer to TGB (undated); NLS Acc. 4338/163 (5)

12. Graham Brown T., De Beer G., *The First Ascent of Mont Blanc*; p. 334

13. Graham Brown T., Early Mountaineering; In Spencer S. (ed.), *Mountaineering*; p. 24

14. Graham Brown T., De Beer G., op. cit., p. 192

15. Meyer H., AJ 63: 82

Chapter 21: Vagabond Professor

1. *Dictionary of National Biography 1961–1970*; p. 151

2. Neil to TGB 10/6/58; NLS Acc. 4338/15

3. Smith to TGB 19/6/57; NLS Acc. 4338/14

4. Lees J., Papers of Johnnie Lees; MHT: GB3075 JRL

5. Quoted in Cruickshank J., *High Endeavours*; p. 56

6. Ibid. p. 55

7. Campbell R., In *Thomas Graham Brown 1882–1965*; p. 7

8. Campbell R., op. cit.; p. 8

9. *The Times*, 30/10/65

10. Cox to Blakeney 16/2/66; BL Add 63123

11. *The Times*, 2/11/65

12. Cox to Herbert 8/11/66; Lord Tangley's papers; AC archive B59.1

13. Blakeney to Tangley 2/2/66; BL Add 63123

Glossary

abseil   technique of sliding down a doubled rope which can be retrieved

aiguille   sharply pointed peak (Fr. needle)

arête   narrow top of a ridge

belay   running the rope around rock or ice axe to secure the climber

bolt   expansion bolt inserted into rock by drilling a small hole

col   mountain pass; gap in a mountain ridge

cornice   overhanging crest of snow

couloir   wide, steep gully

gendarme   pinnacle of rock, typically blocking the way

rappel   French term for abseil

sérac   large block of ice, often unstable

verglas   thin coating of ice

Bibliography

Adrian Lord E., Thomas Graham Brown 1882–1965; *Biographical Memoirs of Fellows of the Royal Society*, 1966; 12: 22.

Anon., In Memoriam; *Alpine Journal* 1973; 78: 282.

Band G., *Summit: 150 Years of the Alpine Club*, London: Collins, 2006.

Basterfield G., The Annual Me(a)lee; *Gritstone Club Journal*, 1925–1926; 2/3: 5.

Bell J., *Progress in Mountaineering*, Edinburgh: Oliver & Boyd, 1950.

Blakeney T., The Alpine Journal and its Editors III; *Alpine Journal* 1976, 81:160.

Bonington C. (ed.), *Great Climbs*, London: Mitchell Beazley, 1995.

Bonner T., *Becoming a Physician*, Baltimore: Johns Hopkins University Press, 2000.

Brendon P., *The Decline and Fall of the British Empire 1781–1997*, London: Vintage, 2008.

Burns T., Sir Arnold Henry Moore Lunn; *Dictionary of National Biography 1971–1980*, Oxford: The University Press, 1986: p. 522.

Busk D., The Young Shavers; *Mountain* 1977, 54: 40.

Calvert H., *Smythe's Mountains*, London: Gollancz, 1985.

Chorley Lord R., T. Graham Brown, *FRCC Journal* 1966; 20: 263.

Collie N., Valedictory address; *Alpine Journal* 1923, 35: 1.

Conefrey M., *Everest 1953*, Oxford: Oneworld, 2012.

Cruickshank J., *High Endeavours: the Life and Legend of Robin Smith*, Edinburgh: Canongate, 2005.

Eccles J. & Gibson W., *Sherrington: His Life and Thought,* New York: Springer, 1979.

Engel C., *A History of Mountaineering in the Alps*, London: Allen & Unwin, 1950.

Evans C., Thomas Graham Brown; *Dictionary of National Biography 1961–1970*, Oxford: The University Press, 1981: p. 151.

Finch G., *The Making of a Mountaineer* (2nd ed.), Bristol: Arrowsmith, 1988.

Goodfellow B., Five Traverses in Dauphiné; *Alpine Journal* 1934; 46: 45.

Goodwin S., The Alpine Journal: A Century and a Half of Mountaineering History; *Himalayan Journal* 2004; 60: 1.

Graham Brown T., The Intrinsic Factors in the Act of Progression in the Mammal; *Proceedings of the Royal Society (B)*, 1911; 84: 308.
> The end results of the treatment of 'Shell-shock'; *Journal of Neurology & Psychopathology* 1927; 8: 146.
> New Expeditions; *Alpine Journal* 1928; 40: 372.
> A New Ascent of Piz Bernina and other climbs in 1930; *Alpine Journal* 1931; 43: 8.
> Col Maudit and Other Climbs; *Alpine Journal* 1933; 45: 231.
> The Alpine Club: 1920–1932; *Alpine Journal* 1933; 45: 120.
> Mt Foraker, Alaska; *Alpine Journal* 1935; 47: 14, 205.
> The Nordend of Monte Rosa; *Alpine Journal* 1941–1942; 53: 281.
> Nanda Devi V. Lessons for the Future; *The Times*, 27/11/36.
> Masherbrum 1938; *Geographical Journal* 1940; 95: 81.
> *Brenva*, London: Dent, 1944.
> Sherrington – The Man; *British Medical Journal*, 1947; ii: 810.

Graham Brown T., De Beer G., *The First Ascent of Mont Blanc*, London: Oxford University Press, 1957.

Graham Brown T., Stewart R., On disturbances of the localization and discrimination of sensations in cases of cerebral lesions, and on the possibility of recovery of these functions after a process of training. *Brain*, 1916; 39: 348.

Greene R., In Memoriam; *Alpine Journal* 1949; 57: 230.

Hallward B., Travels & Climbs in the Alps in 1921, *Oxford & Cambridge Mountaineering*, 1921; p. 42.

Hankinson A., *Geoffrey Winthrop Young: Poet, Mountaineer, Educator*, London: Hodder & Stoughton, 1995.

Hanson N., Courmayeur 1948; *Alpine Journal* 1951–1952, 58: 26.

Hill L., Sir Edward Albert Sharpey-Schafer; *Obituary Notices of Fellows of the Royal Society*, 1935; 1: 400.

Hodgkin R., Masherbrum in 1938; *Alpine Journal* 1998, 103: 218.
   Playing: Robin Hodgkin's Mountaineering Letters 1937–47; published privately 2005.

Houston C., A Summer in Zermatt; *American Alpine Journal* 1936; 2: 483.
   Climbing High; *Appalachia* 1937; 4 (new series): 301.
   Denali's Wife; *American Alpine Journal* 1936; 2: 285.
   Nanda Devi; *American Alpine Journal* 1937; 3: 1.

Howard G., Alpine Uplift; *Alpine Journal* 1949–1950; 57: 1.
   Letter to the Editor; *Alpine Journal* 1949–1950; 57: 564.

Isserman M. & Weaver S., *Fallen Giants*, New Haven: Yale University Press, 2008.

Jones E., Shell Shock at Maghull and the Maudsley: Models of Psychological Medicine in the UK; *Journal of the History of Medicine and Allied Sciences* 2010; 65: 368.

Jones J., Tansey E., Stuart D., Thomas Graham Brown (1882–1965): Behind the Scenes at the Cardiff Institute of Physiology; *Journal of the History of Neuroscience* 2011; 20: 188.

King C.M. & H., *The Two Nations: The Life and Work of Liverpool University Settlement and Its Associated Institutions 1906–1937*, London: Liverpool University Press, 1938.

Letts L., The Alps 1924; *Gritstone Club Journal* 1924; 2 (2): 12.

Liddell E., Charles Scott Sherrington 1857–1952; *Obituary Notices of Fellows of the Royal Society* 1952; 8: 241.

Ling W., In Memoriam; *Alpine Journal*, 151–152; 58: 116.

Lloyd P., Campbell R., Seaton J., *Thomas Graham Brown 1882–1965*, Edinburgh: National Library of Scotland, 1982.

Longland J., Between the Wars 1919–1939; *Alpine Journal* 1957; 62: 83.

Lunn A., Alpine Puritanism; *Alpine Journal* 1949–1950; 57: 341.
   Two Men and a Mountain; *New English Review*; 11: 514.

Magnusson M., *The Clacken and the Slate: The Story of the Edinburgh Academy*, London: Collins, 1974.

Meyer H., The Centenary Reception – a Royal Occasion; *Alpine Journal* 1958; 63: 80.

Mummery A.F., *My Climbs in the Alps and Caucasus*, Oxford: Blackwell, 1936.

Myers C., *Shell-Shock in France 1914–18*, Cambridge: The University Press, 1940.

Pear T., Some Early Relations between English Ethnologists and Psychologists; *Journal of the Royal Anthropological Institute*, 1960; 90: 227.

Perrin J., The Essential Jack Longland, In *The Climbing Essays*, Glasgow: In Pinn, 2006.

Petty W., Easter 1923; *Gritstone Club Journal*, 1923; 1:2.

Ring J., *How the English Made the Alps*, London: John Murray, 2000.

Roberts A., *The Welsh National School of Medicine: The Cardiff Years*, Cardiff: University of Wales Press, 2008.

Roberts D., *Moments of Doubt*, Seattle: The Mountaineers, 1997.

Roberts J., The Attempt on Masherbrum, 1938; *Himalayan Journal* 1939; 11: 50.

Shephard B., *A War of Nerves*, London: Jonathan Cape, 2000.

Shipton E., *Upon that Mountain*, London: Hodder & Stoughton, 1943.

Shipton E. & Tilman H., *Nanda Devi: Exploration and Ascent*, London: Bâton Wicks, 2000.

Smith J.A., *Mountain Holidays*, London: Dent, 1946.

Smythe F., The Red Sentinel of Mont Blanc; *Blackwood's Magazine* 1928; 224: 1.
   A New Route up Mont Blanc Without Guides; *Blackwood's Magazine*; 224: 719.
   The First Ascent of Mont Blanc from the Brenva Glacier and Other Climbs in 1927; *Alpine Journal*, 1928; 40: 58.
   Climbs and Ski Runs, London: Blackwood, 1930.

Smythe T., *My Father, Frank*, Sheffield: Bâton Wicks, 2013.

Southborough Lord., *Report of the War Office Committee of Enquiry into 'Shell-Shock'*, London: Imperial War Museum, 2004.

Spencer S. (ed.), *Mountaineering*: Lonsdale Library Vol. XVIII, London: Seeley & Co, c.1935.

Steele P., *Eric Shipton: Everest and Beyond*, London: Constable, 1998.

Stuart D. & Hultbron H., Thomas Graham Brown (1882–1965), Anders Lundberg (1920–) and the neural control of stepping. *Brain Research Reviews* 2008; 59: 74.

Tangley Lord, T. Graham Brown: A footnote to Alpine history; *Alpine Journal* 1966; 71: 51.

Thompson S., *Unjustifiable Risk? The Story of British Climbing*, Milnthorpe: Cicerone, 2010.

Tilman H., *The Ascent of Nanda Devi*, Cambridge: The University Press, 1937.
  Nepal Himalaya, Cambridge: The University Press, 1952.
  Everest 1938, Cambridge: The University Press, 1948.

Unsworth W., *Savage Snows*, London: Hodder & Stoughton, 1986.
  Everest: the Mountaineering History (3rd ed.), London: Bâton Wicks, 2000.

Waller J., *The Everlasting Hills*, London: Blackwood, 1939.

Warren C., Thomas Graham Brown, FRS 1882–1965; *Alpine Journal* 1983; 88: 252.

Wilson C., Valedictory Address; *Alpine Journal* 1932; 44: 1.

Woolton Earl, *The Memoirs of the Rt. Hon. The Earl of Woolton*, London: Cassell, 1959.

Young G.W., *On High Hills* (3rd ed.), London: Methuen, 1933.

Young G.W., Sutton G., Noyce W., *Snowdon Biography*, London: Dent, 1957.

Acknowledgements

First, my special thanks go to Lindsay Griffin who, on the strength of an acquaintance made over forty years ago on the campsite in Snell's field in Chamonix, has given so generously of his time to write the foreword.

The fun bit of this project was the research; the unexpected pleasure has been the unqualified and enthusiastic help that I received from everyone I approached, and I thank them all. I wish to acknowledge particularly: Francis Graham-Brown, Tony Smythe, Robin Houston, Adam Hodgkin, the late Gordon Parish, Peter Odell, John Russell, Robin Campbell and Bob Pettigrew who shared personal memories and/or material with me; Judith Dray (Cardiff University), Bill Hinde (Gritstone Club), Glyn Hughes (Alpine Club), Chris Sherwin (Fell & Rock Climbing Club), Elizabeth Singh (Royal Medical Society) and Louise Williams (Lothian Health Services) who delved into the archives of their respective institutions; Peter Rowland (Alpine Club) and Joy Wheeler (Royal Geographical Society) who helped source the photographs, and the staff of the National Library of Scotland.

Writing the book proved trying so I am very grateful to David Crane, John Russell and the editorial team at Vertebrate for greatly improving my text. I had not anticipated how absorbing the project would become. I offer apologies and gratitude to my family and friends who endured my obsession with 'TGB'. My wife, Kate, bore the brunt, patiently and supportively; Gareth Jones's interest and encouragement never flagged.

Finally, I thank the following institutions for permission to quote from unpublished material in their possession: Alpine Club, Gritstone Club, Lothian Health Service Archives, Mountain Heritage Trust and the National Library of Scotland.

Index